A Cave
Of Candles

Best Wishes
Dorothy V. Corson

A Cave of Candles
The Story Behind Notre Dame's Grotto
By Dorothy V. Corson

The Spirit, History, Legends and Lore of Notre Dame and Saint Mary's

Homecoming
University of Notre Dame du Lac
Painting by Robert F. Ringel ©

My *The Spirit of Notre Dame* website is
http://www.nd.edu/~wcawley/corson.htm
Web Design by Wm. Kevin Cawley

Please direct questions and comments to:
Dorothy.Corson@comcast.net

Publisher: Dorothy V. Corson
E-Mail: Dorothy.Corson@comcast.net
Web: http://www.nd.edu/~wcawley/corson.htm

Copyright © 2000-2006 by Dorothy V. Corson

Requests for information should be addressed to:
Evangel Publishing House
2000 Evangel Way
P.O. Box 189
Nappanee, Indiana 46550
Phone: (800) 253-9315
Internet: www.evangelpublishing.com

Book Design and Layout: Mark Burford
Technical Director: Greg Corson

Library of Congress Control Number: 2006908917

ISBN-10: 1-933858-11-7
ISBN-13: 978-1-933858-11-1

Printed in the United States of America
by Evangel Press, Nappanee, IN

UNIVERSITY OF
NOTRE DAME

REV. THEODORE M. HESBURGH, C.S.C.

President Emeritus

1315 Hesburgh Library
Notre Dame, Indiana
46556-5629 USA

Telephone (574) 631-6882
Facsimile (574) 631-6877
E-mail Theodore.M.Hesburgh.1@nd.edu

March 13, 2006

Dorothy Corson
South Bend, Indiana

Dear Dorothy:

I have perused your book and think it is a wonderful addition to all of the literature and lore about Notre Dame. I was happy to encourage you as you made this collection of episodes that should be remembered for a long time to come. There are literally millions of people that have prayed at the Grotto since it was created many years ago and it becomes a real focus point of prayer for our students.

I am sure this book will be well received by all who love Notre Dame and its Grotto. Be sure of my best wishes and prayers for continued success in this endeavor.

Ever devotedly yours in Notre Dame,

Father Ted

(Rev.) Theodore M. Hesburgh, C.S.C.
President Emeritus

To My Husband and Son
Jack and Greg
Always My Inspiration

And most especially
To anyone
who has visited the Notre Dame Grotto
and wondered, as I have,
who planned it, who built it, and how it came to be.

© David C. Berta

Note to the Reader

A Cave of Candles: The Story Behind Notre Dame's Grotto began as a personal journal of my research on the history of Notre Dame and its Grotto. A copy of this updated manuscript was destined for a storage box in the University Archives upon its completion. However a curious set of circumstances at the eleventh hour has given it a life of its own, in a way I would never have expected, on the Internet. How it arrived there is a story worth sharing.

It has been said that "everything in life that matters is a mystery." I have pondered those words many times since the first time I heard them. As I've pondered the mystery of the paths my research has taken since I first set foot on that "Trail of Memories" in the autumn of 1991.

My first-person journal of research was completed in the summer of 1994, two years before the Grotto's 1996 centenary. A retired priest friend, Fr. George Schidel, C.S.C., who had been following my research discoveries with great interest, was the first person to read my preliminary manuscript. He asked my permission to share its new-found history with Fr. Theodore Hesburgh, C.S.C. Father Ted, in turn, sent me a beautiful letter of encouragement and directed me to those officials on campus who might be interested in its historical research for the Grotto's approaching centenary. They suggested I make a condensed version of my manuscript in third person focused on Our Lady and the Grotto's influence on the campus, which I completed on August 5, 1995. Six months later, they produced a beautiful illustrated pamphlet containing an essay by James Murphy based on the research in this second condensed manuscript. It was printed by the University for the Lourdes Day celebration at the Basilica of the Sacred Heart on February 11, 1996.

Shortly thereafter, I was compiling a series of oral Grotto stories I had randomly collected during my search to include as an appendix to my journal of research. In the midst of rereading them, it suddenly dawned on me that the quiet memories being made every day at the Grotto were its true history and the most important part of my research was yet to be completed—preserving in their own words—the experiences visitors to the Grotto took away with them.

The Grotto's August 5, 1996, centennial was six months away. I decided to present my idea to Fr. Hesburgh to see what he thought of placing a request for Grotto stories in the ALUMNI Newsletter which would have the potential of reaching many of the 100,000 alumni who received it. All the Grotto stories received would then be preserved, along with my manuscripts, as an archival record of the history of the Grotto for the next 100 years and beyond. Father Ted's response was just the boost I needed: "You'll never know if you don't try. It's a great idea. Tell them I sent you."

When the Grotto stories began arriving, they were all priceless, too precious to be hidden away in a box in the archives, unshared. What to do? I knew publishing them myself, was beyond my capabilities. This time I went to Our Lady at the Grotto for inspiration. "Lady dressed in Light show me the way" was my heartfelt prayer. Immediately, an analogy came to mind. I could abort the whole idea of publishing them or give the idea up for adoption to give them the life they deserved.

The choice was obvious. With the permission of the powers that be at Notre Dame, Mary Pat Dowling, who wrote the Grotto Stories Request for the ALUMNI Newsletter—and is now its editor—compiled and published the research, photographs and Grotto letters I passed on to her and gave birth to a beautiful little book which she named, *Grotto Stories: From the Heart of Notre Dame*, a book that would never have had a life without her. Thanks to Mary Pat, and the help of her Notre Dame Publications book designer, Marty Schalm, miraculously, it was ready in time to commemorate the 1996 Centenary of the Grotto and is now in its fourth printing. If ever there was a miracle associated with the Grotto, it has been seeing that beautiful little book in print for future generations to enjoy.

Now all I had left to do was make a new master copy of my 360 page journal of research, which I had been continuously updating, and get a Kinko copy made of it to go with my condensed manuscript already stored in the archives. My one regret: only a fraction of the research in my manuscript had made its way out into the world.

Unbeknown to me, Our Lady wasn't finished with me yet. To my surprise, Wm. Kevin Cawley, Curator of Manuscripts at the archives, very kindly offered to make the master copy for me on their letter-quality printer. When I returned to the archives a couple days later, he handed it to me and asked a totally unexpected question. In the process of checking the printouts he said he began to read my manuscript, thought it had a "voice," and asked my permission to publish both manuscripts on the Internet. Be careful what you wish for . . . .

As the saying goes, "Never Underestimate the power of a woman," especially the Lady in Blue. Wm. Kevin Cawley, the Curator of Manuscripts she had planted in my path, was also the Webmaster of the University Archives. Fr. Hesburgh's comment on our first visit, "The help will be there when the time comes," had foretold the future. "Our Lady never lets a deed done in her honor go unrewarded." My research at Notre Dame has been blessed by "earth angels" seen and unseen. May Heaven bless all the good people who have been instrumental in helping me tell Our Lady's Notre Dame Story to the world.

Dorothy V. Corson
Lourdes Day, 2000

In the President's Mansion at a southern university is a lovely painting titled, "Above the clouds at Sunrise." On a plaque in the entry hall are these words. "Any great university should have a gem that lifts the soul above the clouds."

At the heart of the University of Notre Dame's picturesque campus, nestled in a gentle hillside among the trees and landscaped lakes, is such a gem—a real group work of art—"that lifts the soul above the clouds."

This peaceful wayside shrine—Our Lady of Lourdes Grotto—has become a place of charm and enchantment for all seasons, a pleasing artistic adaptation to its surroundings, a place for prayer and quiet reflection. May it ever be so, and may it continue to inspire visitors for generations to come.

Please direct questions and comments to:
Dorothy.Corson@comcast.net

Acknowledgments

First, I would like to acknowledge Thomas Schlereth's part in this story. Had it not been for a casual comment he made to me, a stranger, over the phone, this story would not have been written. I had been given his name as someone to contact who was steeped in Notre Dame History. I knew he had written *The Dome of Learning: The University of Notre Dame's Main Building* and *The Spire of Faith: The University of Notre Dame's Sacred Heart Church* and I was hoping he might be writing a third, on the history of the Grotto. With the title, "A Cave of Candles: The University of Notre Dame's Grotto", perhaps? When I asked him if he was going to write another book, similar to the other two, for the Grotto's 100th Anniversary, he said: "No I don't plan to. Why don't you?" It was the inspiration of his unexpected comment, and the realization that probably no one else was going to do it, if I didn't, that prompted my first visit to the University Archives where most of my research on the Grotto was centered.

I would like to acknowledge the continual help, during the past fifteen years, of everyone at the University of Notre Dame Archives, most especially, Peter Lysy, for his cooperation, patience and kindness toward a novice from the first day of my search. Without his guidance and friendly suggestions, I would not have had the courage to get past square one. To Sharon Sumpter, always there, in her calm quiet way, to assist in locating files and explain finding aids. To Wendy Schlereth, whose keen memory and helpful suggestions planted me on many an interesting side path. To Charles Lamb who scanned many of the photographs that enhance the text. To Bernadette Terry, Matthew Steffens, Delores Fain, Nancy Hanson, Marlene Wasikowski, Angie Kindig, Walter Ray, Erik Dix, Matt Wilken and Elizabeth Hogan, all helpful members of an excellent team effort to make researchers feel welcome. And to Kevin Cawley, Web designer and computer guru—who weaved it all together—my heartfelt appreciation. This story would not exist on the Internet and in this book without him.

Also a special thanks to the following: To Rita Erskine at Rare Books and Special Collections, who welcomed me with a special warmth on my first day there, when I felt like a fish out of water, and who has become a very special campus friend. To Bob Ringel, architect, artist, and photographer, who generously shared many of his beautiful photographs of the campus to illustrate this "Trail of Memories." For more of his campus photographs, see the Notre Dame Photo Gallery online.

To Ed Ballotts for sharing his *A Cave of Candles* cover photograph of the Grotto, and to Linda Dunn, for sharing her serene green Grotto photograph on the back cover. For me, Linda's photograph will always be the 1996 Commemorative Centennial photograph of the Grotto. To Rev. James T. Connelly, C.S.C., and Jacqueline Dougherty at the Indiana Province Archives Center, where my search began, who encouraged me to visit the University Archives. To the Sisters of the Holy Cross, a special thank you, for their kind cooperation in sharing their memories. Sister Kathryn Callahan, Sister Rosaleen, and John Kovach, Saint Mary's archivists, were always there to lend an ear and followed my progress with interest. And most especially, to Bob Hohl, Reference Librarian at Cushwa-Leighton Library, Saint Mary's College, for his continual encouragement from the beginning. He always went out of his way to offer suggestions and make me feel welcome.

To Father Schidel, who came along when I needed someone just like him, who was one of my strongest encouragers. He was the first one to critique my manuscript, and did so with infinite care, offering unfailing interest and constructive suggestions along the way.

To Sue Dietl, Head of Access Services at the Hesburgh Library, who arranged a complimentary library card, opening a world of new books to take home that I would never have had the time to read at the library. And to all the unsung Reference Librarians at Hesburgh Library who, like Carol Szambelan Brach, exemplify the kind of help that a reference librarian is always there to provide.

To Mary Waterson and John Palmer in the History Room, and Brenda Loving in Interlibrary Loan at the St. Joseph County Public Library, where I was always warmly welcomed. To Jackson Armstrong Ingram, Archivist, St. Joseph County, who introduced me to those musty old coroner's ledgers. To Terry Frost, whose suggestions, early on, put my computer back in service when the power board went out and was sorely needed. Without it this story would never have been attempted. And last but not least, to Rev. Theodore Hesburgh, C.S.C., Dr. Ralph McInerny, creator of the Father Dowling mysteries, Rev. Richard Warner, C.S.C., Richard Conklin, James Murphy, Ann Korb and Jeanine Van Es who generously offered to read my finished manuscript and offer their suggestions.

There is just not enough space to thank everyone who shared their memories of days gone by; but Victor Couch, Mary Grix and Mary Kintz exemplified the many people I contacted who responded with interest and friendliness.

To one and all, those I've mentioned and so many others along the way who offered their encouragement, I would like them to know that I appreciated each and every piece contributed to the Grotto Puzzle. Bless all of you for helping to make this story possible.

Dorothy V. Corson

****

A special acknowledgment to all those writers
of the past 150 years of campus history
who penned the many descriptive passages
excerpted from their writings which became
a major part of the text of this story.

DVC

On a Trail of Memories

Father Thomas T. McAvoy, C.S.C., former Notre Dame archivist and historian, made this comment about the importance of recording history: "To have a history is to have a name, and the richer the history the more glorious the name."[1] I had barely begun my research into the archival history of Notre Dame and the Grotto, when the richness of its human history—that river of humanity that has flowed through the campus for over one hundred and fifty years—began to surface.

Family stories passed on from generation to generation told of ancestors who were an integral part of the Notre Dame campus. Some helped build the first road from South Bend to Notre Dame, others worked on the Sacred Heart Church, donated the stained glass windows and financed the bell. They brought their horses and mules to help hoist the statue to the Dome after the fire and assisted in building the Grotto.

These same ancestors have descendants who were—and still are—students, faculty, and volunteers on campus. Their remembrances started me on a trail of memories that went back to the very beginning of the University when Indians were still a part of it. Fitting together all the material gathered, and verifying it with newspaper and magazine accounts, was like completing an intricate picture puzzle containing pieces of many people's lives.

Along the way, I found myself encountering interesting stories and intriguing mysteries related to Our Lady and the Grotto, concerning both Notre Dame and Saint Mary's.[2] Because they illustrate how closely connected the two campuses were from their very beginnings, I took the time to check them out and weave them into this story.

What appeared to be the most difficult part of my search—contacting strangers whose names came up in my research—became the most pleasurable. I soon found myself experiencing the reality of Matthew 7:7: "Ask, and it will be given you; seek, and you will find; knock, and it will be opened to you."

Many octogenarians who generously shared their memories with me have since passed away. This story would not be complete without the pieces they added to the Grotto puzzle. Alex Haley, the author of *Roots*, described, so well, their loss to the world: "When an old person dies, it is like a library burning."[3]

As Father Hesburgh expressed it in a letter of encouragement to me, "Keep up your good work on the Grotto. It is a story yet to be told." Now that all the pieces are finally in place, this narrative has become one of those now-it-can-be-told stories that had to wait for the right moment: The Grotto's One Hundredth Anniversary.

— Dorothy V. Corson
August 5, 1996

Oldest Photograph of the Notre Dame Grotto
110 Anniversary, August 5, 2006

Providence smiles on sincere searching
And encourages good energies

— Bob Hohl
Saint Mary's Cushwa-Leighton Library

A Cave of Candles

Chapter 1

Notre Dame and Our Lady of Lourdes

From the day Rev. Edward F. Sorin, founder of Notre Dame du Lac, embarked from Le Havre, France, bound for his mission in the New World, Mary, the Mother of God, was his guiding star.

He relates with wonderment how he found the intimation of her will in the date of the departure of the first colony bound for Indiana on August 5, 1841.

But on the day of our departure, when I opened my new Breviary for vespers, . . . I was struck to see that we were starting on a beautiful festival day of the Blessed Virgin, Our Lady of Snows. The impression I received from the happy coincidence was not to be soon obliterated. I had absolutely nothing to do with the choice of the day. How often have I not thanked her since, for choosing it Herself, as a proof that she wished us to leave for our new Mission under her maternal protection.[4]

Even the visionary Father Sorin could not have envisioned how unerringly she would guide his footsteps to the birthplace of the future University of Notre Dame. Nor could he have imagined how many ways he would find to honor her in the future.

He chose her as patroness of his greatest undertaking, the University itself, and he named the place Notre Dame du Lac, Our Lady of the Lake. And he did not stop until he had her golden statue raised on high looking down over one of the greatest shrines to her anywhere in the New World.

Devotion to Our Lady at Notre Dame was also influenced by something else that took place very early in its history. . . . Word reached the campus of something new and hard to believe that was happening in France. A peasant girl in the mountains claimed to have been visited by the Blessed Mother. . . . Both civil and Church officials were irritated at the affair, for they could see no good reason why such a thing should happen to a girl like Bernadette Soubirous, and many refused to believe.

Across the ocean, however, Notre Dame believed, perhaps because its growth seemed close to miraculous itself. The story of Bernadette's lowliness, poverty and faith were in keeping with its own. It was really the same story: what Our Lady was doing by signs and cures in France, she was working more quietly in America.

Our Lady of Lourdes was quickly accepted at Notre Dame, and honor to her under this title became the dominant Marian devotion on the campus. . . .[5]

The culmination of this early Marian devotion can be seen today in Notre Dame's stone grotto, patterned as closely as possible after the one where Our Lady appeared to Bernadette. This replica of the original Grotto of Our Lady in Lourdes, France, has become a favorite devotional spot on campus. People of all faiths have found rest and peace in this place of quiet reflection; the beauty of its natural setting, the soft candleglow, convey a feeling of warmth and welcome. No tour of Notre Dame would be complete without a visit to this peaceful shrine nestled among the trees in the shadow of the Golden Dome.

Father Sorin's lifelong confidence in Mary's maternal protection is exemplified in this incident that happened two years before his death in 1893. He was very ill, confined to his rooms in the presbytery:

As he lay in his reclining chair he could turn his head and see, through the window, the golden dome and Our Lady surmounting it. He scribbled a note in his shaky hand and addressed it to Father Thomas Walsh, C.S.C., the then president of the University. "This morning, I have been looking at Our Lady. I am now as certain as it is possible to be certain that with the aid of Our Blessed Mother, under whose image we are living, our University will prosper. . . ."[6]

When the youthful Rev. Edward F. Sorin left France bound for America in 1841, he brought with him his own boundless energy and resourcefulness, but above all, his steadfast confidence in Mary and her maternal guidance.

Sorin's Mission in the New World

Father Sorin and the little colony of six Brothers were stationed in southern Indiana when they arrived in the New World. A little over a year later Sorin received his new assignment. It was a prospect that would have daunted any ordinary man.

With empty hands and empty pockets Sorin had agreed to establish in this wilderness a Catholic University. But with what? With an unshakeable faith that she under whose patronage he had begun this work would somehow and in her own time accomplish it.[7]

In the years to come "there would always be one asset Notre Dame could always count on, the courage of Father Sorin."[8]

On November 26, 1842, the twenty-eight-year-old Father Sorin and four Brothers — three more followed at a slower pace with oxen and the laden cart — arrived at the shore of the lake of St. Mary to claim for a school the 524 acres given to them by Bishop Celestine de la Hailandiere.

When they arrived they viewed what appeared, in the heavy winter snows, to be one lake with an Island in the middle. Undoubtedly, the "happy coincidence" of learning the mission site had already been named Ste.-Marie-des-Lacs, and the lake, St. Mary's — by his predecessor, Rev. Stephen Theodore Badin — was not lost on Father Sorin as another intimation of her will.

He mentions the Indians in the area, "There remained only about two hundred Indians, all the others having been removed beyond the Mississippi" and describes Father Badin's impression of what was to become the site of the University:

One day after ministering to the wants of his dear Indians while gazing over the pretty lake on the shores of which

he stood in admiration, a thought flashed to his mind that such a beautiful spot should be secured for God. What a delightful place for an orphan's asylum and a college! Instantly he resolved to buy it. "How well inspired," said he later to Father Sorin, "I was when I entered these 524 acres."[9]

Father Sorin renamed the mission site Notre Dame du Lac, Our Lady of the Lake, in honor of Mary, a name it retains to this day although it now contains two "mesmerizing" lakes:

Here two lakes, fed by never-failing springs, discharge their crystal waters into the river by a westerly flowing rivulet. These lakes were originally surveyed and mapped as one, but the land between them, now dry, was never covered by any depth of water, and in after years its marshy exhalations causing ill health, it was deemed advisable to introduce a system of drainage which converted the original single lake into two, of which the larger covers about 25 acres, the smaller 17. A rising ground between the lakes is still known as the 'Island.' . . . Here reside the members of the order whose duties do not require their constant presence at the university.[10]

These two lakes, [dedicated to St. Mary and St. Joseph], each with its peculiar interest, form the finest feature in landscape of Notre Dame. They are supplied entirely from springs, and their transparent waters wash shores of clean white sand and pebbles, and hide in the recesses multitudes of the finny tribe of every variety, from sturgeon to minnow. They afford rare sport to the pleasure of loving students both winter and summer: bathing, skating, fishing. These lakes cover an area of about forty-five acres, and the groves on their banks are the resort of every species of game known in the country.[11]

St. Mary's Island

The first space on the site dedicated to Our Lady was the island in the already named St. Mary's Lake. St. Mary's Island was the first of many honors bestowed upon Mary leading up to the present Grotto — now a favorite retreat on campus. Columba Hall, a later building on the island, is pictured.

Two years after Sorin's arrival in 1844, the first chapel, which adjoined the Novitiate, was built on the island.

The Community Cemetery

This first winter at Notre Dame turned out to be a very severe one. It seems to have been during this time that Sister Mary of Calvary fell ill, perhaps from living in that drafty log cabin loft; perhaps she had not entirely recovered from the fatigue of the journey from France. She was pronounced dying and received the last sacraments to the great distress of all. Father Sorin, in fact, made a vow that if Sister Calvary recovered, a chapel would be built on the island in the middle of St. Mary's Lake. With that, Sister Calvary did indeed begin to recover, and when the chapel was built in the spring she had the honor of laying the first stone.[12]

This island is necessarily dear to the Order of the Holy Cross; it was the first spot dedicated to Mary and the association of years have added greatly to this endearment. Nearly all the American Brothers look to this spot as their Alma Mater, and here repose the bodies of nearly all who have been called by their Heavenly Father from their work below, to their reward above. Long rows of black crosses continually remind the living associates how their brethren gone before are awaiting them.

This tender affection for this lovely spot has led to its adornment beyond any other portion of the premises.[13]

The little Chapel on the "Island," dedicated to Our Lady of the Lake, was blessed on the 8th of December 1844 and named Most Holy and Immaculate Heart of Mary Chapel. Visitors paddled to the chapel in canoes from the shore of the lake because the neck of land was marshland in the early years:

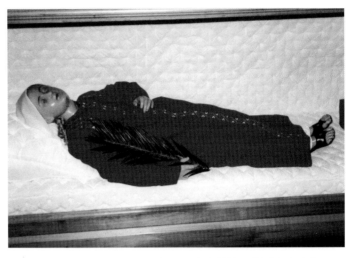

A quaint octagonal Chapel, modest and retired, where the whole community of Notre Dame assembled in times of joy to thank God, and in times of sadness and grief to beg his aid. In 1847, on the 19th of March, it was enriched with the precious body of St. Severa, virgin and martyr, (of the third century) given to the Chapel by Bishop Hailandiere, on his return from Rome in 1845. . . . In this chapel, the Archbishop — then Bishop — of Cincinnati, the Bishops of Milwaukee and Detroit, said Mass with evident delight.

Mrs. Byerley furnished it with a beautiful carpet and Bro. Francis Xavier taxed his taste and skill to the uttermost to adorn the sanctuary. It moves even such cold hearts as ours to listen to good Brother Vincent and other of the more ancient Brothers recount the glories of that dear little Chapel. It is now of the past — but not forgotten. The Chapel of the Portiuncula, with its many privileges, has supplanted it on the

"Island." . . . All those who ever had the privilege of praying in the dear secluded sanctuary, remember it with affectionate regret.[14]

Like many early buildings on the campus this chapel has not survived (the oldest building presently on campus is Old College, pictured, built in 1843.) The replica and bones of the precious body of St. Severa, virgin and martyr, a young girl who was brutally slain in the Roman persecutions because she kept the faith is one of the oldest antiquities at Notre Dame. Her bones and the replica of her body now repose in a glass case among other relics in the Reliquary Chapel of the Basilica of the Sacred Heart.

Other later "adornments" to the Island included the Tomb of Blessed Virgin Mary, and the Holy Sepulcher, which measured eight feet high, fifteen feet long, and six feet wide.

News of Lourdes Reaches the New World

In 1847 the Bishops in the United States petitioned Pope Pius IX to declare the Blessed Mother Patroness of the United States under her title of the Immaculate Conception. On Dec. 8, 1854, Pope Pius IX proclaimed the dogma of the Immaculate Conception in Rome.

Five months later, on April 24, 1855, the cornerstone was blessed and the Academy of St. Mary's of the Immaculate Conception[15] was established. Father Sorin had deeded 50 acres of land, and had given a grant of $5000 for new buildings to the Sisters of the Holy Cross, so they could move their school in Bertrand, Michigan closer to Notre Dame. The convent and school were reestablished on the banks of the St. Joseph River where it is known today as Saint Mary's College.

Three years later, on the 11th of February, 1858, the world began to hear about the apparitions of the Virgin Mary seen by Bernadette at the Grotto of Massabielle in Lourdes, France. The dogma of the Immaculate Conception, proclaimed by Pope Pius IX, was reputed to be a doctrine unknown to the unschooled Bernadette. Yet she said, "the beautiful lady said to her: 'I am the Immaculate Conception.'" In 1870 Notre Dame's, *Ave Maria*, detailed the phenomenon:

The simple facts are these. On the 11th of February, 1858, a humble, ignorant peasant child, named Bernadette Soubirous, being sent by her parents, together with her two companions, to fetch some dead wood by a mountain stream, close to a grotto, known in the country by the name of "The Grotto of Massabielle," suddenly saw in an inaccessible place an apparition, clothed in white and radiant beyond description. This apparition returned at stated times, as it had promised, on eighteen different occasions; it spoke to the child, commanding her to tell the clergy to have a chapel built on the spot; and at its word a miraculous spring burst forth under the hands of the child, in the presence of hundreds of spectators, from the dry hard rock of the grotto, which miraculous source gave sight to the blind, feet to the lame, and healing to the sick of all ages, conditions, and maladies. These miraculous appearances were doubted by the clergy, roused the opposition of the Government, and convulsed the whole country for eight months, when a word from the Emperor left the people in peace to follow their own convictions. From that time until now the number of pilgrims and of miraculous cures have been steadily increasing, and a very beautiful church has been built on the spot indicated by the vision.

The *Ave Maria* also included a review of a book written about it:

Henri Lasserre, Bernadette's historian and author of Our Lady of Lourdes, *has taken almost incredible trouble to verify every fact which he relates. He has given the names and addresses of a host of witnesses both to the original facts and to the cures effected in consequence. The most incredulous man amongst us would be compelled, in the face of such evidence, to hesitate before declaring the whole matter to be the offspring of imagination; while the marvelous disinterestedness and simplicity of the peasant girl and her family, to whom these singular revelations were made, go far to set aside the opposite assertion "that the whole thing was an intrigue, and a pretext to get money out of the credulous." Equally remarkable are the extreme reticence and prudence of the clergy, and especially the Bishop, who was one of the very last to give in his adhesion to the popular belief, and for the first few months utterly forbade his clergy to take any part in the proceedings, or even to visit the grotto. The cry of priestcraft, therefore, falls equally to the ground.*[16]

The Blessed Mother appeared to Bernadette in a humble place, a lowly cave, as Christ was born in a stable. She was a simple peasant girl; even the doctrine of the Trinity was unknown to her. Her use of the phrase, "I am the Immaculate Conception," was to baffle the community, the priests, and those who persecuted her, but they could not shake her faith. She would not change her story. From that moment on Lourdes became a mecca for pilgrimages by the devout and the faithful the world over. News of it spread across the continent into the new world and onto the campuses of Notre Dame and St. Mary's.

The First Replica of a Shrine at Notre Dame

Meanwhile, a year after the phenomenon at Lourdes in 1859, the model and plans for the Chapel of Loretto — which still exists directly behind the present Church of Loretto at Saint Mary's — were brought from Italy by Father Neil H. Gillespie, the brother of Sister Angela of St. Mary's Academy. It was completed the same year. It has the distinction of being the first replica of a shrine built on either campus. It is a facsimile of the original "House of the Incarnation" where Gabriel, the angel of the Lord, announced to Mary the birth of Jesus — the Son of God. According to legend, it was transported by angels from Nazareth to a shepherd's field in Loretto, Italy.

Father Gillespie was one of the first students who entered the University of Notre Dame. In June 1849, he became one of the first two graduates to receive a Bachelor of Arts degree from the University.

Two years later, in 1861, the first replica of a shrine at Notre Dame, The Portiuncula Chapel of Our Lady of Angels, was built on the "island." It took the place of the island chapel, the first of many early shrines on campus, dedicated to Mary throughout the University's early history. It was removed in 1858 along with the first Novitiate.

The Chapel in Assisi, Italy was originally known as St. Mary of the Angels because of local reports of angelic visitations. It was probably built in the tenth or the eleventh century, but was abandoned late in the twelfth century. The young Francis repaired it in 1207. There St. Francis received his vocation and founded his first order. He died there in an adjacent cell in 1226.

This facsimile was yet another "adornment" on the "island." It was erected when the Holy Cross Community obtained the canonical establishment of the

Portiuncula indulgences at Notre Dame. In the years that followed, throngs of pilgrims visited the little Portiuncula Chapel on August 2, the Feast Day of Our Lady of Angels, to gain the plenary indulgences.

The Portiuncula Chapel, dismantled in 1898, was just the beginning of a conscious effort by Father Sorin to encourage pilgrimages to Notre Dame.

Many years later, Notre Dame's famous resident sculptor, Ivan Mestrovic, was associated with another Portiuncula Chapel.

In his early career when Mestrovic was working as both an architect and a sculptor, he built an Our Lady of Angels Chapel to keep his promise to a young shipowner's daughter, Maria Racic Banac. Before she died, after two other members of her family died in rapid succession, she asked her mother to have Mestrovic "build me a tomb and console me with the thought that death is just a shadow." As an answer to Maria, the artist inscribed on the bronze bell hanging from the cupola: "Know the mystery of love and thou shalt solve the mystery of death and believe that life is eternal."[17]

Mestrovic sculpted many works of art on campus. Of his sculptures honoring Mary, the "Pieta," now in the Basilica of the Sacred Heart, and "Woman under the Cross," Mestrovic said: "All speak of the supreme sacrifice which is also a promise of salvation to those that recognize immortality imprisoned in every soul in love with eternity."

The *Ave Maria*

After the Civil War was over in 1865, Father Sorin, ever open to new ways to honor our Lady, decided to establish a printing shop so that a devotional periodical could be printed. He appealed to Alfred Talley, a printer from Chicago, to help him establish it.

On the 1st of May, [Mary's month] 1865, in collaboration with the Sisters of the Holy Cross, Sorin launched the national magazine to promote devotion to our Lady. He called it, *Ave Maria*, which means "Hail, Mary," and referred to it as "Our Blessed Virgin's Journal."

Volume One, Number One of *Ave Maria* was printed and circulated with the aid of the Sisters. Under Mother Ascension's direction, they set type, read proof, folded and sewed by hand the *Ave Maria* (and later the *Notre Dame Scholastic*)[18] Talley conducted the publication of the first volume from his home on Juniper Road. It was printed by hand press. By the time Volume Two went to press Notre Dame had purchased a steam power press. The *Ave Maria* magazine, which was published until 1970, carried regular notices of numerous cures both physical and spiritual through a regular column under the title of The Association of Our Lady of Sacred Heart, a devotion promoted for years by the Holy Cross fathers through the *Ave Maria*. The *Ave Maria Press* has been in continuous operation ever since. In 1962-63, they began publishing books and other devotional materials.

Alfred Talley continued as foreman of the *Ave Maria* office until his health failed. He resided at the Juniper Road farm until his death in 1870. The handsome house he built within a mile of Notre Dame is still there. It was awarded landmark status in 1975. Boulders from the land on which it was built were later used in the building of the 1896 Grotto.

The First Church and Main Building — 1866

On May 31, 1866 the Archbishop of Baltimore, Martin J. Spalding offered prayers over a new 12-foot statue [smaller and painted not gilded] of the Blessed Virgin under the title of the Immaculate Conception. The statue was placed on a pedestal atop the building's wooden dome, clad with tin sheeting and painted white. A contemporary guidebook reported it was "surrounded by a light and graceful belvedere, whence a view of great extent displays the panorama of prairie scenery, and whose lofty and protected platform serves as a landmark by day."[19]

After the Our Lady of Sacred Heart statue was solemnly blessed, the two feet six inch crown created for the twelve foot statue was taken by Sorin, on August 30, 1866, to be blessed by the Pope. The request was honored and the crown blessed by Pope Pius IX on September 18, 1866. However, upon Sorin's return, it was decided that the crown was too perishable to be left to the elements and a decision was made not to use it as originally intended. The statue was never crowned; instead, the crown was placed in the college parlor to be viewed by the public.

On his way to Rome to have the crown blessed by the Pope, Father Sorin wrote about Mary and the dedication in a letter from Europe. It was dated August 29, 1866, and published in the *Ave Maria*:

I was indeed very happy to hear repeatedly, since I left home, of the visible evidences of protection which Notre Dame and St. Mary's continue to receive from Our Lady of Sacred Heart. I knew that after all we tried to do for her on the 31st of May [the dedication], she would in return give us new proofs that she notices every effort to honor her. The memory of that solemnity is so deeply engraved on my mind, that my memory could serve as a cliche fifty years hence, were I to live so long. It follows me everywhere; and whenever I kneel before a shrine of Mary, I love to present that pious and immense assembly, gathered from every quarter of the States, that every one of them may be blessed for his or her share of devotedness on that day for the glory of the Holy Mother of God.[20]

The first Sacred Heart Church, built in 1848, was replaced with a new one in 1871. The 1866 Main Building, which was destroyed by fire in 1879, was replaced by the present Main Building with its larger (golden) dome and statue built in 1879.

Chapter 2

Lourdes Movement Begins at Notre Dame

In 1869, Rev. Edward Sorin announced the council's decision to build a new Church to replace the old one. Joseph M. White's history of the Sacred Heart Parish sheds additional light on Sorin's ongoing interest in making Notre Dame a mecca for religious pilgrimages:

A printed brochure proclaimed to the public the Holy Cross community's aim, decided by its local council the spring of 1869, to build a new church to surpass their inadequate one. In naming the church, it is interesting to note the new title "Our Lady of the Sacred Heart of Jesus." The old place of worship was definitely dedicated to the Sacred Heart of Jesus at the beginning. But a growing devotion to Our Lady at the university accounts for adopting a different but related name for the proposed church. One manifestation of Marian piety was Sorin's collaboration with Holy Cross Sisters in launching the national magazine Ave Maria in 1865 to promote devotion to Our Lady. Another instance was to place a statue of the Virgin atop the dome of the new college building completed in 1866.[21]

By the decree of Pope John Paul II, the Vatican named this second church built at Notre Dame a minor basilica on November 23, 1991. The church can now use the title the Basilica of the Sacred Heart.[22]

Father Arthur Hope wrote a pamphlet in 1958 entitled: "Sisters of the Holy Cross at Notre Dame." He was allowed, by Sister Mansuetus, to read the Sisters' Chronicles which were kept in a tremendous volume labeled

"Record." From it, he took items of interest to reproduce in the pamphlet. Among them was this interesting excerpt which discloses St. Mary's contribution to the proposed new church at Notre Dame which replaced the first one completed on May 25, 1848.

Sometime in 1866 or 1867, permission was given Mother Angela by Father Sorin to carry out a project very dear to her heart: namely the erection of a church at St. Mary's [which she planned to name Our Lady of Sacred Heart]. She went to work with a will and with the aid of Sister Mildred, hundreds of letters were sent out to the wealthy patrons of St. Mary's soliciting donations for this object, and promising many spiritual benefits and a share in a Perpetual Mass to the benefactors.

Meanwhile, Very Rev. Father Sorin went to Europe [1869] and Father Granger, hearing of Mother Angela's success in making collections, wrote [a very interesting letter] to Father General [Sorin][23] relating to the subject — suggesting to him that the church should be erected at Notre Dame, that Mother Angela could not fulfill the promise of the Perpetual Mass, etc. Mother Angela yielded to Very Rev. Father General's request, and gave Father Granger $3,452.00 which she had collected.

This was a great blow to many of the Sisters who had set their hearts on having a church at St. Mary's. In this, as in other things, Father General's strong will dominated, and St. Mary's had to be content with having inaugurated the movement.[24]

The *Ave Maria*, launched in collaboration with the Holy Cross Sisters, was already a popular national publication. The Association of Our Lady of Sacred Heart, formed soon afterward, seated at St. Mary's and advertised in the pages of the *Ave Maria*, was quickly gaining new members.

The Our Lady of Sacred Heart Association was also taken over by Father Granger. Its "seat" was transferred from St. Mary's to Notre Dame when building began on the new Our Lady of Sacred Heart Church. Favors granted by Our Lady of Sacred Heart to members of the association reported in the *Ave Maria*, encouraged more readers to become members and donations were sent for the building of Our Lady of Sacred Heart Church at the University of Notre Dame.

Lourdes Water Arrives at Notre Dame

The first discussion of the Grotto of Our Lady in Lourdes, France appeared in the *Ave Maria* in January 1870. It was an extract from the *London Lamp*. The following month, *Ave Maria* serialized an English translation of Henri Lasserre's *Our Lady of Lourdes* which Father Edward Sorin had sent from France.

Lourdes water shipped from France to Notre Dame encouraged even more donations ($5 to $50) to the new church at Notre Dame through cures published in the *Ave Maria*.

In 1871 the cornerstone for the church of Our Lady of Sacred Heart was laid. Over the next ten years contributions from grateful users of Lourdes water would be used to finance the church building. The church would become free of debt in 1888.

Our Lady of Lourdes had made her arrival on the Notre Dame campus and Catholics throughout the United States became interested in obtaining the miraculous water. Cures by Lourdes water, rather than from membership in the Association of Our Lady of Sacred Heart, began to be published.[25]

The Confraternity of Lourdes office on campus, which was established in 1874, continues to fulfill requests for Lourdes water. The Lourdes office custodian, Brother James Lakofka, also fulfills many requests to light candles at the Grotto from people who are unable to go there in person. Many requests come from alumni living too far away to visit, from parents for students, and from professor's wives for their deceased husbands who loved the Grotto.

First Pilgrimages made to Lourdes, France

In 1873 Father Sorin and Mother Angela made separate pilgrimages to Lourdes, France. They were both impressed and sent back mementos of their visit.

On June 21, 1873, Sorin sent a six foot statue of Our Lady of Lourdes from Paris for the Juniors.[26] He described it as "the finest representation we have ever seen." It arrived on November 1, 1873, and was placed in the large parlor.[27] Later, the St. Mary's section of the *Scholastic* reported that Father Sorin and Mother Angela arrived from Europe on September 13, 1873. It included this added bit of news:

In a few weeks there will be forwarded to St. Mary's from Paris, a life-size marble [later corrected to "terre cuite" and plaster cast] statue of Our Lady of Lourdes. [The Bernadette statue arrived earlier].[28]

The fate of Father Sorin's 1873 Lourdes statue is unknown, but the one Mother Angela brought back 123 years ago is in Lourdes Hall at Saint Mary's today, along with the one of Bernadette.

First Lourdes Grotto at St. Mary's Academy

In 1877 an interesting entry[29] appeared in the *Scholastic* concerning a Grotto at St. Mary's:

There are already three representations of the Grotto in the United States, one at the House of the Sisters of Notre Dame in St. Aloysius parish in Washington, D.C., one at the House of the Sisters of Charity at Yonkers, and one at St. Mary's at Notre Dame, Indiana.[30]

In August of 1878 another description of this early St. Mary's Grotto appeared:

The facsimile of the Grotto of Lourdes at St. Mary's Academy comes nearer the original than any that she has seen in either this country or in Europe. Miss Jamison resided for some time at Lourdes, during a tour made by her to Europe, and of course her opinion carries much weight.[31]

An entry in the St. Mary's Academy section of the *Scholastic* in December of 1874, indicated a Grotto at St. Mary's had been in existence for several years:

The lovely Madeira vine at the Grotto of Lourdes has been shorn of its fragrant blossoms.[32]

Historians and archivists on both campuses knew of no evidence of any Grottoes on either campus before the present one at Notre Dame in 1896, yet these two items suggested there very definitely had been one at St. Mary's.

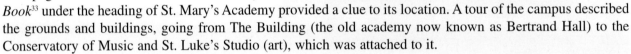

Two pages at the end of an 1880 *Class Day Book*[33] under the heading of St. Mary's Academy provided a clue to its location. A tour of the campus described the grounds and buildings, going from The Building (the old academy now known as Bertrand Hall) to the Conservatory of Music and St. Luke's Studio (art), which was attached to it.

After leaving the State road, leading from South Bend to Niles, for more than a quarter of a mile, maples, sycamore and poplars shade, and hedges of Osage orange and lilacs [many now gone] border the broad carriage drives and pleasant walks that lead to St. Mary's Academy . . . .

Passing the GROTTO OF OUR LADY OF LOURDES which separates the Academy from the Convent, we will mention attractive features belonging to the grounds, among which . . . ."

Elderly nuns had no remembrance of a Grotto on the grounds passed on by Sisters now deceased. There was also no archival evidence to support the existence of an 1870s Grotto at St. Mary's.

Statues in Lourdes Hall

Then one Sister happened to mention there was an Our Lady of Lourdes statue in Lourdes Hall at Saint Mary's. She suggested that the Grotto might have been on the building site of Lourdes Hall. "If that were so, and it had been dismantled," she said, "perhaps the statue of Our Lady was then placed in the new building and that is why it was called Lourdes Hall."

On the third floor of Lourdes Hall, there was a six by ten foot hallway alcove facing the grand staircase. A life-size statue of Our Lady of Lourdes stood on a simple pedestal. Behind it, was a narrow stained glass window with bits of purple color predominating. Facing the Our Lady statue was a smaller statue no one had mentioned, a life-size kneeling statue of Bernadette! The alcove was bare except for the statues. The graceful polished grand staircase, worn smooth by the many footsteps of students and nuns in bygone days, was centered on a long hall. One stairway led to the north hallway and the other to the south hallway.

Had the statues always been there or had they come from somewhere else? Several buildings were now all attached in a U formation. The center of the U has been called the "teardrop" because that was where the Sisters said goodbye to one another before leaving on missions to far away countries. Could the Grotto have been between the buildings before they were attached?

The new addition, now called Lourdes Hall, was built at St. Mary's in 1871-72. It was originally called "the academy wing."³⁴ Its design was borrowed from a sketch of the hospital where Mother Augusta tended the wounded during the Civil War. She was impressed with the building and asked a wounded soldier to do a sketch of it for her. The St. Mary's Sisters were well represented during the thick of the war, as were the priests at Notre Dame who were chaplains.

The *Scholastic* index showed no entries about this early St. Mary's Grotto. Paging through them backwards, from the date of the Class Day Book entry in 1880, was made a bit simpler by the fact that any writings about St. Mary's were at the end of each issue.

This puzzling unindexed entry appeared in the September 1879 issue:

The Grotto of Lourdes has been replaced by a simple curtained alcove [the one at the head of the Lourdes Hall grand staircase]. The beautiful statue of Our Lady of Lourdes stands on an ornamented pillar, and the window back of the statue is shaded by purple hangings. The statue of Bernadette has been painted anew.

In his late instruction, Very Rev. Father General said that Bernadette Soubirous was chosen to be the recipient of the great favors she enjoyed, because of her singular innocence. He said that the majesty of innocence had power to make strong men tremble. He mentioned a new French publication respecting this little peasant girl, and promised its early translation into English.

*Bernadette was chosen because Mary is the Mother of him who came to be a sign of contradiction to expose the empty pretensions of pride and place to reverse the false values of the world, to manifest the mysteries of His Kingdom to little ones and hide them from the wise and the great.*³⁵

The French publication about Bernadette mentioned by Father Sorin is the aforementioned book, *Our Lady of Lourdes*, written by her official historian, Henri Lasserre.

On May 28, 1870, another review of Lasserre's book was reprinted in the *Ave Maria* entitled, "Pilgrimages in the Pyrenees and Landes." It was written by the same reviewer, Denys Shyne Lawlor:

It is impossible to read this account of the gifted author's sojournings in the "Land of visions" — without feeling the heart throb with increased devotion and love for our ever Blessed Mother. . . . We tread with him the winding banks of the Gave . . . or kneel in the Grotto of Lourdes, where, in our own day, wonderful visions have been granted to the simple and pure-hearted little shepherdess, Bernadette. . . .

I do not know in the whole range of modern literature any work that exceeds Notre Dame de Lourdes *in eloquence of description, accuracy of detail, accumulation of proof, force of reasoning and earnestness of conviction. No honest-minded person can peruse it carefully and refuse to believe that the Blessed Virgin did personally appear at the grotto of Massabielle to Bernadette Soubirous, and that she confirmed her apparition by numerous miracles.*³⁶

Father Sorin must have been involved with the Grotto of Lourdes at St. Mary's and knew it intimately in the years before it was replaced.

Several maps of the Notre Dame Campus³⁷ included drawings of the St. Mary's campus as well. One, an 1878 St. Joseph County map, was an overall view of the land surrounding the campuses, including the Notre Dame lakes and the St. Joseph River behind the St. Mary's Academy. The others were Sanborn maps³⁸ for 1885 and 1891, detailed drawings of buildings on both campuses used for fire insurance purposes.

The Sanborn maps showed the 265 foot long building called Lourdes Hall was divided by a grand staircase. There were student classrooms on one side of the staircase, and the Sisters' refectory, chapel, and convent, on the other. The significance of the wording in the *Class Day Book* — "Passing the Grotto of Lourdes which separates the academy from the convent" — suddenly became clear. The Grotto, thought to be outside, had been inside all along — in Lourdes Hall! But how big was it, and what had it looked like to warrant it being labeled "nearer the original than any seen in either this country or in Europe?"

Letter Describes St. Mary's Grotto

Another unindexed article, "Some of St. Mary's Shrines," in the October 1877 issue of the *Scholastic* supplied the answer in the form of a letter sent to them for publication. It included a detailed description of the Our Lady of Lourdes Grotto, located indoors in Lourdes Hall, at St. Mary's Academy — the first grotto for pilgrimages on either campus.

As we left the Chapel the Sister said: "We have another shrine, the perfect facsimile of Lourdes. It stands between the Convent and the Academy." "I shall be delighted to see it; for last week, at Sadlier's, in New York, I purchased a book, written by Henri Lasserre, giving a full description of the Grotto and its history." "Indeed!" replied the Sister; "our Mother Superior met with the author four years ago [1873] when at Lourdes." "Did she witness any of the wonderful miracles which take place so frequently?" "I heard her speak of two to which she was an eye-witness. . . ."

"Our Mother Superior had ample opportunity to examine every part of the world-famed shrine, and ours is correct in every detail, not a crevice even missing. She had the good fortune also to meet at Paris the artist who had made the statue of the Blessed Virgin, which is according to the description given by Bernadette, and now marks the exact spot where the apparitions took place. She immediately ordered one exactly the same size as the one at Lourdes, and a lifelike statue of Bernadette, to place in the facsimile she intended to erect, which is just one half the size of the original."

We had now ascended to a long corridor, which runs the whole length of the edifice, 250 feet in length, and opposite to the grand staircase, in a large alcove fronting, is the Grotto, to all appearance like a rock. From the descriptions I had read, I should have recognized it even if I had not been told what to expect. The entrance is in the shape of a crooked arch; the rock sloping back from the entrance becomes narrower on either side; above, to the right is a niche-like orifice; a wild rose springing from a fissure in the rock at its base; tangled brambles extending their roots into the crevices of the rocks. In the niche is the statue spoken of above. The long white robe falling in folds suffer her feet to appear, reposing on the rock; on each of them is a rose of bright golden hue; a girdle of blue, knotted in front, reaching almost to the feet, and a veil descending as far as the hem of her garment. A chaplet of white beads hang from her hands. Above her head is inscribed in golden letters: 'I am the Immaculate Conception.' (This was the answer given by the Apparition to Bernadette when she asked her name.) Kneeling at the base of the rock is a life-like statue of Bernadette in peasant costume; a dark worn dress, and white capulet which covers her head and falls behind; a kind of kerchief covers her shoulders, sabots on her feet. [This statue is now painted all white.] She looks towards the Virgin, her whole countenance expressive (as mentioned by Lasserre) "of the majesty of innocence." In one hand she holds her

beads, in the other is usually placed a lighted candle, during novenas which are often asked by devout clients of our Lady, and a lamp is kept burning before the statue for special intentions. An altar is inside the arched Grotto, to represent the one at Lourdes. To the right of the altar, and nearer to the front, is a small receptacle to represent the fountain from which the miraculous water flows. A small iron railing is placed along the whole; on the outside is a stone ledge where all who pass kneel for an instant. I was so intent in examining this truthful and beautiful representation that I had not noticed the absence of one of the Sisters, until she came back and placed in my hand a small package, saying: "Mother Superior begs you to accept, with her compliments, a few vials containing some of the water which she obtained herself from the fountain at Lourdes. . . ."[39]

Mother Angela had definite plans for the statues she had shipped from Lourdes the year before. She placed them in an indoor replica of the Our Lady of Lourdes Grotto she built in Lourdes Hall in 1874.

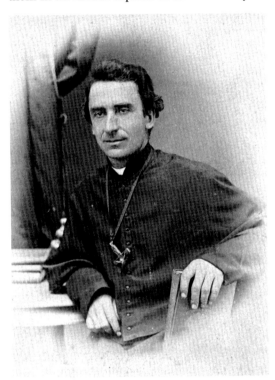

Sacred Heart's Lady Chapel

The work on Notre Dame's new Our Lady of Sacred Heart Church was progressing, slowly but surely. It would take another fourteen years before all the chapels were completed. Meanwhile, in 1874, about the same year Mother Angela built her indoor Grotto, Father Sorin's nephew, Rev. Auguste Lemonnier, died.

Reports of his death indicated that the present Lady Chapel with its Madonna in Sacred Heart Church, was to have been an Our Lady of Lourdes Chapel, a memorial to Fr. Lemonnier in fulfillment of his deathbed request of Father Sorin. Father Lemonnier was president of Notre Dame when he died on October 31, 1874.

In a letter to the community, Father Sorin writes of Father Lemonnier's last request of him:

. . . But there is one thing in particular which, as a last request, I feel bound to respect; a dying friend's wish presents itself to the living with a special sacredness, claiming, as it were imperiously, an undelayed satisfaction. It was on the eve of his death, as your Reverence is already aware that he entreated me not to refuse the Blessed Virgin the fulfillment of a promise he had made her with your consent and mine, viz., to erect here, if he should be restored, a Chapel of Our Lady of Lourdes: "For," said he, "although I am not going to be cured, I owe her more for dying as I do, then even for a longer life."[40]

The first library was named for Father Lemonnier. Timothy Howard speaks of him in glowing terms: "Innocence, gentleness, and purity, had a wonderful attraction for his soul. There was nothing which he touched that he did not beautify. He was 35 years old when he died."[41]

The proposed memorial chapel was described in the *Scholastic*:

The Lemonnier Memorial Chapel dedicated to Our Lady of Lourdes will be 45 feet x 32 feet . . . in keeping with and in the rear of, the new church. It will be decorated with stained glass windows, and ceiling. It is the intention of the projectors to make it the richest and most beautiful part of the Church of Our Lady of Sacred Heart. Work to be commenced this season as soon as the old church can be taken down to make room for it. In all probability, this Chapel of Our Lady of Lourdes will be, more than any other, the devotional shrine to which inmates and visitors will hourly repair to pray. There before the altar will be kept a constant supply of the precious water from the miraculous grotto in France while along the walls will be hung the ex votos which many pious souls may send in acknowledgment of favors received or solicited.[42]

Donations to Lemonnier's Our Lady Of Lourdes Chapel were regularly listed in the pages of the *Scholastic* and the *Ave Maria* from the time of his death. Other interesting items in the church concerning Father Lemonnier and Lourdes also came to light.

The Sanctuary Lamp

From Sorin's first pilgrimage to Lourdes, France in 1873, the focus at Notre Dame centered on Our Lady of Lourdes. The *Ave Maria's* announcement of the arrival of a sanctuary lamp, in 1875, was more evidence of a desire on Sorin's part to honor his nephew's deathbed request. It was completed on December 8, 1874, shortly after Lemonnier's death. The *Scholastic*[43] also refers to a lamp being presented to the church in memory of Fr. Lemonnier at this same time.

This sanctuary lamp is an exact replica of the one in Lourdes, France. It is the only sanctuary lamp displayed in the church today. It was refurbished during the last renovation, which was completed in 1992.

The *Ave Maria* described "the wonderfully beautiful Lamp, a gift of the Dioceses of Vivers and Valence, France, to the Shrine of Our Lady of Lourdes, France."

It is a masterpiece of true religious art, designed by M. Bossan, the eminent architect, and executed by M. Armand Calliat, one of the first goldsmiths of France. As the shrine of Our Lady of Lourdes at Notre Dame is to have a similar artistic gem from the same maker, a compendious account of the Lamp may not be considered uninteresting. A detailed description follows with the mention of the wording on the "circlet of the crown . . . which adorns, without concealing, the crystal chalice which contains the oil. The circlet of the crown is blue, with the inscription, in Latin: "In Him was Life and the Life was the Light of men."

The jewels adorning the dragon figures are also described in detail with this added:

Between these brilliant figures there are three shields blue, with a golden representation of scenes in the Nativity of Our Lord wherein He manifests Himself, by light, — to the shepherds, the Magi, and in His own Divine Person. . . . Three beautiful chains of golden leaves, flowers and blue globules, attached to the dragons' necks, meet above in the inner centre of a reflecting crown, composed of the monogram "A.M." (Ave Maria) interlaced with the cross and six broad leaves. From the bottom of the Lamp hang two golden pendants, connected about the middle by a medallion on which there is the following inscription:

THE LAMP
HAS BEEN PRESENTED TO THE SANCTUARY OF
OUR LADY OF THE SACRED HEART
AT NOTRE DAME, INDIANA
BY THE DEVOTED FRIENDS OF JESUS AND MARY
IN AMERICA,
AS A TOKEN OF THEIR FAITH AND BURNING LOVE,
TO KEEP WATCH IN THEIR NAMES
AND PERPETUATE THROUGH THE DAY AND THROUGH
THE NIGHT THEIR
ADORATIONS, THEIR PRAISES, AND THEIR SUPPLICATIONS
BEFORE THE AUGUST SACRAMENT OF THE ALTAR.
DECEMBER 8, 1874.[44]

This exquisite sanctuary lamp is filled with the finest Italian olive oil and is kept burning day and night in the sanctuary of the Basilica of the Sacred Heart. Another source describes how the lamp was made larger for Father Sorin.

Armand Caillat made a lamp for Father Sorin five centimeters larger than the Lourdes lamp and in every way an improvement on the first and today this genuine work of art hangs before the main altar in Sacred Heart Church. Few members of the Community realize how beautiful this lamp is, because few have ever had a close enough look to see its exquisite workmanship.[45]

In the intervening 14 years it took to complete the remaining chapels, the original plans for the large chapel dedicated to Our Lady of Lourdes, in Father Lemonnier's memory, were modified. An altar and a stained glass window depicting Lourdes[46] were added to the church instead, and the newly completed chapel with its Madonna statue became the Lady Chapel.

The years 1874 and 1875 were filled with events associated with the Blessed Virgin, some of them sad. On November 14, 1874, two weeks after the death of Father Lemonnier, acting president of Notre Dame Father Gillespie passed away. Sixteen years had passed since he brought back the plans for the replica of the Chapel of Loretto shrine at St. Mary's in 1858, the first replica of a shrine on either campus. His body was laid out in the Chapel. He is said to be the only one accorded this privilege.

Of all the chapels about Notre Dame and St. Mary's, Loretto was his favorite, and it was fitting that when his soul had fled to heaven his body should be laid out in this sweet place. The blessed candles were interspersed here and there among the many beautiful hot house plants and by these candles alone was the little chapel lighted.[47]

A statue of Our Lady of Consolation which Mother Superior brought from Luxembourg a year after his death, was placed in the Chapel of Loretto on September

28, 1978. It honors Mary, the protectress of Luxembourg, the Mother who ever since the 16th century has given so many proofs of her watchful care over the city, guarding it from pestilence and the arms of enemies.

The Blessing of the statue was the occasion of a very interesting ceremony in the convent chapel.

Sorin presided assisted by Fathers Granger and Corby. Very Rev. Father Corby made a few remarks on the devotion to the Holy Mother of God, and the proper respect and relative honor due to all religious symbols, marking the great distinction between the adoration and veneration given respectively to God and the Blessed Virgin.[48]

With appropriate ceremony, the statue of Our Lady of Consolation was carried on a tastefully decorated stand. A candlelight procession wound round the avenues and parterres near the academy and along the bank of the St. Joseph River.

Chapel of Loretto Receives Solid Silver Star

In that same year, 1875, another item of special interest linked to this Blessed Virgin statue concerning Father Sorin appeared in the *Ave Maria*:

Chapel of Loreto.

In the Chapel of Loretto, at St. Mary's Convent, Notre Dame, Indiana, is suspended a star of pure silver, with the following inscription: "Ave Maris Stella; Dec. 24th, 1875," just above the head of the statue of the Blessed Virgin. Crowning her brow with its quiet radiance, it proclaims its touching history while arousing new confidence in the protection of the "Gentle Star of the Ocean." This beautiful and appropriate votive offering was made by Miss Eliza Allen Starr, in thanksgiving for her preservation through the dangers of her voyage to Europe. The date it bears is that of the landing in Havre of the steamship L'Amerique, after the memorable and disastrous breaking of her shaft in mid-ocean on the 21 of November, 1875. The perils of a disabled ship on the high seas, the tempests, the suspense, the starvation, the pestilence triumphed over, together with the prompt and miraculous discovery made by the gallant ship of rescue, the welcomed Ville de Brest, were providences most gratefully accorded to the intervention and loving patronage of "Mary, Star of the Sea," to whom the voyage was confided.[49]

The Blessed Virgin is called the Star of the Sea, says St. Thomas, because as sailors are guided to their port by the polar star so Christians are guided in the voyage to eternal glory by Mary.

Sorin also Rescued from Disabled Ship

Father Sorin was on the same ship. Their miraculous rescue was depicted in a painting that once hung in the Sacred Heart Church. A letter written by him aboard the steamer that rescued them, Ville de Brest, was published in the *Scholastic*: The Ville de Brest was sent by the French Transatlantic Steamship Co. to cruise for the Amerique. They started looking for her on November 24, 1875, and sighted her on December 5th, but because of rough seas were not able to get close enough to effect a rescue until a week later, on December 12. She was towed into Queenstown harbor and thence to Harve and arrived December 17, 1875. Excerpts from Sorin's description of the rescue follow:

The officers of this vessel deserve the highest praise for their noble and persevering efforts to save us. They suffered extremely in keeping themselves at a proper distance during the gale which lasted a whole week after our first meeting. . . . I saw the "Ville de Brest" crossing us starboard, scarcely twenty feet from our bow, whence a single sea would have dashed her against us. . . . Five minutes later both steamers were tossing and rolling at a distance of half a mile from each other, which position remained the same for a full four days, the storm in the meantime continued with unabated violence [after the rescue]. The events which transpired on board will not be soon forgotten. Miss Starr had never before passed through such an ordeal. She went down bravely enough half the length of the rope ladder along the side of the big boat, but when she reached the lower boat I could see she was still alive by the sign of the cross she was making and repeating. Ah! She is a Christian woman.[50]

Eliza Starr was closely connected with both Notre Dame and St. Mary's. When her artist's studio in Chicago was destroyed during the Chicago fire, in 1871, she was invited to reside at St. Mary's as the head of their art department. She returned to Chicago in 1878, but still commuted to St. Mary's to teach. Many of her stories and poems are in the early *Scholastic* and *Ave Maria* magazines in the stacks at the Hesburgh Library. In 1885, she became the first woman to receive the Notre Dame Laetare medal for her many artistic contributions.

Although the solid silver star no longer adorns the statue in the Chapel of Loretto, several items belonging to Eliza Starr are displayed in the Heritage Room, the convent museum in Bertrand Hall. Among them, are her rosary, and a beautiful egg-sized cameo of the Blessed Virgin, which was blessed and given to her by the Pope.

In 1881, Eliza Starr wrote a lovely poem about the University:

Notre Dame as Seen from the Saint Joseph River

The purple air, the misty hills;
The meadows, green with hidden rills;
The grove, that screens from curious gaze
Its silent, meditative ways;
The lake beyond, its placid eye
Blue as the arch of vernal sky;
The church, and chapel spires that claim
The Virgin's favor, with her name;
How, like a thought of peace, the whole
Takes calm possession of the soul.

By E.A.S.[51]

Notre Dame as Seen from St. Mary's Lake

If Sorin had been lost at sea, would it have altered Notre Dame's destiny?

Chapter 3

Sorin Builds First Grotto at Notre Dame in 1878

During the years 1876 and 1877, no major events related to the Blessed Virgin or the Grotto were recorded. Then references to an early Grotto being built by Sorin appeared in several 1878 entries. One entry, which confused Sorin's 1878 grotto with the present one, reported it had taken 18 years to build and was completed in 1896. The present Grotto was completed in three months.

A few earlier mentions of work in process on Sorin's Grotto were published in the September 29, 1877 *Scholastic*:

It is the intention of Father Sorin to erect a facsimile of the original [Lourdes Grotto] with the exception of the immense rock 200' high. The hill at the rear of the church presents every advantage for a facsimile which he wishes to reproduce with scrupulous exactness as regards, height, length, depth etc. Ever since his first visit to Lourdes in 1873 his resolution to satisfy the wishes of pious pilgrims and visitors in this respect has constantly increased. Being there is quite a concourse of pilgrims at Notre Dame from time to time the facsimile of the wonder-working Grotto cannot fail to be an object of attraction to all who visit the place.[52]

Scholastic: April 6, 1878

Work on the imitation of the Grotto Of Lourdes, just to the Northwest of the new church has commenced in a little wooded dell regarded as one of the charming spots at Notre Dame.[53]

The dedication of an earlier Grotto built by Sorin was reported in the *Scholastic* on August 22, 1878.[54] It was a brief entry. No description of the ceremony was included.

More paging through the *Scholastics* revealed that two days before the 1896 dedication of the present Grotto, the *Scholastic* reported:

Removal of tower-like niche which sheltered Blessed Virgin on site of old Grotto was effected, after the statue had been placed in the new Grotto. When [the] statue was taken away the niche meant nothing and was a disfigurement.[55]

If the statue fit in the new Grotto, then the old Grotto niche must have been similar in size to the present one, but why were there no pictures of it?

A folder in the University Archives contained an article written for the Columbian Jubilee Celebration in 1892. It included a brief description of an earlier Grotto built at Notre Dame by Sorin in 1878.

As we leave the Seminary grounds and turn eastward toward the University, our path lies along the shore of St. Mary's Lake, on the opposite bank of which we see the barns, stables, and numerous small buildings that constitute the "home center" of the great farm.

Our path has now led us to the foot of a little hill, and we are agreeably surprised, as we are brought face to face with a facsimile representation of the Grotto of Lourdes, beautifully sculptured out of the side of the declivity. The rocks are there portrayed, while underneath is the gurgling fountain. To one side, lifted on high, is a beautiful statue of Our Lady of the Immaculate Conception, encased in an octagonal frame, the sides of which are glass, supported by stone pillars. At a little distance is the kneeling figure of Bernadette, in her quaint, pleasing Breton dress, praying to the Virgin of the Apparitions. To the left of this lovely spot is a square, three-story building — the residence of Very Rev. Father General Sorin and his assistants. It is the mother house of the entire Congregation of Holy Cross — the great center whence issue those directions that regulate the affairs of the order extended over the world. Such are some of the principal features of Notre Dame — the Pride of the West . . . .[56]

This octagonal building description of Sorin's 1878 Grotto, in turn, registered as a building. The Sanborn maps of the 1880s, which had drawings of buildings on the campus, showed a small circle, labeled Grotto, in the corner of the church and sacristy. Since only buildings were indicated on the Sanborn maps, a cave-like Grotto like the present 1896 Grotto would not have been noted on them.

Thomas Schlereth's 1976 book[57] on the history of the campus included photographs from the 1880s showing the church and presbytery before the chapels were added. One photograph showed just the top of an odd shaped building. It had to be the octagonal building referred to in the "Jubilee" article. Unfortunately, the photo was too indistinct to view clearly, even with a magnifying glass.

A more intense search through the archival photographs of the church and presbytery grounds finally turned up a photograph that had gone unnoticed before: A large picture[58] of the front of the Sorin Grotto, dated November 22, 1886! It was between the presbytery and the church, about ten feet from the present sacristy steps, rather than at the bottom of the hill where the present Grotto is now. Subsequently, it has turned out to be the only clear photograph in existence depicting Sorin's Grotto, the first one built at Notre Dame. It is the photograph at the beginning of this chapter.

This photograph pinpointed the exact location of the octagonal building, its size, and how far away it was from the present Grotto. Unfortunately, the photograph was cropped leaving out the area below it. There were no photographs of the lower part of Sorin's original Grotto to show what it looked like. The photograph showed only what must have been a cement representation of the arch of the Grotto cave, below and to the left side of

the "octagonal frame." The written description of the portion that was not visible, "the rocks are there por-trayed, while underneath is the gurgling fountain," would seem to indicate it was not the exact replica of the Lourdes Grotto Sorin intended it to be.

The words "tower niche" and the fact that it was removed because "it no longer served a purpose" were now explained. What had been referred to as a "tower niche" was this quite large octagonal, glass-enclosed building.

Until his death in October of 1893, Sorin viewed his Grotto and gardens from the windows of his presbytery rooms. His windows faced south toward the Grotto and the sacristy, and west toward the garden area which would now be the top of the present Grotto. A hedge of evergreens bordered this elaborate garden. On the other side of the hedge the present Grotto cave was carved from a small hill that faced St. Mary's Lake. This new location proved to be the ideal spot for it.

Father Sorin speaks of his 1878 Grotto in one of his *Circular Letters* written on board the "St. Germaine" on his way home from France. It was written on June 4, 1883.

Then, again, I wished in real eagerness to convey to you something of my petitions, and thanks, and tears of happiness, as your representative at the Grotto of Lourdes for the more than three days that we spent there, undisturbed, alone with her! Yes: alone with her! and yet with everyone in turn of the dear family, and at times with the entire little family; and she, from the celebrated Rock, looking down attentively and motherly upon each and all, and that usually four times a day, and from one to three hours each time. Never can I forget this fourth pilgrimage to the Immaculate Mother. . . . Two hours before we left, 8,000 men had arrived from distant points, and were on their knees, in earnest supplication before their Heavenly queen; 25,000 are often seen at a time in the same act of devotion; a million, at least are expected this year. Hundreds of miracles will probably be the result and the reward of this universal and ever-increasing piety. May Heaven be praised for this glorious and saving sign among us poor mortals!

It must be a great consolation for us at Notre Dame to possess such a neat and exact facsimile of the real Grotto of Lourdes. I will visit it oftener than I ever did, and hope many others will do the same. Dear Brother Vincent, you will come and join me there, on fine days, will you not? You know Lourdes; you will show us how much you love it . . . .[59]

Another Grotto Mystery Solved

Sorin's circular letter contained the only known written reference he ever made to his 1878 Grotto. In it, he seems to stress the point that it was *such a neat and exact facsimile of the real Grotto of Lourdes.*

However, there were indirect references to it made by others that seem to suggest that it was not the close replica of the Grotto he had planned to build, which may explain why Sorin's Grotto was also replaced seventeen years later when he was no longer around to object.

There appears to have been a bit of a mystery associated with both the earlier St. Mary's Grotto and the one Father Sorin built in 1878. No one living had ever heard of them and no books written about the campus recorded their existence.

The following excerpts from a variety of sources may explain somewhat this mystery. They also confirm that St. Mary's Grotto was Mother Angela's own inspiration.

An article was written for the *Baltimore Catholic Mirror*, by the same woman mentioned earlier, Mary Regina Jamison. Coincidentally, she visited both Notre Dame and St. Mary's on August 22, 1878, the day Father Sorin's Grotto was dedicated. That same day she described St. Mary's 1874 Grotto as "nearer the original than any she has seen either in this country or in Europe."

In this second article written at the same time, under the title "An Indiana Academy," Mary Regina Jamison

described St. Mary's and made this interesting observation about Grottoes:

To sanctify all these natural enjoyments of the campus, there is a spiritual atmosphere pervading the whole place that would rejoice the heart of Father Faber: plenty of beautiful oratories in the house and about the play-grounds, a Grotto of Lourdes, and a facsimile of the Holy House of Loretto. Although an indoor arrangement, the grotto is the first correct reproduction of the real Grotto of Lourdes that I have seen in America. Many churches and religious houses have so-called grottoes, but they are only handsome oratories, entirely unlike the rocky spot where our Immaculate Mother appeared to Bernadette. . . . At an early date the Mother Superior intends having a grotto in the Academy grounds at a spot on the river bank [in the glen] closely resembling the natural situation of the Grotto of Lourdes. No doubt many devout persons who find it impossible to cross the ocean will then gladly make a pilgrimage to St. Mary's Grotto.[60]

Could viewing Sorin's new octagonal shrine-like Grotto have triggered Miss Jamison's remarks about inaccurate oratories? If she had seen both Grottoes at the same time and pronounced the earlier St. Mary's Grotto as the closest replica to Lourdes in United States or Europe, what had the rest of Sorin's first Grotto looked like, and why hadn't she mentioned it?

The area allotted for the original 1874 St. Mary's indoor Grotto must have been more than three times the width of the present six by ten foot alcove, now narrowed by two closets placed on each side of it. The Lourdes statues stand alone in the small alcove. They are now silent witnesses to what must have been, from descriptions of it, a warm and appealing depiction of the Our Lady of Lourdes Grotto at St. Mary's.

The river bank in the glen was ideally suited for the outdoor Grotto Mother Angela planned to build. It was very much like the site of the Lourdes Grotto in France. The disappearance of St. Mary's Grotto eight months after Father Sorin's was dedicated — and the abandonment of Mother Angela's plans to build a grotto in the glen — seemed to parallel the situation ten years before. The Church name, Our Lady of Sacred Heart, and the funds Mother Angela had already collected for their proposed church, were turned over to Father Sorin to build the new church at Notre Dame in 1869. St. Mary's had to be content with having inaugurated the movement.

In a letter to Father Sorin, she speaks of her reason for doing so; in order that "a great monument to our Blessed Mother [a new church] can be erected in the United States."

I now *feel satisfied,"* she wrote, *"this should be at Notre Dame in preference to St. Mary's."* She concluded: *"After a while I am sure (if Providence does not grant other means) that you all at Notre Dame will help to put up a chapel in which we will be able to have Mass the year round."*[61]

Perhaps Mother Angela (or Sorin) also felt there was no need for two Grottoes for pilgrimages. Having "satisfied" herself that the Grotto of Our Lady of Lourdes "should also be at Notre Dame in preference to St. Mary's," she had hers dismantled eight months after Father Sorin built his. Once again, St. Mary's had to be content with having inaugurated a movement — an Our Lady of Lourdes Grotto for pilgrimages on campus.

An excerpt from Sister M. Georgia Costin's, *Priceless Spirit*, sheds more light on the subject. She quotes Mother Compassion who "continues into a matter for which Mother Angela has been both praised and blamed:"

Mother Angela regarded Very Rev. Father General [Sorin] as God's representative and obeyed him as such, and taught all her Sisters to do the same. No matter how much it cost her or how different her opinion was, as soon as she learned his will she submitted to it without a murmur . . . .[62]

The Mater Admirabilis Statue

History records many interesting written references to Father Sorin's beautiful way with words, his obvious devotion to Our Lady, his indefatigable spirit, and also his determination to have his own way.

Possibly the ultimate example of this audacious aspect of Father Sorin's personality turned up in an 1873 *Scholastic*:

It seems that Very Rev. Father General in one of his rambles through the studios of Rome came upon a marble statue which an artist was about finishing. It was Mater Admirabilis [Mother Most Admirable]. The subject represents the Blessed Mother in deep meditation, sitting by her spinning-wheel. It has always been V. R. F. Sorin's favorite representation of the Blessed Virgin. Of course he wanted it — wanted it, right away. There was only one little obstacle to his getting it. The artist regretted to inform him that the statue was intended for the Holy Father. Well, this was rather an obstacle. Many a one would have given up the idea of ever getting the Mater Admirabilis. Not so Father General. He recommended his petition to the artist himself, and on his side prepared for a vigorous attack. But we will let him relate the incident. After speaking of several objects of art which he has purchased in Rome he speaks of this statue in a letter home:

The second is marble, a Mater Admirabilis, which was being made for the Pope: Today at 11³/⁴ a.m. we go to a private audience: if I can prove to the Holy Father that I love very much his chosen model, etc., he may let me carry it away: I am preparing my speech.

July 2 — Yesterday, at last, I had an audience, more delightful, if possible, than any of the nine audiences I received before. The Holy Father was more of a father to me than I had ever seen him since twenty years. A few moments afterwards, the artist, one of the first sculptors in Rome went to the Vatican with his splendid Mater Admirabilis to present it to his Holiness as a token of his veneration. (I have the following little incident in writing, from the sculptor himself.)

"But, most holy Father," said the artist, "here is the card of an American Missionary who came to my studio while I was finishing this your graceful and favorite design; I told him it was for your Holiness. I was giving it the last touch; he looked at it none the less attentively. It appears, most Holy Father, it pleased him so much that he declared he must have it. Those Americans are so positive!"

I answered; "if his Holiness permits!"

"Ah! — Padre Sorin! — certainly, with pleasure. I bless it for him; let him have it."

Sorin ends his letter with, I have the pleasure to announce to you that it is to be shipped this morning for Notre Dame [August , 1873].[63]

While it was an amusing incident, it left little doubt of his penchant for realizing his goals. Joseph White, author of the Sacred Heart Parish history, recounts another example of Sorin's philosophy when a close examination revealed a foot-long crack in the old church's largest bell:

Sorin reported that "a wise head" — probably Sorin himself — "trusting more than the rest in the Blessed Queen of the place" suggested that the broken bell be replaced by another, four times, or even five times larger, positively declaring that, while few persons would feel inclined to subscribe anything for an ordinary bell, many would be delighted to contribute for the acquisition of an extraordinary one.[64]

With characteristic determination he pursued the effort and raised the funds for the bell which required four men to ring it. It arrived the summer of 1867, but turned out to be too large for the early church. It was placed a short distance away in a separate ground level belfry. While it may have been comical at the time, ten years later it was perfectly suited for the new church where it resides to this day impressing everyone who has seen it.

This uncanny ability Sorin had to triumph in the end was very like what has been attributed to an atmosphere on campus: "a certain force — an energy allowed each person to perform on a level higher than usual. It came to be called the God loop. It provided good luck when least expected."[65]

It was Father Sorin himself who said, "There are moments when a vigorous stand upsets the enemy!" The enemy to Sorin was fire, pestilence, lack of funds, and anyone who didn't want to do things his way. He also said, "You can only do good by risking it." And risk it he did, on many occasions. As Father Hope put it, "There were times when Fr. Sorin was just one jump ahead of the sheriff." Yet it does seem that many of his bold actions were the result of pushing his faith to the limit to prove to himself, and others, what unbounded faith can accomplish.

As Father Hope has said, "It is not wholly irreverent to say that Father Sorin was a tyrant. Tyrannical he was and no doubt, many were the toes stepped on. But all, in all, his energy was so great, his vision so clear, his personality so impressive, that the imposition of his will cannot be said to have been a bad thing."[66]

What he is said to have lacked in common sense, he made up for with a terrific imagination. His boundless energy emanates from words written by him and about him. It has been said that, "The world steps aside for a man who knows where he's going," Sorin certainly had that quality.

Yet he became an instrument of Providence because he was a man who just wouldn't give up on what he believed to be his mission in life. And because he felt his dream was from and for Our Lady, he was willing to go where no man had gone before in fulfilling that mission. In that respect alone — today's University of Notre Dame has proven — he was a man of destiny.

Another example of Fr. Sorin's perseverance was his appointment as Postmaster of a Post Office at Notre Dame. In his *Chronicles* he wrote: "The regular passage of the mail coach would make the college better known, and causes the public highways leading to it to be carefully maintained." [quoted in Arthur Hope, *Notre Dame 100 Years* (Notre Dame: University Press, 1948), p.74] It would also bring revenue for the college. On January 6, 1851 after a prior attempt failed, Fr. Sorin was made Postmaster of a postal station at Notre Dame. His interest in the upkeep of the roads around Notre Dame also prompted him to seek and gain an appointment as Inspector of the Public Ways.

Evidence of the site of the original Notre Dame Post Office still remains today in the hitching rings shown in these photographs. Undoubtedly, Sorin himself used these same hitching rings. They are located in a group of pine trees about 100 feet east of Sorin's statue in front of Hurley Hall.

Sorin was not alone in his mission, nor in his determination to fulfill his goals. Mother Angela — whose very presence at Notre Dame, according to Father Hope, was a "religious hijacking" by Sorin — was on her way to join another religious order when Father Sorin convinced her to join the Sisters of the Holy Cross. History records that she also had her own unique destiny to fulfill and her own characteristic way of accomplishing it.

A similar reference to Mother Angela's own strong personality is in a collection of letters at the University Archives. This unguarded forthright estimation of the human side of Mother Angela's personality is interesting in terms of the universality of human nature. It was written by a general's wife, a reliable source, who was related to Mother Angela and knew her intimately. The general's wife was writing to her husband about their daughter's forthcoming trip to Europe and Mother Angela's wish to go with her. She speaks of their daughter and her "unwillingness that she not be harassed by her presence."

She would embarrass and annoy her in many ways . . . for Mother Angela is unreasonable in her demands upon others and she is moreover totally ignorant of the duties of those not in her own sphere. . . . Please do not intimate that I have written in this way.[67]

Had some of Sorin's forceful personality rubbed off on Mother Angela?

The general's wife apparently accomplished her aim. The letter was written in 1873 the same year the General's daughter, Mother Angela and Father Sorin went separately to Europe and the Grotto of Lourdes, each with their own traveling companion. It was during this same trip, in August of 1873, that Sorin went to Rome and talked the Pope out of his Mater Admirabilis statue.

The *Scholastic* reported that another Mater Admirabilis statue was received at St. Mary's a month later on September 13, 1873. It was sent from Europe by Mother Angela during that same trip. Father Sorin's was marble and Mother Angela's a pleasing and colorful painted statue. The existence of Father Sorin's is unknown, while the one Mother Angela sent home is still located near the south window of the 4th floor hallway of Bertrand Hall.

As the stories told about Sorin have served to humanize him, it seems only fair that this one hundred and twenty-two year old slice of life be shared to humanize Mother Angela. Perhaps it is also only fair to conclude, that

Notre Dame and Saint Mary's might never have existed without two such strong autocratic personalities to found them.

Father Sorin, himself, mentioned the importance of recording a true unedited history in his own reflections recorded in his *Chronicles*:

. . . If these annals are to be considered as a truthful history they must either speak the truth or be silent, unless it be understood that they show only the fair side. But that would not be doing justice to the institute, nor even to the actions of Providence; because unless we see the obstacles and the difficulties of all kinds that have been met, it will not be possible to appreciate the triumph of grace. Moreover, those miseries contain lessons and warnings which will at least not be useless for our successors.[68]

The association of Father Sorin and Mother Angela was covered very nicely in Sister M. Georgia Costin's book, *Priceless Spirit*. "Sorin saw the great design; Angela supplied the details. He was the architect, she was the contractor."[69]

Sorin's gardens viewed from the windows of his presbytery rooms, now
the top of the present Grotto.

Chapter 4

Our Lady is on the Dome!

On April 23, 1879, eight months after Sorin's Our Lady of Lourdes Grotto was dedicated, the second Main Building was destroyed by fire. An eye witness to the atmosphere during the 1879 fire gives a firsthand account.

The force of contrast has been strikingly illustrated by two circumstances connected with the fire. One is the tall chimney of the steam-house, which seems so very tall since the college has disappeared from its front. Standing without relief among the little buildings that are left, it seems to have suddenly shot up into the blue sky. The other contrast to which we refer is the striking of the clock in the Church tower during the burning of the College. At twelve, at one, and at two the solemn strokes were sounded as usual, but with almost supernatural effect upon the ear, as if the clock of eternity were knelling the conflagration of the globe and the destruction of all things. Time marked its ceaseless course through the terrible burning, even as it had done in the hours of peace, study and prayer. We shall never forget that bell, unruffled and peaceful, as it was heard, and barely heard, amid the crackling and roaring of the flames, the falling of walls, the noise of the engine, the rushing and hissing of water and the loud shouts of men — the peaceful but appalling sound of these sweet church bells striking the hours of God's ever passing time, His quiet, all-embracing Eternity.[70]

In the concept of God's ever passing time, it is sobering, to be reading those words more than one hundred years later.

Tom Schlereth's book on the main building, *A Dome of Learning*, reports the fate of the Blessed Virgin statue atop the first dome:

The fire spread rapidly across the roof to the base of the wood and tin dome which, when its supports burned away, collapsed under the weight of Sorin's beloved statue and carried the fire into the building's interior.[71]

The 1879 *Scholastic* also reported another work of art destroyed in the fire:

Among the many precious works of art destroyed in the College Chapel by the late fire was the solid silver ostensorium, two and a half feet high, elegantly chased and embossed, which was a gift to Rev. Fr. Carrier from ex-Empress Eugenie. All that remains of this once beautiful object are a few lumps of molten metal found in the ruins.[72]

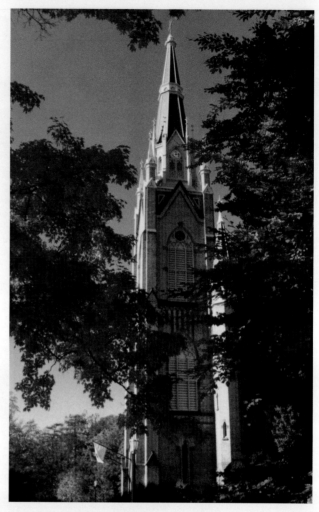

Once again, Father Hope records Sorin's characteristic spirited response to the disastrous fire: "I wouldn't care, even if we had lost everything! We will begin again! The Mother of God cannot be defeated!" As Father Hope put it, "It was like a grand pep talk between halves."[73]

Whatever the odds were, Sorin always knew he could count on Our Lady.[74]

The Rededication of the New Notre Dame

Because of delays, the rededication of the "New Notre Dame," planned for September 8, 1879, the Feast of the Nativity of the Blessed Virgin, was postponed. A solemn High Mass was celebrated on that day instead, at the beginning of the school session, less than five months after the fire. Rev. W. Corby, President of the University, addressed eloquent words of instruction and wisdom to the students.

Education without religion or moral training, is a very dangerous thing. It is like a sharp tool in the hands of an infant. The tools in themselves are good, fit for use by those who know how to handle them, but destructive to those who know not how to use them — even death dealing, at times, to the infant. So education without moral training is one of the most dangerous instruments used by the enemy of man's salvation for a greater destruction — death to the souls of men.

Every day we read of crimes, . . . not committed by the uneducated only; no, but by those who had received an education above the common, but devoid of moral training. . . . While these men's intellects were well trained, the heart and the morals were neglected. . . . It is time for the educators of the country to take this matter into consideration. The sooner they do, the sooner we may look for a nation of citizens whose lives will be an example of truth, honor, justice, and all that makes men noble. . . . It must therefore be the aim of all true educators to develop the moral as well as the mental faculties in those committed to their charge.[75]

Stories abound about the new colossal statue of the Blessed Virgin created for the new Dome. It arrived on campus in the summer of 1880. It was placed on the front porch of the newly constructed Main Building — a Lady in waiting — until the Dome was prepared to receive her statue. For three years she adorned the porch awaiting ascent to the top of her pedestal on the finished Dome.

Many local families have passed on family remembrances of ancestors who helped hoist the statue to the Dome, as many farmers of the day must have done. Records show they often joined forces in assisting their neighbor, Notre Dame, with tasks that required man and horse power. Similar stories were passed on regarding the building of the present Grotto.

One descendent of an alumnus of those days, Mary Roemer, remembers hearing a family story of how the statue of Our Lady was brought by wagon from the train station pulled by a team of six or eight white horses. "Sounds like a fairy tale, doesn't it," she said. She explained that it was just a long ago remembrance. She had no way of knowing where it came from.

It's a story that could easily have been true. The heavy statue would have been transported from the train station by wagon. Such a momentous ceremonial occasion might have warranted a team of all white horses.

No confirmation of her story has been found, but another amusing anecdote about an uncompromising Father Sorin turned up in an unpublished manuscript in the University Archives. It was written by the first Father J. W. Cavanaugh. He describes Father Sorin's vision of Our Lady atop a Golden Dome and his unrelenting efforts to accomplish it.

When the council repeatedly refused Sorin the Dome and Our Lady, Father Sorin rose and with a fine blend of dignity and indignation gathered up his breviary and his pajamas, or whatever was used for pajamas in those days, and started to St. Mary's. Over there just off the regular parlor was a small room called by the irreverent the "Puppy-hole," in which Father Sorin often retired to recite his office without distraction. Father Sorin took up his post there and remained for two weeks like Achilles skulking in his tent, declaring that never would he return to Notre Dame until he was allowed to carry out his plans for the big dome carved with a beautiful figure of Our Lady.

In desperation the members of the council decided that they had better yield. A committee was sent to St. Mary's with their hats in their hands to beg Fr. Sorin to return, assuring him he could have his dome.

There will be those, of course, who will find something less than perfect in the religious attitude of Fr. Sorin throughout this episode. It is fair enough that they should have their opinion. Others will marvel at what seems to be the uncompromising spirit, the hardheadedness, the obstinacy of a man, whose great role of a founder and builder of a college in a wilderness must have been a reasonable compromise. Whoever looks at the beautiful campus now and considers how different the whole thing would appear without the dome will hesitate to entertain either suggestion. The truth is that the dome upon the Administration Building assembles all the other buildings on the campus around it and contributes to each a dignity which, otherwise, it would not possess.[76]

Raising the Statue to the Dome

The work of raising the statue to its present position was skillfully accomplished by Mr. Alexander Staples, of standpipe fame,[77] who engineered putting it on the Dome. It took two days. The 1879, *Scholastic* published a description of the statue:

We have received a description of the proposed statue of our Lady which is to adorn the new University, and which the young lady graduates[78] *of St. Mary's Academy generously proposed themselves to contribute as their crowning gift to Notre Dame. The model of the statue is that adopted by our late Holy Father, Pope Pius IX, in 1854, on the occasion of the solemn proclamation of the dogma of the Immaculate Conception (erected by Pius IX in front of the Propaganda College in Piazza di Spagna in Rome). The material will be of highly polished bronze, sixteen feet in height, the crescent with the serpent beneath, and a starry crown above. Nine of the stars will be seen over and on either side of the head. By day the statue itself and its circle of stars will glitter in the*

sunlight, an object of beauty for miles around; and by night the nine stars will be lit with the electric light, and thus be a beacon of beauty from a still further distance. As the head will be 186 feet above the earth [sources vary on this; 197 feet seems to be the correct figure],[79] it is evident that the jets of light will be seen by night all over the neighboring city and for a great distance on the various railroads entering here.

The young ladies of St. Mary's have therefore undertaken a beautiful task, a labor of love, in thus placing our Lady's statue in mid-air, as Michael Angelo placed the faultless Grecian temple above St. Peter's, a thing of beauty to rest and shine there, a joy forever. May their labor of love be rewarded, here, with the success of the object which they have in view, and afterwards with the sweet memory of the noble deed which they have accomplished, and may our Blessed Lady look upon them with her brightest smiles when, as the shades of night come on, her beautiful statue lights up the landscape of Notre Dame and St. Mary's![80]

Marion McCandless in her book, *Family Portraits*, reports on this project which was proposed the same year the St. Mary's Alumnae Association was founded, in 1879. She then mentions the fact that this first project proposed by them was accomplished only in part by the alumnae.[81] It is not clear from surviving records if others at St. Mary's made up the difference or whether Sorin obtained the rest from other sources.

Tom Schlereth in his book, *A Dome of Learning*, states that it was "purchased largely from bequests from Mother Angela Gillespie's Holy Cross sisters, women students and alumnae of Saint Mary's Academy."[82]

Another source seems to validate Schlereth's statement:

Mother Angela sent a circular letter to the Sisters commanding, not requesting, each of them to raise twenty dollars toward the restoration of the main building at Notre Dame. Gifts poured in from friends, alumni, merchants, other educators, benefactors of all ages, places of residence, and economic levels. The Saint Mary's Academy alumnae officers began collecting funds to put a bigger statue on a bigger dome. The new building opened on time in September, not complete, but usable.[83]

In 1883, the *Scholastic* described in detail the placing of the statue on the Dome:

The great event of the past week was the placing of the colossal statue of the Blessed Virgin on the Dome of the University. . . . As announced in the Scholastic, *a short time ago, the exterior work of the Dome was finished, and everything was ready for the statue. On last Monday afternoon, the statue was lowered from the front porch and brought to the rear of the College. There it was allowed to remain until the apparatus necessary for raising it to the summit of the Dome could be prepared. Everything was ready by Wednesday noon and that afternoon, slowly but surely, the grand figure ascended to the roof of the College. On Thursday work was resumed, and at length, at five o'clock p.m., amid the ringing of bells, the statue was seen to rest firmly and securely on its grand pedestal.*

The statue is the work of the late Mr. Giovanni Meli, of Chicago, and is the largest of its kind in the United States. It stands sixteen feet in height and weights 4,400 lbs.

"The statue is on the Dome!" was the general exclamation last Thursday night. Few and simple were the words, yet they contained a wealth of meaning. They announced the accomplishment of long-cherished desires of the heart, the filling up of a void long too open at Notre Dame, the crowning act in the public expression of honor to her under whose patronage this Home of Religion and Science is placed.

Notre Dame — "Our Lady." These two short words speak volumes in explanation and praise of the motive which has led to the erection of this glorious monument to the Mother of God . . . . More than three years have glided by since Notre Dame passed through its fiery ordeal, and the time was well employed in preparing for the erection of a monument which would be, as far as loving hearts and willing hands could make it, a fitting expression of gratitude, and the most glorious of its kind in the country.

And now these desires are realized. Today this grand statue, so familiar to the visitor and student at Notre Dame, stands upon her magnificent throne, and, with extended arms, gives the assurance of the continued protection of her whom it represents.[84]

The golden dome was finished on September 26, 1883. The following month the statue of Our Lady . . . was hoisted, on a trough by block and tackle, to its throne 207 feet above the earth. One year later her crown and crescent were electrically illuminated thus making Notre Dame the first college to use such lights. Edison had discovered the incandescent globe on October 21, 1879 after

Student waving from Dome

spending two years testing over 6,000 substances and spending $100,000 in search of the proper filament. It is said that the Notre Dame statue of Our Lady became also the first airplane beacon light visible in five states.[85]

A picture of the "circle of electric lights crowning her head and the moon at her feet" appeared in the first Notre Dame yearbook, the 1906 *Dome*. A poem from the same era describes Our Lady's crown and crescent, "emblazoned in a halo of Electric Glory."

> Night comes and sets thy beacon in the skies
> A woman starry-crowned, with starry eyes,
> That watch forever with a solace meet,
> Above the glimmering moon beneath her feet.[86]

When floodlights were introduced that would adequately illuminate the statue, the crown and crescent were removed, and Our Lady was forever to be seen as she is today, aglow with light.

The Gilding of the Dome and Statue

The Dome and statue were accomplished in 1883. A year later the crown and crescent were added. Three years later, in 1886, the Dome and Statue were gilded for the first time.

Father John W. Cavanaugh's unpublished manuscript described the reception Sorin received when he announced the gilding of the Dome and the Statue:

Later, in 1886, Father Sorin decided that at last his old dream might be completely realized by the gilding of the Dome. A gift of two thousand dollars made this possible and the happiness of the founder was complete.

I remember hearing him make the announcement at commencement from the stage of Washington Hall. There were many, of course, who turned up their noses at this also. It was another extravagant bit of pious sentimentality on the part of the old man, they said. The truth is it was cheaper than paint . . . and lasts longer. To put up the scaffolding alone for one painting of the dome would cost five hundred dollars. Paint would have to be renewed every few years. As a matter of fact, the gold leaf on the dome lasts from fifteen to twenty years and it is considerably cheaper than paint would be. Thus, once more, was the dream of the aged peer justified by the rude figures of commerce.[87]

Professor James Edwards, who was on campus at the time, placed several annotations correcting and amending the pages of Timothy Howard's, *A Brief History of Notre Dame du Lac*, an early history of the campus. A note in the front of the book, signed by him, confirmed these knowledgeable additions. One penciled note opposite Howard's description of the Dome provided a piece of information not commonly known:

The dome, as is well known, is surmounted by a colossal statue of the Blessed Virgin illuminated by an electric crown and crescent. The gold for the gilding of the dome was contributed by a devout client of Our Lady.[88]

The name Professor Edwards penciled in the margin stated Mary Phalen, Mother Angela's mother, was the devout client. It was one of Mrs. Phalen's last gifts, one among many. Mother Angela Gillespie died March 4, 1887, two years after her own Church of Loretto on the campus of St. Mary's was finally realized. Her mother followed her in death six months later on December 10, 1887. Mrs. Phelan also financed Washington Hall which is still used as a music and entertainment center.

There's an interesting parallel to Fr. Sorin's dream of having a golden lady, on a golden dome, dedicated to Our Lady. An excerpt from the October 1884 issue of the *Scholastic* refers to the Statue of Liberty, then nearing its completion, destined to be placed in the New York Harbor two years later:

It may perhaps seem strange to some that we should make any attempt at enthusiasm about the erection of a simple statue. But let us consider for a moment what an enthusiasm is there not spreading throughout the United States . . . in regard to the placing of the statue of "Liberty enlightening the world" — in the New York Harbor. We grant there is a reason for it and a good one. It is because . . . the prevailing idea among the masses of our countrymen is that they realize the benefit of a free government and are willing to do anything that may give fitting expression to their sentiments. Should it then seem strange, that we here at Notre Dame, imbued . . . with Christian sentiments, and recognizing unmistakable evidences of the intervention and protection of the Mother of the world's Redeemer — should be just as enthusiastic about any outward expression of homage and gratitude towards her?[89]

The Statue of Liberty — proposed as a gift to the United States by France to commemorate its Independence — had been the dream of its designer, Frederic Auguste Bartholdi, since 1871. It was a topic of worldwide interest until it was completed eleven years later, on May 21, 1884. It was shipped to the United States in 1885 where it awaited its dedication upon the completion of its pedestal.[90] Bartholdi's efforts to create the Statue of Liberty paralleled Sorin's struggles. Sorin's own words after the sad destruction of the Main Building by fire in 1879 express that same kind of indomitable spirit that never gives up:

The fire was my fault, he concluded. I came here as a young man and founded a university which I named after the Mother of God. Now she had to burn it to the ground to show me I dreamed too small a dream. Tomorrow we will build it bigger and, when it is built, we will put a gold dome on top with a golden statue of the Mother of God so that everyone who comes this way will know to whom we owe whatever great future this place has.[91]

Perhaps Father Sorin's even bigger dream might have been spurred on by the colossal vision of another Frenchman, Frederic Auguste Bartholdi, who also wouldn't give up on his dream. It was typical of Sorin that his Lady was placed on the Dome and dedicated in September of 1883, three years earlier than Barthodi's "Lady Liberty." Its final gilding occurred on September 22, 1886, a month before the Statue of Liberty was dedicated on October 28, 1886.

In 1884 Father Sorin envisioned the completion of his dream which was finally accomplished in 1886, he died seven years later:

The exterior of the beautiful Dome of Notre Dame is now finished, thank God! and not a dollar expended on it will ever be regretted. It is the grand feature of the place — one of the chief ornaments of the West. But, beautiful as it looks, it is scarcely anything compared to what it will soon be, when covered, as originally intended, with the heavy and imperishable gilding of the purest gold which will reflect magically through the day the rays of the sun, and at night turn darkness into bright light, from the electric crown of twelve stars with which the whole figure of the Blessed Virgin is to be clothed, typifying the prophecy: And there appeared a great wonder in heaven: a woman clothed with the sun, and the moon under her feet, and on her head a crown of twelve stars (Apoc., xii, i). What a beautiful sight! — one that has never been seen in this country.[92] — *Sorin*

The *Scholastic* reported another approval: "Signor Gregori who is quite familiar with the best domes in the world is delighted with the new Dome of Notre Dame."[93] Signor Gregori was the artist who painted the interior of Sacred Heart Church. He also painted the inner Dome and the murals on the main floor of the Administration Building.

Once again, history had proven what a visionary Sorin turned out to be. As early as 1844, Sorin had envisioned his Lady on the Dome when he wrote:

When this school, Our Lady's school, grows a bit more, I shall raise her aloft so that, without asking, all men shall know why we have succeeded here. To that lovely Lady, raised high on a dome, a Golden Dome, men may look and find the answer.[94]

In the 1993 *Dome*[95] the first close-up color photograph of the statue on the Dome was published in the yearbook. The delicately modeled face, the exquisite drapery of

Our Lady's gown, the crescent moon and the serpent visible at her feet were captured on film by Bill Mowle. Such detail could only have been guessed at before from a distance. It is a beautiful statue and a most unusual photograph.

Another brief poem in the *Scholastic* celebrates her glowing image:

Silent she stands, Our Lady of the Light
Whose mercy keeps a watch upon the waters;
Over our hearts, by day or dreamy night,
May she hold sway, Fairest of Daughters.[96]

Chapter 5

The Missing Empress Eugenie Crown

Two weeks after the gilding of the dome was completed, on October 6, 1886, the *South Bend Tribune* reported a "Bold Burglary At Notre Dame." It described the theft of two crowns from the church during the time the chapels were about to be added:

An entrance was effected into the church by prying off some of the boards of the wooden partition back of the altar which was placed there temporarily while the work of extending the church was in progress. . . .

The larger crown was famous all over the country for its intricate workmanship and beauty of design. It was made in France by order of certain donors in this country, for Notre Dame, and was known as 'the Crown of the Blessed Virgin.' It was first exposed to view at the time of the raising of the statue of the Blessed Virgin on the old university building in May, 1866. At the time thousands of people formed in line and passed by the glass case in which the crown reposed, to look at it. Rich in wrought gold and silver and resplendent with jewels it was a work of art, once seen, never to be forgotten. Its exact cost was never known, but it reached several thousand dollars. The duty alone was $943 in gold, equal then to nearly $2500 in greenbacks. This crown rested under the dome of the old university building, in a glass case, in a room especially fitted for it, until the church of the Sacred Heart was built, when it was taken there and thus escaped the fire, which in 1879 caught near the dome and destroyed the old university. In the church of the Sacred Heart this crown was suspended at one side of the grand altar, over the image of the Blessed Virgin, where it was seen and admired by thousands of *people from all parts of the world, and where it hung until stolen last night by miscreants, whose impious hands destroyed its beauty forever.*

The other crown was a small one made in this country and it originally cost $100.[97]

Father Joseph Carrier, who brought the large crown from France, described it in detail in an 1866 *Ave Maria.*

Five workmen were constantly employed during three months in making the crown, and twelve for two weeks. The large crown weighs 52 pounds and contains twenty-three and a half pounds of pure silver, and one and three fourths pounds of gold. It measures twenty inches in diameter at the base, two feet four inches in the middle, and and is two feet six inches high.

The sixteen medallions at the base representing the Fifteen Mysteries of the Rosary, and the cipher of the Blessed Virgin Mary, are beautifully enameled (scenes), and cost one hundred francs each [the names of the thirty "generous and noblehearted persons," who each paid $100, are engraved on the casings of the medallions].[98]

By a quirk of fate, after the robbery, two off duty policemen saw two suspicious men about to board a train out of town. When they arrested them, the crowns squashed beneath their jackets fell to the ground completely shattered.

Although considered irreparable, the crown was eventually restored by a Chicago silversmith and reposes to this day in the Guadalupe Chapel at the Basilica of the Sacred Heart. The smaller crown was at first thought to be the Eugenie crown, but turned out to be the $100 solid silver crown.

The larger crown and the Eugenie Crown were among many gifts brought back from France by Father Joseph Carrier in 1866. The Empress Eugenie crown was described as being made "of solid gold, studded with precious stones and inlaid with pearls. It rests on the head of the statue of Mary Immaculate. It was presented by the Empress Eugenie of France in 1866."[99] It is believed it escaped being stolen because it was on a statue on a hanging pedestal in another part of the church.

Napoleon and Eugenie had given many valuable gifts to Notre Dame over a period of years (among them the solid silver ostensorium lost in the fire). It was their hope that Notre Dame would become an outpost of French culture in the new world and the gifts were to help that dream come true.

The Forgotten Crown[100]

The Empress Eugenie crown, which had escaped the burglary in 1886, was sent to the campus laundry for safekeeping while the chapels were being completed. There it supposedly reposed, hidden away and forgotten, a most unlikely yet reasonable place to conceal it, where it would be in the care of the Sisters who ran the laundry. After all, what thief would look for it there?

After an indefinite period of time it surfaced at the laundry. Mistaken as a stage prop, an imitation, it was borrowed for an altar decoration during the nocturnal devotions, then used in numerous plays on campus. As long

as there were devotions and plays, there was a use for the crown. The crown, sadly depleted over the years, was later reported to have been used as a prop in Washington Hall and local South Bend plays, but it was always returned to the attic at Holy Cross Hall for safe keeping.

As years passed and it was no longer needed it faded into deeper obscurity. It was awarded no special significance until, as the story goes, it was too late to rescue it. It remained at the Holy Cross Seminary until it was dropped and shattered after reposing on a peg in the boiler room for a number of years. The crown, stripped of its beauty and fame, reportedly was cast off during one of the housecleanings at Holy Cross.

The University found out the tragedy of the Eugenie crown some years later; the first hint came from Holland in a letter written by an employee of the University.

The incident went like this: One of the university employees happened to find some of the jewels that had fallen from the crown. He picked them up as so many pieces of glass and saved them. Later, when he happened to return to his native Holland for a vacation, the "pieces of glass" were among some of his souvenirs. Upon his return, his sister saw the jewels and thought that it would be a fine trick to show them to her fiance and make him jealous. They looked like diamonds.

Fate made the young man a jeweler's apprentice and the "pieces of glass" once more appeared as valuable diamonds. When word reached Notre Dame, it was too late. Someone remembered that the old crown had been cast aside.

In spite of a diligent effort to sift through the ashes, remains of it or its jewels were never found. A more detailed description of the story is in Chapter 12, *A Cave of Candles: The Story Behind the Notre Dame Grotto* on the Internet. An article, written by Richard Gerbracht in 1953, — "The Forgotten Crown,"[101] — recounted the story, the above incidents, and the probable fate of the missing crown:

From the ash pile it went to the dump truck, then to the lake. Thus, the crown of the Empress Eugenie, wife of Napoleon III, Emperor of France, was to become part of the most valuable ash pile in the history of Notre Dame, destined for a watery grave, its ashes reputedly dumped somewhere in St. Mary's lake.

The Completion of the Sacred Heart Lady Chapel

It took fourteen years after Father Lemonnier's death in 1874 to finish the church and the remaining chapels. During that time the original plans to dedicate the large chapel in Father Lemonnier's memory were modified. Father Sorin built his Grotto of Our Lady of Lourdes in 1878. Subsequently, an altar below the painting of the Lourdes Grotto, and a stained glass window depicting The Immaculate Conception,[102] were added to the church. The newly completed larger chapel, graced with its Madonna statue, became the Lady Chapel instead.

The next event of importance concerning the Blessed Virgin, the new church and Lourdes, was the completion of Gregori's painting of the Our Lady of Lourdes Grotto in the church. A detailed description of the large painting was printed in the *Scholastic* on September 8, 1888.

Probably the largest representation of the apparition of Our Lady of Lourdes that exists anywhere was lately finished by Signor Gregori in a Gothic angle of the church of the Sacred Heart at Notre Dame over an altar dedicated to the Immaculate Conception. It represents the fifth apparition. The Blessed Virgin stands over a cleft of the rock; the Rosary is suspended on her wrist, and she is about to make the Sign of the Cross. Bernadette kneels at her feet, gazing upward and holding a lighted taper. The stream in the foreground, the rocks and foliage are skillfully painted, and so true to nature as to deceive those entering the church at the main door. The painting is 12 feet wide below and twice as high.[103]

The Lourdes altar under the Grotto painting was later removed during one of the renovations.

Over the years, many articles written about the church identified the crown on the Madonna statue in the new Lady Chapel as the Empress Eugenie crown. It had already been missing from the church for some time.

During the month of April, 1889, eight months after the Grotto painting was completed, three brief entries described the arrival of the Madonna statue destined for the Lady Chapel. They were small, but they were evidential in proving the crown on the statue was definitely not the Eugenie Crown.

On April 6, 1889, this interesting entry appeared:

A new and artistic statue of the Madonna and child has been placed in a niche in the small tower back of the Minim's chapel in the church. Very beautiful effects are produced by the variegated colors of the windows surrounding the statue.[104]

No one among the elderly priests on campus had ever heard of the "Minim's Chapel." The chapel described above had always been referred to in the church as the Holy Angels Chapel, or more recently, the Laetare Chapel. In an 1878 *Scholastic* entry,[105] was the confirmation: "Sodality of *Holy Angels* 1st organized 1857 by Gillespie in 1875, was *changed* from Junior to *Minims Dept.*"

On April 20, 1889, another entry appeared: "The Senior Archconfraternity have purchased a handsome statue of the Blessed Virgin which will be placed in the church during the month of May when the students attend May devotions."[106]

On June 2, 1889, yet another, confirming mention: "The new pedestal for the statue, which members of the Archconfraternity recently received from France, is a real work of art."[107]

These three brief entries in the pages of the *Scholastic* verified the origin of the present Madonna statue. It was a gift of the Senior Archconfraternity, was made in France, was placed in its niche in 1889, and is still there today 104 years later.

This information put to rest false statements made in early written sources, that referred to the Crown on the statue in the Lady Chapel as the 1866 Empress Eugenie Crown. The crown on the Madonna is embossed gold. There are no jewels in it, which alone would prove it is in no way connected with the missing Empress Eugenie Crown.

During the last renovation of the church, completed in 1992, the Madonna statue was removed from the niche and repainted. Those who saw it up close have confirmed it. The crown was not separate; it was part of the statue. When it was repainted during the renovation, the crown and other gold areas on the statue were newly gold leafed.

When the statue was removed from its niche to be refurbished, several three dimensional heart-shaped gold boxes made of brass, containing prayers and petitions, were found under the pedestal. The oldest among them had seven petitions. One petition, signed by Father Sorin and dated 1876, was a heart made of paper like a small valentine with a picture of the founder. A second one, dated 1878, was from a Sister, signed M.P.B., asking for a happy death. Another, dated 1885, included prayers for someone's mother.

Duly noted, they were returned to the niche with the renovated statue, along with several new petitions, there to reside for perhaps another one hundred years. With the disparity in the dates, speculation naturally followed. Where were they before they were moved there in 1889? Could they have once been in the octagonal tower niche of Father Sorin's original 1878 Grotto?

Petitions were also found in hymnals and under the carpeting of the church near the altar when it was removed during renovation. A slip of paper with what was thought to be the names of early craftsmen who had worked on the church was also found. This is not an uncommon practice among tradesmen. Even today, masons have been known to write their names on a piece of paper and drop it, like a time capsule, into the opening of a cement block or behind a brick.

It is practically certain that at the time of the robbery in 1886 the Eugenie crown was safe. It was hidden away after the robbery to be returned later. Probably no one at the time suspected that it would take almost another three years before the chapel interiors were completed. Perhaps, when the time came to replace it, no one remembered where the crown had been hidden or what had happened to it. The statue it was on had been removed from the church three years before, so there was no reason to look for it. Thus, a new Madonna statue was ordered for the new Lady Chapel.

Since the Empress Eugenie crown has never been found, and there is no other crown like it anywhere in the church or on the campus, regrettably, "The Forgotten Crown" story seems to be the only plausible explanation for its disappearance. It has been thoroughly researched and nothing has been found to contradict it being a true story.

A similar little known incident, filed away in the same Sacred Heart Church folder in the University Archives, adds further credence to the story. This incident was reported in an article published in the 1933 *South Bend News Times*:

A six-foot hand-wrought bronze crucifix, the gift of Napoleon III of France to the University of Notre Dame was "discovered" Saturday by workmen preparing scaffolding for the renovation of the Gregori frescoes in Sacred Heart church.

Someone in the dim past, evidently confronted with the need for an altar crucifix for the apsidal chapel, entered upon the west side of the adoration chapel, and placed the crucifix behind the altar. There it stood, no one knows how many years, with only the plain top of the cross showing above the back of the altar. The exquisite design of the carved base could not be seen. No one remembers when the cross was first "missed." Its "disappearance" is paradoxical in that hundreds of people saw it during the years it was lost.[108]

The last line of the above newspaper story could have been written about the Empress Eugenie crown. Its disappearance was also paradoxical. Many people also saw it and handled it during the years it was lost. Fortunately, in the case of Napoleon's crucifix, it was more happily concluded. It is now displayed in the Quadalupe Chapel in the Basilica of the Sacred Heart.

A Living Legacy

The Empress Eugenie Crown and the six-foot bronze crucifix were among many beautiful gifts given to early Notre Dame by Napoleon III and his Empress Eugenie. However, they were all surpassed by another extraordinary gift they were not even aware they had given. It was to become a living legacy — an intangible gift — that would benefit people at Notre Dame and throughout the world. For centuries their names were destined to be linked with the Our Lady of Lourdes Grotto at Lourdes and Notre Dame:

Ultimately, Emperor Napoleon III himself intervened to have the barricades removed from the grotto of Massabielle.

Their part in the drama that unfolded at Our Lady's Grotto at Lourdes in 1858, links them forever with its mystery.

These facts were confirmed, not only in the 1875 book, *Our Lady of Lourdes*, written by Bernadette's historian, Henri Lasserre, but also in Franz Werfel's book, *The Song of Bernadette*, based on Lasserre's book 80 years later, which became a classic award winning film.

Lasserre records this episode at the Lourdes Grotto during the time it was barricaded and guarded. The Mayor of Lourdes issued a proclamation. The public was forbidden access to the Grotto. Anyone trespassing on the Grotto grounds or taking water from the Spring would be prosecuted according to law. "Illustrious personages," Lasserre relates, "sometimes transgressed the limits of the enclosure":

. . . a lady had passed the boundary a few paces behind and had gone to kneel against the barrier of boarding

which closed the Grotto. From between the opening of the palisade she was watching the miraculous Spring gushing forth and was praying. What was she demanding of God? Was her soul turning itself towards the present or the future? Was she praying for herself, or for others who were dear to her and with whose destiny she was charged? Was she imploring the blessings' and protection of Heaven for an individual or a family? No matter.

This woman engaged in prayer had not escaped the vigilant eyes which represented the policy of the Prefect, the Magistracy and the Police.

The Argus . . . rushed towards the kneeling woman. "Madame," said he, "nobody is permitted to pray here. You are taken in the very act; you will have to answer for this before the Fuge de Paix, presiding over the Correctional Tribunal, and without appeal. Your name?"

"Willingly," said the lady, "I am the wife of Admiral Bruat, and Governess of His Highness, the Prince Imperial." . . .

No one in the world had a higher respect for the social hierarchy and established authorities than the formidable Jacomet. He dropped his accusation.

Lasserre does not pursue this interesting factual account further. Werfel, however, eighty years later, proposes — perhaps by Lasserre's account or further research — that Madame Bruat by her very admission that she was the Governess of the Imperial Prince, may have been there at the bidding of her Mistress the Empress Eugenie in behalf of the two-year-old Crown Prince, only child of Napoleon III and Empress Eugenie, who might have been ill. And that perhaps the very devout Empress Eugenie's influence may have had a great deal to do with the Emperor's change of heart from stoic disinterest to immediate action. A decree was dispatched "directing that for the future the people should be allowed perfect freedom of action."

Lasserre describes the jubilation:

The town of Lourdes was in a great state of emotion. During the afternoon, the crowd kept going to and fro on the road leading to the Grotto. The faithful, in countless throngs knelt devoutly before the Rocks of Massabielle. They sang canticle, and recited the litanies of the Virgin. Virgo potens, ora pro nobis. They quenched their thirst at the Spring. The believers were free, God had achieved a victory.[109]

Napoleon III and his Empress Eugenie, without knowing it, had given their first gift, an everlasting one, to the University of Notre Dame — the Our Lady of Lourdes Grotto.

Our Lady had inspired a peasant girl, and moved an Emperor and his Empress — worlds apart from one another — to make a difference in the lives of millions of people. Without their actions, the Grotto at Notre Dame would not have existed, because there would have been no Our Lady of Lourdes Grotto in France to inspire it.

Bernadette's experience is expressed in a beautiful hymn at the end of an undated 19th century book about Lourdes. The beginning seven verses and its ending follow:

A Hymn at Lourdes

The hour had come for evening prayer;
The Angelus chimed on the chilling air.

Ave.

A hidden Angel walked and met
The unwitting steps of Bernadette.

Ave.

Across the mountain stream she hied.
A wind in the valley rose and died.

Ave.

Sudden it shook her, sudden it fell.
She saw the Virgin on Massabielle.

Ave.

She saw the tender and gentle face
Crowned with light that filled the place.

Ave.

It was the Mother of God who smiled
Like her own mother on the child.

Ave.

Clad in white was the Lady chaste,
A ribbon of Heaven around her waist.

Ave.

The sick, the mourner, the forgiven
Come to Lourdes on their way to Heaven.

— Unknown[110]

Bernadette was 35 years old when she died. In the movie, *Song of Bernadette*, her faithful parish priest speaks to her at her bedside:

You are now in Heaven and on earth, Oh Bernadette.
Heaven chose you . . .
Now there's nothing you can do except choose Heaven.

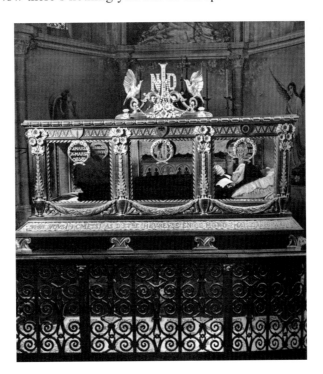

Alain Woodrow concludes an impressive article in the 1994 *Catholic Digest* entitled, "LOURDES, More Popular Than Ever," with this moving tribute:

Bernadette was not theologically sophisticated. But she nevertheless grasped the essential message of the Gospel. "See how simple it is," she said on her deathbed at Easter, 1879. "All you need is love." That is the true miracle of Lourdes.[111]

Sister Lourdes and Sister Bernadette at Notre Dame

Two Sisters of the Holy Cross, Sister Lourdes and Sister Bernadette, spent most of their religious lives on the Notre Dame campus. For 59 years Sister Bernadette baked the altar breads and cut them for the chapels. Sister Lourdes worked in the kitchen at Carroll Hall for 62 years. Their names and the dedicated lives they led marked them to be included in the story behind the Grotto.

Sister Lourdes arrived at Notre Dame in 1874, the same year the first Grotto was built in Lourdes Hall. A description of her life and death on campus could have been written about Saint Bernadette, who lived the same very simple life of service. She spent most of her life going between old Carroll Hall in the Main Building and the convent chapel, pictured below, a distance of less than 100 feet.

Her devotion to Notre Dame was remembered in the 1936 *Notre Dame Alumnus*: "Sister Lourdes dies at 85."

Death on January 12 touched lightly a noble soul, revered in the memory of thousands of Notre Dame men the world over — Sister Lourdes, C.S.C., 85 years old, the "coffee urn Sister" of the old kitchen. Her story is a simple one. . . . She had spent her entire religious life at Notre Dame. In that time she left the campus only two or three times. She set herself to do one thing humbly and generously — to please God in every thought and word and act. She was assigned to try to please God in the Notre Dame kitchen. Thousands of Notre Dame men, priests, brothers, professors and students — in every part of the world rise up and call her blessed. Sweetness and kindness itself, she knew only two places in her long life, one was the kitchen near Carroll Hall where her motherly heart and lovely smile dispensed buns and soup and a "handout" to countless minims and juniors and seniors and the other was the convent chapel.

She did only one thing; she pleased God and Him alone. Only the immortal Father John W. Cavanaugh, who preceded her to Heaven could adequately describe this valiant Notre Dame woman:

To the priests who attended her in her last illness, it seems more fitting to ask the students to pray to her than for her. For 72 hours she lay dying and conscious till the very last. She was just pleasing God. Her only words were ones of thanks for His blessings. She did not have the shadow of even the least worry. If God wanted to take her in 11 seconds, all right; if He wanted her to linger on for 11 years more, all right. She died in Christ's peace with a smiling good-bye to Notre Dame.

May her powerful prayers [and those at the Grotto, her namesake] help Notre Dame and the sons of Notre Dame do the one thing necessary — to please God in every thing.[112]

Carroll Hall in the west wing of the 1879 Main Building was named after Charles Carroll (1737-1815), the only Catholic and the last surviving signer of the Declaration of Independence. His cousin, Bishop John Carroll (1735-1815), the first Roman Catholic bishop in the United States, ordained Rev. Stephen Theodore Badin, the first priest ordained in the United States. It was Fr. Badin who organized the Mission and Indian Orphanage at Ste. Marie des Lacs — the future home of Notre Dame.

Sorin had a great admiration for America and its patriots and he honored them by naming halls on campus after them. Brownson and Carroll Halls, housed in the new Main Building, date back to the huge fire. For years the students of the university lived the common life of the dormitory — dressing on the first floor, studying on the second and sleeping on the third.

In 1943, during the war years, Carroll Hall in the west wing and Brownson Hall in the east wing of the Main Building were vacated. When the Holy Cross Sisters who lived at Notre Dame went back to St. Mary's in 1958, Fr. Hesburgh carried on Sorin's tradition by renaming the building that had served as their convent Brownson Hall.

Later across St. Mary's Lake, Dujarie Institute, built as a Brothers' house of studies in 1906, was vacated by the Brothers when they established Holy Cross College. Its new name, Carroll Hall, was borrowed from old Carroll Hall in the Main Building. It became an undergraduate dorm in 1977 where, it was said, "its isolation from other campus dorms promoted camaraderie between students . . . and a real family atmosphere."

And so, old Carroll Hall — the domain of Sister Lourdes, the "coffee urn Sister" — still lives on in memory across St. Mary's Lake near Redbud Island. It is the focal point of this peaceful scene taken from the lakeside benches directly across the road from the path leading to the Grotto.

Sister Bernadette and Sister Lourdes were not alone in their devotion to their duties at Notre Dame. An account of the work of the Sisters at Notre Dame under the direction of Mother Ascension is mind boggling:

Mother Ascension was gifted with exceptional powers for organization. During her administration the convent at Notre Dame presented the efficiency and productiveness of a small factory. The amount of work accomplished is inconceivable. The Sisters did the baking and cooking for the whole institution. They set type, read proof, folded and sewed by hand the Ave Maria and the Notre Dame Scholastic. They cared for the poultry, milked the cows, and made butter and cheese. They tailored the suits, cassocks, and habits. They laundered and mended the clothing. They wove the table linen, manufactured mattresses and window shades, knit socks and underwear, made the vestments and baked altar bread for Notre Dame and the nearby missions.

Fr. Sorin's will was the will of God to her, and often she followed it at the cost of great personal sacrifice.

At her funeral, Father Hudson's eulogy captured the essence of Mother Ascension's Christian dedication:

All Christians direct their course to the same Divine End, yet each soul approaches God by its own uncharted path. To attempt to follow Mother Mary of the Ascension on her quest of God is to be lost in labyrinthine ways. Only of this can one feel confident, that at last, after many wanderings, she reached her heart's desire. . . . to the end she was devoted heart and soul to the interests of Notre Dame.[113]

In a pamphlet honoring the Sisters of the Holy Cross at Notre Dame, written at the time the convent was closed in 1958, more evidence of the Sisters devotion was cited:

Once, many years ago, when Father Matt Walsh was president, he was determined to show the Sisters that their services were highly appreciated. He approached their Superior and made known his desire to do something for the Sisters. What would they like? What could he do to show them that the priests were grateful for the part they were playing in Notre Dame's welfare?

The superior demurred, and said she would ask around among the Sisters for their opinion. When Father Walsh went back to find out their wishes, the superior said to him: "Father, most of our nuns never get outside very much. Hardly any of them have ever seen Lake Michigan. We thought a little outing up to the Lake might be a happy diversion. But we don't want to cause any . . . ."

Father Walsh told her that was just fine and they would arrange it to suit their convenience.

So one summer day, as many of the nuns as could be spared got into automobiles, some of them for the first time, and were driven off to the blue waters and refreshing breeze of Lake Michigan. Father Walsh, seeing how delighted they were, could only exclaim "What a very little thing they ask for all their months and years of service!"[114]

More than one priest has mentioned that Notre Dame would not have been here without the dedication and devotion of the Sisters of the Holy Cross at Notre Dame.

How appropriate that Notre Dame was blessed with a Sister Bernadette and a Sister Lourdes to grace the Grotto with their presence.

Chapter 6

SECLUDED SPOT WHEREIN THE VERY AIR, WHISPERS AMONG THE TREES A VESPER PRAYER.

Planning Notre Dame's 1896 Lourdes Grotto

On October 31, 1893, All Hallows' Eve, "eve of all the holy ones' day," in the wake of declining health, Very Rev. Edward Sorin, C.S.C., founding father of the University of Notre Dame, took his last breath on earth.

Mother Ascension, who was devoted heart and soul to the interests of Father Sorin and Notre Dame, was with him. So was Father John W. Cavanaugh, who describes his last moments:

I remember seeing Father Sorin as he lay dying in his own bedroom attached to his suite on the first floor of the Presbytery. He was breathing heavily. His cheeks glowing with each recurring breath. There was little change in his aspect except that his eyes moved furtively about the room up and down and towards the side almost constantly. At the same time, I noticed that very frequently, even in his unconscious condition his gaze erected for a moment on the pretty little statue of the Blessed Virgin which had been set upon a small table at the foot of his bed. Those in the room were the venerable Mother Ascension, who had been such a true friend and helper to Sorin, Brother Columba, his faithful nurse during the months and years even of his illness, a little novice who was there to be useful in whatever way she could, and Father Zahm who held Father Sorin, literally in his arms, as he breathed his last.[115]

The University prepared for his funeral on All Saints' Day. He was buried on All Souls' Day. In his *Chronicles*, Sorin had noted with wonder the significance of his departure from France to "this new world" on the Feast Day

of Our Lady of Snows in 1841. He would have
been equally pleased that he departed from this
life under similar significant circumstances.

In *Notre Dame One Hundred Years*, the
author, Father Hope describes his funeral:

*Archbishop Elder of Cincinnati preached the
sermon. His words were a great comfort. He
very likely exaggerated a bit when he said he
did not "think that in all our country, nor in
any single country, there is a place where one
single man has transformed a savage wilderness into such a city of splendor and culture as
this University of Notre Dame." He found a
vibrant response in the hearts of his listeners.
He made the most of the fact, also, that Father
Sorin's death had occurred on the last day of
October, a touching symbol, he said, of Father
Sorin's two great devotions — his confidence in the Blessed
Mother to whom October is dedicated, and to the Poor
Souls, for it was the eve of November that he had died.*

*. . . when all was ready the coffin was lowered into the grave.
Only the autumn leaves, brown and rustling, whispered in
the silence. He would have been eighty, they said, had he
lived until spring. He was so great a man that no one, on that
occasion, cared to think of his shortcomings.*[116]

Timothy Howard speaks of the Sorin he knew in his later
years:

*The richest of all the gifts received by Fr. Sorin on this
solemn Jubilee feast [1888] is that which Fr. Sorin has himself given to religion — his own life. And this gift, like the
grain of mustard, has grown, flourished, and sent forth leaf,
bud, blossom, and fruit, until Notre Dame today is among
the fairest of all the beautiful gardens planted in the wilderness of America.*

*The snows were now transferred to his noble brow, to his
flowing beard, both worthy to adorn a prophet's head. Only
the dark eye of genius, only the strong mental grasp, the
immortal youthful hope and the childlike faith, marked him
as the same courageous and far-seeing priest that had planted
the cross in the wilderness, and beside the cross built up this
dwelling place of religion, art and science.*[117]

It would not be an exaggeration to conclude, that Notre
Dame might not exist today without the distinctive personality

and character of its founder and his unwavering faith in Mary. To the end, Father Sorin's whole being was focused on the Blessed Virgin. Notre Dame du Lac was everything to him because Our Lady — the Mother of Goodness — was everything to him. He was a man with a mission — the keeper of the flame of her faith.

When Father Sorin died, that flame was passed on to Rev. William Corby, former Chaplain of the Irish Brigade during the Civil War. A statue depicting him giving general absolution to soldiers going into battle at Gettysburg stands in front of Corby Hall on campus. A soldier after the war told his wife, "he felt as strong as a lion after that and felt no fear although his comrade was shot down beside him."[118]

Father Corby accomplished what Father Sorin wasn't able to achieve, a more exact replica of the Grotto of Lourdes, a place of prayer and meditation for all who wander, by accident or design, into her presence on the Dome and at The Grotto.

The influence of Father Sorin's penchant for doing everything bigger and better has not been wasted on his successors. Each in his own way has carried on that tradition. Sorin was never one to do anything half way. He was always topping himself in honoring Our Lady. First the small bell was replaced with a huge one, the organ with a much finer one, the first church and main buildings with bigger and better ones, and the Dome and its statue of Our Lady, with even larger versions.

How pleased he would have been to know that Father William Corby was about to carry on that tradition in building a bigger and better Grotto at Notre Dame, one that has so surpassed Sorin's that his has been literally forgotten. Nonetheless, Father Sorin was as responsible for the Grotto being there as if he had been on the scene, as he surely must have been, in spirit.

Father Corby's Trip to Lourdes

In 1895 the University was fifty-three years old. Father Sorin had been gone two years.

Father William Corby, provincial at the time, made a trip to Europe. He visited the Grotto of Our Lady of Lourdes with a desired request. One year later, in the spring of 1896, the *Annals of Lourdes* magazine detailed the outcome of that trip — the inspiration to build a larger more exact replica of the Lourdes Grotto at Notre Dame.

The *Annals* chronicled events associated with Lourdes, France. Volume 1 was published at Notre Dame in 1885. Volume 72, the last one published, was printed in 1949. The *Annals* printed letters regarding cures effected with the use of Lourdes water, here and abroad, as well as articles pertaining to 19th century piety and pilgrimages. It also included the announcement of plans to build the 1896 Notre Dame Grotto:

Grotto of Lourdes at Home of The "Ave Maria"

For many years it has been the cherished desire of the best and most devoted clients of Our Heavenly Queen to see erected a Grotto of Lourdes at Notre Dame. . . . Notre Dame the Home of the Ave Maria, Notre Dame the home of Mary to whom all the grounds are dedicated, to whom all the buildings are dedicated, to whom is given all the credit of the work done here for the past fifty years. Mary is sole superior at Notre Dame and for a thousand other reasons this is the most suitable place in the new world for a real Grotto of Lourdes, and a place of pilgrimages . . . . Many go all the way to France to visit the grotto and they do well; but many can not go and the next best thing for these is to visit the grotto reproduced at Notre Dame. . . . [119]

Mary and the School Colors

Another aspect of Notre Dame's dedication to the Lady in Blue is mentioned in an article written by Lelia P. Roby in 1891:

It is interesting to know that the college colors are yellow and blue; in heraldry, yellow is light and blue is truth. [120]

The school colors for both campuses honor Mary. Saint Mary's colors are the traditional ones associated with Our Lady — sky blue and white. The archives on both campuses reported that very little was known about their meaning. Their original symbolism was apparently lost in history along with this early 1890s reference to the school colors.

The following information regarding the school colors chosen to represent Notre Dame and Saint Mary's shows that all the attributes listed with these colors are also associated with Mary:

BLUE Truth; the Intellect; revelation; wisdom; loyalty; fidelity; constancy; chastity, chaste affections; spotless reputation; magnanimity; prudence; piety; peace; contemplation; coolness. . . . Christian: Heaven; heavenly truth; eternity; faith; fidelity; the colour of the Virgin Mary as Queen of Heaven.

GOLD — The sun; divine power; the splendour of enlightenment; immortality. . . .

WHITE . . . White is associated with both life and love, death and burial. In marriage it symbolizes death to the old life and birth to the new, while in death it represents birth into the new life beyond. . . . The purified soul; joy; purity; virginity, innocence; the holy life; light; integrity.

YELLOW Christian: As golden sacredness; divinity; revealed truth; 'the robe of glory'; used for feasts of Confessors.[121]

Notre Dame's Blue and Yellow, and St. Mary's Blue and White are emblematic of everything Our Lady represents.

Sometime, undoubtedly after the Dome and Statue were gilded, Notre Dame's colors, Blue and Yellow, became Blue and Gold. The first evidence of this appeared in an account of a pilgrimage to the Grotto in 1896. It describes the badges that were worn: "The badge was a circle with a picture of the Grotto, suspended from a blue and gold ribbon hanging from a gilt bar."

It is interesting to note that St. Edward's University in Austin, Texas, was also founded by the Holy Cross order. It was established while Sorin was still alive and founded by him. It also explains why St. Edward's Day was always a special celebration at Notre Dame during Father Sorin's lifetime.

This item of special interest about the school colors for both universities appeared under the heading, "St. Edward's, King and Confessor," in a 1965 copy of *The Tower* yearbook:

We recognize Saint Edward, King and Confessor, during the celebration of the 900th anniversary of the foundation of Westminster Abbey by our patron saint on Holy Innocents' Day, 1065. Father Edward Sorin, founder of Notre Dame and St. Edward's Universities, held King Edward as his patron saint. Blue and Gold, the royal colors of the king, are the colors held dear by the two educational institutions. The death of Saint Edward is commemorated on October 13, his feast day. This day has been celebrated at Saint Edward's University since the founding of our university in 1881, Austin, Texas.

A 1995 newspaper article also illustrates how devotion to Mary inspired one person to bless the lives of others:

The estate of Mary Frances McNamara gave $1.2 million to establish the McNamara Scholarship Fund in the Notre Dame Law School. A Chicago Public Schools teacher who died last year at age 99, McNamara wrote in her last will and testament, "Through my lifelong devotion to Mary Our Mother, I have been blessed with a long productive and happy life. . . . In thanksgiving, I bequeath all of the rest, residue and remainder of my estate . . . to her university, the University of Notre Dame du Lac . . . for the purpose of establishing more funded scholarships in the Law School."[122]

Father Corby's Promise

Excerpts from the June Annals, described Father Corby's promise to build a Grotto at Notre Dame:

Grotto of Lourdes at Notre Dame, Indiana

. . . About a year and a half ago our Provincial, Father Corby, desired a great favor for the benefit of his Community in the United States. He started at once for Europe, and after attending to some important business in Rome, directed his steps to Our Lady of Lourdes, France, where he celebrated Holy Mass, said some fervent prayers, and then placed his desired request in the blessed hands of Our Lady of Lourdes. Then and there he promised, with God's help and the help of friends of Mary, to build at Notre Dame a Grotto in honor of the Immaculate Conception, if Mary would grant him his request. On the first day of May, 1895, — Mary's own Month — he was informed by cable that his request was granted. This convinced him that the favor was obtained by the Immaculate Lady of Lourdes. During the whole year after, he had in mind the promise he had made to the Blessed Virgin, but a combination of circumstances prevented him from fulfilling his promise. He resolved, however, to begin the work this Spring, and late in April, 1896, he wrote a friend in the East to help him build the Grotto. Strange to say, this friend responded promptly with a handsome donation, and it came on the Eve of the first day of May, just as the exercises of the Month of May were about to commence. This he looked on as an additional proof of Mary's gracious and maternal kindness. Moreover, it seemed to be a sanction on her part of all that had been done. First, the spiritual favor was announced as granted on the first of May; and second, the first generous donation for the building of the Grotto came on the first of May. This is to say then on her part, "You asked a favor of me and I granted it. Now, I will help you to fulfill your promise, to build me a Grotto, and I send you on the first of May, — my own month — money to enable you to begin at once." Mary, evidently, from what we have experienced, wants a Grotto at Notre Dame. This we see from the simple facts mentioned above. When in France, at Lourdes, Father Corby was presented, by the Superior of Lourdes, a model of the Grotto made of metal to build by. He also brought with him the exact dimensions of the Grotto at Lourdes, and he intends to reproduce at Notre Dame, a facsimile, the exact size of the original. . . . The work on the foundation of the Grotto has commenced, and we hope to see it finished by the 15th of August next — feast of the Assumption.[123]

The friend who responded to Father Wm. Corby's appeal for help in financing the Grotto was Rev. Thomas Carroll. His letter to Father Corby, on April 28, 1896, is preserved in Father Wm. Corby's correspondence in the archives of the Holy Cross Order at the Indiana Province Archives Center. It confirmed that Father Carroll paid all the Grotto costs, about $2,500. Carroll left this proviso to Father Corby in that letter:

. . . provided you on your part, carry out all that you promise. As you say, I may end my days at Notre Dame under the shadow of the grotto. Favor I wish inscribed on the marble slab, that the blessed Mary, Our Lady of Lourdes may obtain for me the Grace of a happy death.

Father Wm. Corby acknowledged Father Carroll's generous gift with these prophetic words of appreciation:

. . . You will have made many good investments; but likely this [is] the best you ever made. With the prayers of the community and the maternal care of Mary, you, I hope will be richly rewarded in time and in eternity.[124]

Although Rev. Thomas Carroll's marble donor plaque is weathered and worn now, those words are still discernible on it. An 1896 article written after the Grotto was completed tells more about the man who financed it.

Rev. Thomas Carroll of Oil City, Pa., was a student here in 1855. He was ordained in 1859. His name, to those at Notre Dame who have never met him, has come before him, for it is inseparably linked with the history of our beautiful "Grotto of Lourdes," which his beneficence made possible.

Father Carroll has been an indefatigable builder. To him is due the honor of erecting one of the 1st Catholic churches and presbyteries ever reared in South Bend — old St. Patrick's. To this man's generosity Notre Dame owes one of her most beautiful, most faith-inspiring scenes, a shrine to which not only we at Notre Dame, but others from outside, carry burdens and go away relieved.[125]

When the site for the new Grotto was chosen in 1896, it had already been hallowed by memories:

Just behind the presbytery is a little wooded dell which has always been regarded as one of the charming spots at Notre Dame. For years the pilgrims from Kalamazoo and Jackson have chosen it as a resting place after their long journey; it has been a favorite walk with visitors at all times; and during the spring and autumn those who live at Notre Dame seek it instinctively for its coolness and attractiveness. It is where the Grotto has been built.[126]

A good many families in town were related, in one way or another, to one common ancestor — Louis Hickey — who was also linked to Notre Dame. His obituary in the *Scholastic* carried this mention of his many years of service to Notre Dame:

He was an intimate friend of Father Sorin and his life was closely connected with the University. He cut the first road from Notre Dame to South Bend and spent 40 active years in building Sacred Heart Church and other University buildings. He helped place the big bell in the church tower and his name is inscribed on it. On account of Mr. Hickey's close friendship with the founder of the order and out of respect for a life well spent the huge bell was tolled Tuesday morning."[127]

The huge bell is engraved with the names of all those who contributed to its cost, many of them local residents. Louis Hickey also donated a stained-glass window in the Church.

Thomas Hickey II, a descendant of Louis Hickey, shared more information about the Hickey family, the townspeople, and their connection with Notre Dame. He laughed and said it was an old family saying that "if you stood on a corner long enough you'd meet someone related to a Hickey." It is a saying that could also be applied to Notre Dame. Stand on a street corner long enough and you would meet someone associated with Notre Dame. The Hickey family is still closely affiliated with Notre Dame more than one hundred and fifty years later.

The search for more information about the building of the Grotto was made easier by a chance encounter with a local resident, Mary Kintz. She shared the history of her husband's ancestor, Peter Kintz II, and of the land they owned within a mile of the University of Notre Dame.

Her husband, Elmer Kintz '27, another Notre Dame Alumni, watched Notre Dame grow — right from the bottom to its very tops — since 1902. He was born across the street where his folks lived for 50 years. His father learned carpentry working on the Campus and he studied architecture when he enrolled at Notre Dame. He was general superintendent and "the key man" in the construction of the mammoth Athletic and Convocation Center. He "showed visitors around like a proud papa" and told how "you could put Stepan Center in the middle of the track in 'the spare' arena." The story goes that he also saved the crumbs from the workers lunch sacks and spread them out for the pigeons and a duck who were wintering in the upper girders. That was one way Elmer Kintz watched out for the transients who called the A & C Center their home-away-from-home. Elmer's two sons were also alumni of Notre Dame.[128]

In the first page of the Kintz genealogy was this interesting information, "Peter Kintz II, took rocks from their farm and *built* the Notre Dame Grotto." Her husband's grandfather was a farmer and his sons were carpenters.

In those days area farmers were skilled at carpentry and stone masonry in building barns and stone foundations. Mary Kintz said it was a common practice to pitch in when something special was going on at the campus. According to family legend, they had also taken their horses to Notre Dame to help hoist the statue to the Dome of the new Main Building after the fire.

Genealogy records by their very nature are often incomplete, and information passed on, even among family members, can sometimes be recorded inaccurately. Had they actually built the Grotto or had they helped build it? Mary Kintz agreed that it could have been, "helped build" rather than "built."

Proving that statement would be very important in reconstructing the events of the summer of 1896 when the Grotto was completed.

Chapter 7

People and Events Associated with the Grotto

One item of particular interest on file at the Indiana Province Archives Center was a December, 1953 letter of correction,[129] written by Father Joseph Maguire to Father Thomas T. McAvoy, the University Archivist at the time. It disputed a number of commonly held beliefs about the Grotto's history and became a benchmark for all the research that followed.

Father Maguire was ordained in Sacred Heart Church in December of 1896, the year the Grotto was built. He was one of the few people alive in 1953 who had known Father Sorin. In the first part of his letter to Father McAvoy he states :

My dear Father McAvoy:

After reading the account of the Grotto as printed in the recent publicity sheet, I felt I should write a word or two for your files correcting the mistakes and that you could have the correction for future use. I did send, some time ago, an account to the Provincial who said he would add it to the files but perhaps no one thought of looking there for the information. So here is the story: Father Sorin may have expressed a wish for a grotto and he may have made one somewhere on the grounds but I never saw it or heard of it. If he did construct one, he probably built it on the grounds of the Sisters.

The first effort to build a grotto was made by Father William Corby in 1896 when he was Provincial. Father Sorin died in 1893. Father Carroll of Oil City, Penn., supplied not only part of the money but all of it — so I was told — as an expression of his devotion to Our Blessed Mother. . . .

It soon became evident that very little was known about the Grotto as it approached its one hundred anniversary. Father Maguire had written his letter to correct these false impressions, but it must not have gotten beyond the archives to correct future interpretations of people who weren't around at the time. Most people still believe the present Grotto was built by Sorin.

Father Maguire's letter, although it was not completely accurate, touched on previous unknown aspects of the building of the Grotto which assisted in the research of its actual construction.

Father Maguire's letter goes on to say this about the site of the present Grotto:

The spot chosen was not a "beautiful dell" but an old midden where everything from old shoes and tin cans or what have you were thrown — just a dump heap. When it was decided to build the grotto there old Brother Phillip had his crew clean up the rubbish before the work was begun. The boulders were gathered from our farm and the others surrounding it.

The "little wooded dell" reference appeared to be a common description of the area behind the church from the early 1870s until 1896. This would have been eight years before Sorin built his 1878 shrine-like Grotto directly behind the church. During those times pilgrimages involving as many as 1200 people were made to the numerous shrines in the area of the Portiuncula Chapel, the last stop being the Sacred Heart Church.

Seventeen years before the present Grotto was built, this item appeared in the June, 1879 issue of the *Scholastic*. It was two months after the disastrous fire that destroyed the Main Building. It explains the paradox:

The rubbish of the burned buildings after the fire was taken to fill the low ground west of the church and presbytery and the charcoal was put in barrels while the loose mortar was gathered and spread on the roads.[130]

The *Scholastic* also speaks of the "much admired artificially trimmed cedar trees which were scorched on one side that were bound to go" and how "the familiar cut forms look lonely enough turned upside down with *other rubbish near the lake.*"

Father Maguire had been right about the rubbish though he did not know its origin or that it had been buried under the construction site of the new Grotto.

With this key information, it was evident where all the curious items Father Maguire mentioned in his letter had come from, the rubbish from: the 1879 fire in the Main Building. Probably everything imaginable was dumped behind the presbytery, then dirt fill was piled on top of that before the wooded area was re-landcaped. When the cave was carved out of the slope of this refurbished area seventeen years later, to build the second Grotto, the rubbish was unearthed. The spot chosen by Corby to erect the new Grotto was described as a "beautiful wooded dell." Conversely, it also turned out to be "just a dump heap" like the site of the Lourdes Grotto itself that was said to be a dumping place and repository for all manner of refuse.

On the left side of the path north of the Grotto, along the road from the Main Building, is what appears to be a rock outcropping from the earth. The partial words, "thday Gift," are carved on the portion visible above the ground. Could it have been part of some kind of statuary, possibly a *birthday gift* to Father Sorin, that was thrown out a window during the fire and broken? Since it is apart from the main cavern of the Grotto, it may have been in a dumping area left undisturbed by the building of the new Grotto.

At the top of the steps, along the left side of the path from the Grotto leading to the Church, is another rough hunk of what appears to be white marble. It has a curious symbol carved on it . It could also have been part of something else, or was put to use for practice carving.

An excerpt from another 1896 *Scholastic* article entitled, "Where Peace Is," describes the area designated for the new Grotto:

This was Father Sorin's garden, created for him by the hands of his children in Christ. Once upon a time, . . . the ground sloped down from the west wall of the church to the water's edge, thirty yards distant; and after the garden was planned, it took many tons of earth to build the broad terrace. But it was all "for Father General," and the work grew apace. Rose bushes sprang up, and flowers of all sorts. Then came the great fire and the plot was suddenly widened. The lake was driven backward.

Much fill must have gone on top of the rubbish from the fire as the grounds around Father Sorin's garden were landscaped and improved. Seventeen years went by, then in the spring of 1896:

The workmen came with picks and shovels, a month or two ago, to chop in the garden's lower edge a niche for the new grotto of Lourdes . . .[131]

More Pieces in the Puzzle

With Father Maguire's letter as a guide, more pieces in the puzzle of the story behind the Grotto began to fit into place. A picture of the times and the people involved when the 1896 Grotto was erected, began to take shape.

Financial entries in an 1896 ledger[132] at the University Archives listed the expenses for the present Grotto. The first entry appeared on June 6, 1896: Item No. 1113, $500 "pd. on contr." to Gill the contractor. Further on was another $500 entry with the names McCoy and Gill etc. The existence of a John Gill, masonry contractor, was verified in the 1896 City Directory.

So Peter Kintz and his sons had not actually built the Grotto. Instead, they must have "helped build it" upon delivering their stone to the Grotto. An entry in the same ledger listed "Milk and Meat" sold to the campus by the Kintz family near the time the Grotto was being built. This item confirmed their close ties to Notre Dame.

Researching this family's history and their relationship to the campus added the names of more people and events associated with the building of the Grotto. It also involved more and more unexplored areas — plat books, census records, old 1896 newspapers, and records of deeds in the recorder's office at the County-City Building.

These records proved invaluable in "fleshing out" the history of the University and the farm families surrounding it in the last quarter of the 19th century. They supplied more evidence of the interaction between townspeople and Notre Dame and St. Mary's from earliest times.

While browsing through those old records this pensive poem spoke from the pages of an old Scholastic, like a voice from those bygone days. It was written one hundred and twenty-three years ago:

A Hundred Years to Come

Who'll press for gold this crowded street
A hundred years to come?
Who'll tread your church with willing feet
A hundred years to come?

Pale, trembling Age, a fiery Youth,
And Childhood, with his brow of truth;
Of rich and poor, on land and sea,
Where will the countless millions be
A hundred years to come?
We all within our graves shall sleep
A hundred years to come;
No living soul for us will weep
A hundred years to come:
But other men our land will till,
And others then our streets will fill,
And others' words will sing as gay,
And bright the sunshine as to-day,
A hundred years from now!

— By Coz[133]

It is interesting to find the "Who" in Coz's poem embodied in this generation one hundred years after the 1896 Grotto was built.

More Notre Dame connections began to appear in digging more deeply into the Kintz family heritage. Cecelia Kintz, a daughter of Peter Kintz II, was the mother of Carmelita Roemer who was the mother of Mary Roemer and James A. Roemer, the present Director of Community Relations at the University of Notre Dame, and the grandmother of Congressman Tim Roemer. All are alumni of Notre Dame along with many others in their family. James Roemer said the story of his ancestor, Peter Kintz II, helping to build the Grotto had been passed down on his side of the family as well. It was Mary Roemer who recalled the story of the statue being delivered from the train station by a team of white horses.

Sister Cecile Marie Luther, former principal of St. Mary's Academy, and Sister Helen Therese Matras, Holy Cross Sisters at St. Mary's Convent, are both descended from this same Peter Kintz family and both told the same story. Sister Cecile Marie recalled the many times she had gone to the Grotto and said the same prayer: "Dear Lord up above, do you remember when my Grandfather Peter Kintz brought huge big boulders from his farm to build this Grotto so that Our Lady could be honored on this spot? Blessed Mother be sure to bless Peter Kintz and all his descendants."

Sister Helen Therese's grandmother, Mary J. Lacose, married Maglorias Madra (Merit Metras). They were one of the first couples to be married in the Log Chapel, on September 29, 1856. He was the first layman Father Sorin hired to teach French at Notre Dame.[134]

Another descendent of the Kintz family, Victor Couch, great grandson of Peter Kintz, also confirmed that farmers did masonry work on foundations, and carpentry in building barns, and many worked at Notre Dame in the winter when they were not farming.

His memories encompassed a maze of South Bend family names that touched Notre Dame and St. Mary's in countless ways and went back well over one hundred years. He, himself, has been an usher at Notre Dame Games for 52 years. He also remembers ushering for Rockne games, in 1928-29, when he was a 2nd class Boy Scout and there were wooden bleachers. He continues to farm ten acres of his family's land, located a mile North of the Notre Dame, and says the ground is still full of big rocks and boulders.

It was soon evident why this family had close ties with the University of Notre Dame and how they, and many other surrounding farm families, were connected with the doings on campus. He produced his abstract for the 80 acres of Kintz property, once part of the original 230 some acres of Talley land, which told a story in itself. It was from this property that Peter Kintz and his sons hauled boulders to be used in the Grotto.

Alfred Talley, born in 1809, was the printer Sorin brought from Chicago to assist him in launching the *Ave Maria* in 1865. The first issue was printed in his home on Juniper Road. His home is still there, though it is now missing its cupola. It is a large red brick two-story house[135] on the East side of Juniper Road, near Cleveland Road, about a mile North of the University of Notre Dame. An 1875 Atlas drawing of the Talley House and farm is at the head of this chapter

According to the Historic Preservation Commission of South Bend, Indiana, the house received Landmark status in June of 1975, when it was bought by its last owner. It is still in the same family. It was purchased by the last owner's son, P. Reiley O'Connor.

HANEY'S HOUSE.
The "Oliver" of the Olden Days.

Another lovely old home in the Roseland area, now only a memory, was pictured in *The Dome* with the words "The Pie House" written under it. Erma Helmen Post penned this interesting explanation of its connection to Notre Dame. "The Haney House was a favorite stopping place for Notre Dame Students. Back in those days students were not allowed to go into South Bend on their afternoon off, which was Thursday. Mrs. Haney's oldest daughter Kate started catering to a few students by serving them a cut of pie or cake with milk or coffee. Her popularity grew and on Thursday afternoon or on any other holiday, you would see students coming and going. It proved profitable to her and helped the family income which had been severely cut when the two grandsons she had helped her mother and father raise left the farm for more desired careers of their own. The Haney house was spacious and in inclement weather there was always room in the big dining room to care for the wants of the boys. The fame of the "The Pie House" was known all over the United States and in foreign countries just because one ambitious woman with a lot of Irish humor, knew how to bake good pies.

When asked if he'd ever heard of "The Pie House," Father Carey's eyes lit up in remembrance. "Sure do," he said. "That was the old Haney House. Used to go there every Thursday. You could get a cut of pie or cake and a glass of milk for a dime."

The Kintz Family Enters the Picture

The southern portion of the Talley/Chirhart property ended just south of the Toll Road on Juniper Road. Juday Creek meanders through the southwest corner of the property. In the late 1800s the creek was simply referred to as The State Ditch. Earlier yet, on an old 1863 map, it was designated as Sheffield Creek.[136]

In 1888, the county decided the creek needed to be straightened, dredged and widened. The people who owned the land the creek passed through were to be taxed accordingly. Jacob died in 1885. Mary Talley Chirhart and her children were disturbed at this charge and forfeited the land rather than pay the taxes. Father Thomas Walsh, then president of Notre Dame, bought the 80.10 acres containing the creek at a Sheriff's sale on May 5, 1888.

On January 5, 1891, Father Walsh sold the property to Peter Kintz II and his wife Mary on a Warranty Deed. The loan was secured with a payment of $1600 on January 5, 1891, with the remainder to be paid in four promissory notes with a 7% annual interest. The deed was paid off on December 15, 1900, and the University of Notre Dame released the mortgage to Peter and Mary Kintz.[137] Kintz Drive, on the east side of Juniper Road, runs down the middle of the 80 acres of land they bought from Father Walsh.

The Kintz genealogy refers to a Kintz son who worked for the Summers family for a year to help pay the mortgage. Gabriel Summers was into real estate and farming. He owned adjacent land south of the Toll Road, now Indian Village, and west of Juniper known as Summers Woods and Oakmont Park.[138] In later years, much of the Summers land was bought by Notre Dame. An 1863 map shows that Sorin once owned the portion of land along Juniper Road now known as Indian Village.

When Peter Kintz died, his 80.10 acres of the original Talley/Chirhart land was passed on to his surviving eight children, each receiving 10 acres. Some time in the late 1930s, 10 acres owned by Cecelia Kintz, who was married to James Luther, were bought by Alden Davis, a Notre Dame Professor, one of her boarders. He purchased the old Summers barn and moved it from the Indian Village area to its present site south of the old Talley/Chirhart home on the creek at the corner of Juniper Road and Kintz Drive. It was remodeled into the picturesque dark brown rustic homestead that now graces the winding path of Juday Creek. As late as the early 1950's sheep could be seen grazing on his grounds. As the story goes, he eliminated lawn mowing by using them to keep the grass clipped. The present owners, William J. and Linda Conyers, have added their own charming touches to the Conyers Cottage. An arched Monet bridge constructed by William J. and his brother, Father Richard J. Conyers, C.S.C., now graces their water gardens.

Many early priests, most especially Sorin, financed their religious endeavors by buying and selling land. It was a skill they passed on to one another. An article entitled, "Stories of Two Remarkable Priests – Benoit And Sorin," by Bishop John M. D'Arcy, explains how Father Julian Benoit founded St. Augustine Parish on what is now the grounds of the Immaculate Conception Cathedral in Fort Wayne:

In addition to the Cathedral, he bought land for churches and built churches and schools throughout the area. Yet he died penniless. How did he do it? Indeed, during his later years, Pope Pius IV, aware of his business sense, asked him this question: "How do the priests in America make their living?" Father

Benoit, from his early days in Fort Wayne, saw that money was being made in land speculation. So he would buy land, very reasonably, and later sell it for a profit. With the money he received, he would buy further land for churches and, indeed, build churches.[139]

The article goes on to mention that Father Benoit and Father Sorin were good friends. When Father Sorin was in deep financial trouble at Notre Dame, he turned to Father Benoit for loans. This land speculation must have been a skill Sorin also learned and passed on, as President Walsh's purchase of sheriff's sale land and its resale to the Kintz family, at a tidy profit, indicates.

The family story is told that Peter Kintz's youngest son, Ott, as a very young lad, weeded and replanted, with a hand planter, the corn that had fallen or been eaten by crows in the field where the Athletic and Convocation Center is now. The older Kintz sons worked as carpenters at Notre Dame and, as the family story goes, hauled stone and worked at the Grotto as part payment on the mortgage with Father Walsh; a reasonable assumption since the Grotto was being built midway in the mortgage.

This was not an uncommon practice. One man paid for his son's college education by building the spire of the church.[140] Another entry in the *Scholastic* refers to the building of the original church:

An appeal was made to the few Catholics around, if they could or would do a little — most of them were poor, many not very fervent. However a subscription was made: it was paid in labor.[141]

One sentence in Father Maguire's letter also mentions this practice. Speaking of the building of the Grotto he says:

The boulders were gathered from our farms and others surrounding it.

Confirmation of the above statement was offered by Father Joseph Rogusz. He remembers being told by Brother Peter Claver Hosinski, (1872-1958) that he and other Holy Cross Brother novices hauled stone for the Grotto.

In the same 1896 ledger, a $26.35 payment is recorded for stone brought to the campus by the contractor, John Gill. Two other unnamed entries were paid $5.90 and $51.60 for 8³/₅ cords of stone at $6.00 a cord. Stone was measured like wood then. A pile of wood 4 feet wide by 4 feet high by 8 feet long was a cord. These two unnamed entries might have been stone brought by the Kintz family and their payment was applied to their mortgage. Unfortunately, there are no University records of payments on the Kintz mortgage, by cash or barter, still in existence to verify this family story.

Stone was also brought on a stone boat by O. P. Stuckey, who was paid $13.66. O. P. Stuckey's home and barn, now gone, were located north of the Francis Branch library and the Greek Orthodox Church on Ironwood Road. The old Stuckey School stood on the Northwest corner of Ironwood and Douglas surrounded by a fieldstone wall, all of which has long since disappeared. In 1890, O. P. Stuckey and his team of horses were killed, struck by lightning in a field on his farm. However, he had a granddaughter named June Turnock. She became June McCauslin, the Financial Aid Director at the Notre Dame Campus for 18 years until her retirement. She also passed on another family story. Her Grandfather Turnock plastered the interior of the Dome.

Many area families were well represented in their donations to the stained glass windows and bell. The family of Peter Kintz donated a stained glass window for the church and gave money for the bell. Louis Gooley, related to the Kintz family, also donated a stained glass window for the church and contributed toward the bell, as did the Chirhart family who owned the Talley land. Another member of the Gooley family was said to have hauled the clapper for the bell to Notre Dame in his mule cart.

A reference to the donation of one of those first stained-glass windows was printed in an 1876 *Scholastic*. It records another bit of history and also explains why it was a special privilege to be associated with a church in this way. It appeared under the title, "Gift of the Edward Mulligan Family:"

The above inscription, printed in large characters on a golden scroll at the bottom of a stained-glass window in the new Church of Our Lady of the Sacred Heart, brings back to our minds "the Ages of Faith," when crowned heads and princes of Christian blood, as well as the common faithful of inferior rank, esteemed it a singular and precious privilege to see their names immortalized, as it were, the moment they were accepted to be recorded on the walls or pilasters, or on stained-glass windows in the House of God.

Thus, indeed, many a name has been handed down from remote antiquity, to the notice and praises of subsequent centuries, which otherwise would have been long since totally forgotten.

In those happier days of piety, it was justly considered a greater honor to leave such lasting evidence of generous munificence towards God's own House than large estates, or coffers filled with gold, or the coveted wealth the end of all which was so soon to be met in a coffin, save what was done for God's honor and glory.

Time then, as ever, often made woeful changes in human fortunes, and frequently, as even now, great landlords fell from the pinnacle of high offices and honors to the ordinary walks of society; and yet, when reverses had leveled all, the stained glass of a modest or of a grand Church, revealed and transmitted to succeeding ages the lovely evidences that such a family had left an imperishable record of their religion, and their grandsons and nephews could walk into their generous ancestor's temple without a blush, if they had preserved their faith, or keep their heads down, if they had abandoned it. Thus it is that honorable names, long since gone from our midst continue to speak to their descendants the eloquent language of their glorious Faith.

We feel rejoiced that the honor of the first one of these magnificent and classical windows has been secured by the pious family whose name is there inscribed for ages. Mr. Edward Mulligan, now deceased, has left a family worthy of himself. Thirty-five years ago, [1841] to his last moment in 1868, he remained Father Sorin's best friend. His memory is held in esteem and affection by all his acquaintances, and it will be a pleasure to see in this stained-glass window the evidence that his family hold in honor the virtues which he left them as a rich legacy.[142]

Mary Grix, another local resident, said her great grandfather, Patrick Mulligan, owned a 200 acre farm that went from U.S. 31 to Laurel Road. The family purchased the land in the early 1800s. Mary is still living in a home built on his land. He also loaned money to Notre Dame in the early days and his name is engraved on the bell. When he died the church was draped in black. She said he was very fond of the Grotto and never left the campus after church on a Sunday morning without stopping to say a prayer and take a drink at the fountain.

It was now very much in evidence that many farmers and townspeople of the day helped their neighbors, Notre Dame and St. Mary's.

Chapter 8

The Builders and Architect

John Gill was the man recorded in the financial records as being the contractor of the Grotto built in 1896. Charles McCoy, who was also listed in the 1896 ledger and was one of his brickmasons, simply vanished from the census records. This was not unusual for the 1890s. All census records, nationwide, as well as other records were lost in a fire. Property he owned was sold in 1900 to an unknown woman for one dollar. He was never heard from again. He seemed to have appeared for the building of the Grotto, lived within a block of John Gill on Main Street, and afterward left town for parts unknown.

John Gill, however, was a different matter. In an old 1884 campus work ledger, twelve years before his contract on the Grotto, there was a surprising entry with his signature at the bottom of it: "Hired John Gill to work on St. Joseph Farm for 1 year for $170.00."[143]

The first Gill listed in the telephone book proved to be his grandson, Oren Gill. His property, coincidentally, is adjacent to the Notre Dame campus. He confirmed that he was indeed the grandson of John Gill, and the son of Lawrence Gill, who were both brickmasons. "My grandfather was a masonry contractor," he said, "and my father a mason, but though I tried, I never got the hang of it and settled for something else." He was surprised to learn that his grandfather had the contract to build the Notre Dame Grotto. He was non-Catholic, he said, as his grandfather had been, and he had never heard it mentioned before.

Oren Gill was in his eighties and had no children. He said his brother, who died in 1954, had one child, a daughter, Judy Ladd. She lives in South Bend and was an art teacher at a local high school. She was a Catholic convert, he said, and he was sure she'd find the information most interesting. She was delighted and found it hard to believe that no one in the family knew about it.

John Gill also seemed to have disappeared from the city directory in the late 1890s. Another phone call to his grandson revealed more information. He had disappeared from the city directory because he had moved to the county. Oren Gill related a childhood memory of going out on a buckboard with his brother and sister to see his grandfather who lived on a farm. Oren Gill chuckled as he related how his grandfather had a touring car. When he was a little boy, he remembered his grandfather telling him how "it went 52 miles an hour and two feet off the ground."

The county recorder's office produced evidence that John Gill had indeed prospered after building the Notre Dame Grotto. His family was amazed at the land he had owned, now prime property in the Granger area. It was at about this time, 1913, that he moved to California. On June 22, 1923, John Gill, the contractor on the Grotto, died in California; he had a stroke while changing a flat tire.

Other Masons Who Worked on the Grotto

Boleslaus Luzny and Victor Callicrate were added to the names of masons who worked on the Grotto. Family legend holds that these two men also helped build the Grotto, but there are no surviving records to confirm this. However, both men were listed as working masons in the 1896 city directory and both families were connected with the Notre Dame campus.

A local South Bend writer, Bernard Pinkowski, a friend of Boleslaus Luzny's daughter Clara, confirmed their story. He said she worked in the Notre Dame Main Building most of her adult life. She was also godmother to his child. Many times, he said, she sat at their dinner table and told of how her father helped build the Grotto. She mentioned the huge supporting stone at the base of the Grotto which her father always pointed out to her as one he had positioned there. Father Francis Luzny, a Holy Cross priest, now deceased, he said, was also related to this family. He often repeated the same story.

Another person interested in the Grotto, Leonard Preuss, was another descendent of the Luzny family and an employee on campus. He was looking for evidence that his great uncles had worked on the Notre Dame Grotto. He supplied more interesting pieces in the Grotto puzzle.

He sent obituaries and a newspaper article confirming their family stories:

The Luzny brothers were brought to South Bend (in 1881) from Germany (Polish Province) by the Oliver family to work on the Oliver home . . . . Frank Luzny, his brother Boleslaus, and his cousin Roman worked on the Studebaker and Oliver mansions. They had their trade from the old country.[144]

Boleslaus' first job when he arrived here from Poland was at the University of Notre Dame where he was hired by Rev. Edward Sorin, C.S.C., founder of Notre Dame.[145]

A 92 year old grandson of Victor Callicrate said he was told that his grandfather Victor Callicrate, and two of his sons worked on the Grotto. The Callicrate name is also associated with Notre Dame. One of Callicrate's sons, Dominic, was captain of the 1907 football team.

He then added another bit of campus lore. In his day, he said, the community cemetery for the religious was called "Boot Hill." The dictionary gives this interesting definition: "a cemetery in or near a frontier town of the old West." And the meaning of frontier? "The farthest part of a settled country, where the wilds begin." In Sorin's time it definitely applied, since the cemetery is on a hill in the frontier town of Notre Dame, Indiana. In Sorin's time, this region was known as the Old Northwest.

The remembrance of another local resident, Molly Sullivan, produced the names of two more brickmasons who worked on the Grotto. These two new names provided even more interesting details of the events unfolding in the summer of 1896 when the Grotto was being built.

Molly was a teacher of English Literature at St. Mary's Academy and Saint Mary's College. She also has her own special connection with Notre Dame's early history. She is the daughter of a Notre Dame English Professor, Richard Sullivan, now deceased, and she lives in a charming little cottage on Juniper Road less than a mile from Notre Dame. This little cottage is also steeped in Notre Dame history. Molly explained that it had once been a large chicken house on the campus, one among two, that were moved and remodeled as homes when the University began building east and north of the campus in the 1920s. A Chinese man, who owned the China Gardens, bought it from the University in 1919 and she bought it from his widow some years ago.

She said a friend of hers, who was a brickmason, often told of how his father and grandfather worked on the Grotto. This man had died, but she said his sons were brickmasons and she was sure they would be able to offer many more details she might not remember.

His son, Nick, very willingly shared his family history. He explained that being a family of brickmasons, it was common practice to pass on stories while working. He had heard the history of his grandfather and great grandfather on a number of occasions. They were skilled stonemasons who came from the old country together. They were known as church masons and steeplejacks then. Their passage was paid by Judge Gary and had to be paid off as indentured servants.

When they arrived in Gary, Indiana, they were put to work in the steel mills. They soon found themselves taken advantage of and abused, so they escaped and headed south, stopping in South Bend along the way. While in South Bend, they worked on the Tippecanoe Place, Copshaholm, the house across from it, and St. Paul's Church. They were also hired as masons to help build the Notre Dame Grotto. Their names were Nick and Lod (Ladislaf) Kowalski.

He said his father told him that he was told by his father and grandfather that two or three people died while the Grotto was being built. The Grotto had collapsed a couple times before the problem was solved and there was a problem with a large stone in the back of the niche, though he didn't recall what it was. He also remembered something about the huge boulders being unsuccessfully held in place with timbers.

His remembrance confirmed another item Father Maguire mentioned in his 1953 letter of correction:

I do not know who the builder was but he had quite a problem when he came to the roof. Many said it could not be built of such rocks; it would collapse. Finally it was decided to try it anyway and a wooden form was constructed, the roof 'keyed.' From its appearance today the work was one hundred percent perfect.

The number of masons reputed to have worked on the Grotto was growing. John Gill, the contractor, and his mason Charles McCoy, were the only ones noted in the Grotto expense ledgers. The others were Boleslaus Luzny, and possibly his brother Frank, Victor Callicrate and his sons, Nick and Lod Kowalski, and Peter Kintz and his sons. Peter Kintz, a farmer, was the only one not listed as a mason.

John Gill must have hired extra men and paid them in cash, as was customary at that time. This would account for the additional names not being on record. The sons may have worked along with their fathers as laborers. This would not be an unusual number for a project that big and heavy. Manpower would have been needed, masons as well as laborers. Generally, one laborer works with two masons. In this case, the huge boulders might have required extra hands and horses. These extra hands might have been supplied by farmers, like Kintz and his sons, upon delivering their stone.

Two Deaths Associated With The Grotto

If there were two or three deaths associated with the Grotto, it would be recorded in the 1896 newspapers. And if the Grotto had collapsed, it might also be mentioned. Four months of newspapers, from May through September, would cover the time the Grotto was being built. There were many unusual stories, but none of the deaths recorded were associated with the Grotto.

What the world was like almost one hundred years ago, and what the weather was like, added more details to the Grotto story. The temperature reached 102 degrees during the time the Grotto was being built. An unusually hot summer spawned violent thunderstorms. A horrendous tornado in St. Louis left hundreds of people dead. The most common accidents recorded were with runaway horses.

The first mention of the Grotto appeared under the heading, "New Grotto Of Lourdes." It was a brief announcement. "The contract has been let for a new Grotto of Lourdes at Notre Dame to cost about $2,500. It will be constructed entirely of stone."[146]

OFT HAVE WE WATCHED THY SOFT BLUE EVENING SKIES, BENDING ABOVE AS LIKE A MOTHER'S EYES.

There was no other mention of the Grotto while it was being built in any of the four local newspapers. Only a brief mention was made of its dedication in August. However, there was a reference to a Michael Presho who had been injured while unloading a wagon of stone. It happened at Notre Dame, so it had to be at the Grotto:

Michael Presho was engaged in hauling stone to Notre Dame this morning. A large stone had been taken from the front end of the wagon, allowing another large one to remain in the rear. This overbalanced and threw Presho at least 10 or 12 feet into the air. He fell, striking on the wagon gearing and sustained internal injuries. It was thought he was injured fatally, but his physician has hopes of his recovery.[147]

The *South Bend Tribune* also reported two drownings in the St. Joseph Lake on the Notre Dame campus during the month of June. They occurred within two weeks of each other. The brickmason's son's words took on a new meaning. "Two people died while the Grotto was being built" didn't have to mean at the Grotto itself in the process of building it. If two people had drowned nearby in the St. Joseph Lake, someone working on the Grotto would have said, "two people died while the Grotto was being built." In this case, it would mean in close proximity to their work on the Grotto.

There were a possible three people in the brickmason's story. He had said two or three, he wasn't sure. Perhaps, the third man, Michael Presho, who was injured at the Grotto, had not survived. This also might explain why there was some doubt about a third death. Perhaps these two masons who worked at the Grotto had not known the outcome of what must have appeared to be a fatal injury.

The city directory for the subsequent years revealed that Michael Presho had survived what had been described as a serious injury. He was listed as a teamster, a name given to men who drove teams of horses in 1896.

Although nothing in the records verified that these two Kowalski men were masons who worked on the Grotto, their knowledge of the deaths was proof positive they had been there. No one else would have had this information to pass on.

One of the two drownings was Brother Michael Desmaison, an elderly basket weaver who lived on campus. He had gone to the lake to collect reeds for basket making and had somehow stumbled, fallen in, and drowned. He was found the next day in 18 inches of water by a newsboy walking along the lake.[148]

The research on these drownings led to the discovery of another interesting item of information. In the early days, St. Mary's lake was called "Blue Lake." A descendant of Timothy Howard, author of *A Brief History of the University of Notre Dame du Lac*, about Notre Dame's first fifty years, verified this little known fact. He then added another. The St. Joseph Lake was known as "Mud Lake." He wasn't sure how they got their names. In the case of St. Mary's Lake, he thought it might have referred to the beauty of the lake or because it was the color of blue associated with Our Lady. St. Joseph Lake, he said, could have been dubbed "Mud Lake," by the students because it was the swimming lake and had a muddy bottom.

The second drowning, about two weeks later, was a 19-year-old seminarian from Ireland, Lawrence Parnell. He had been swimming in St. Mary's Lake alone. It was believed he had a heart attack or had been entangled in the weeds. In one newspaper, this interesting mention was added to Lawrence Parnell's obituary. "He had a sister who was a Holy Cross nun, Sister Othelia, at St. Mary's."[149]

An elderly Sister at St. Mary's Convent remembered a relative and supplied her address. A niece, Sister Eutropia, was still living at 92, at St. Catherine by the Sea in Ventura, California. A letter from her provided another glimpse of what was happening on the campus, during the summer of 1896, when the Grotto was being built.

I was only in the mind of God in 1896 when the sudden and sad death of my uncle, Lawrence Parnell, occurred. I met Sister Othelia for the first time in 1920 in New York after crossing the ocean en route to the Novitiate at St. Mary's. The visit was short but we did full justice to our get together and that same summer we visited Lawrence's grave . . . talked of their rewarding summer in 1896, and their fond goodbyes.

After their visit, she returned to Eureka, Utah, and the sad news reached her a short time later. She was not able to return for the funeral. Thank God, He does heal our sorrows with the passage of time. She was a lovely lady, my aunt, and a good friend. She died in 1952.[150]

A visit to his grave in the seminarian section of the Holy Cross Community Cemetery was like reaching back in time. These poetic words from an old *Scholastic* speak of those bygone days:

The flowers of the heart that blossomed then, have never fully faded away. They are still there to be revived and freshened by the dews of memory and the tears of grief.

It is difficult to even begin to fathom the number of feet that have trod the paths from here to there, the wealth of memories attached to every corner of the campus, all the human history that has left its imprint on the University grounds in more than one hundred and fifty years.

An Architect Associated with the Grotto

With each point clarified in Father Maguire's 1953 letter, more evidence was added to the story behind the Notre Dame Grotto.

Another name was suggested by a local resident. "Call Alice Hennion," she said, "Many times, I've heard her tell the story of her grandfather being the architect on the Notre Dame Grotto. She would be able to give you more information."

The name Robert Braunsdorf was added to the list of those associated with the Grotto, this time supplied by his granddaughter, Alice Hennion. Alice is the wife of a George Hennion, a retired Professor of Chemistry at Notre Dame. She offered a most important piece in the Grotto puzzle from family remembrances. It hardly seemed likely that an architect would be needed, but it was a clue worth investigating.

Alice related how her grandfather was a well known builder, a renowned New York architect of his day. He was hired to build Studebaker's Tippecanoe Place and St. Paul's Episcopal Church in cut granite fieldstone. He also built many other buildings and homes in the area, as well as on the Notre Dame and Saint Mary's campuses. It is possible the front entrance to the Saint Mary's College, which was built in 1897,[151] was also his work.

Father Maguire's letter of correction, mentioned earlier, in which he states, "Many said it could not be built of such rocks; it would collapse" — and the brickmason Kowalski's remembrance of the stones collapsing when the timbers were removed — had confirmed her story.

Another relative, James Braunsdorf, provided more evidence of this same noted Braunsdorf architect. He then told the story passed down on his side of the family. He said that because of his previous work for the University, he was called in as a consultant to assess a problem they had with the collapse of the Grotto. Two prior attempts had been made. After the boulders were cemented and the timber supports to hold them in place were removed, they had collapsed under their own weight. Braunsdorf redesigned it, solved the problem — probably gratis — and the work proceeded on schedule. This would account for no financial entry being in the ledgers under Braunsdorf's name. In addition to building many buildings on both campuses, Robert's sons,

Walter and William Braunsdorf, were both minims at Notre Dame.

The St. Stan's Grotto — a replica of the Notre Dame Grotto — was built at the St. Stanislaus Church in South Bend in 1962. Bill Buckles, the son of the man who built it, was a mason who worked on it. He explained that it was built using a 24-inch-wide carpenter's arch as a form for the rock arch of the cave opening. The form was removed when the mortar had set. Perhaps Braunsdorf, who had been a carpenter, might have done the same thing.

At St. Stan's Grotto, beneath the wood carpenter's arch made to support the opening of the cave, he said, a huge mound of fill dirt was added to the proposed size of the interior of the cave. Stone was positioned on the carpenter's arch, and on top of the packed dirt mound beneath it. This formed the shape of the ceiling of the interior of the cave. Mortar was then poured around them. Once that had hardened the dirt inside the cave was removed exposing the rocks in the ceiling of the cave.

The dirt extracted was then placed on top of the cemented stones to form the hillside that had not been there before. Ivy, trees and shrubs were planted on this mound, above and behind the Grotto, giving it the appearance of the natural hillside seen at the Notre Dame Grotto. It was a safe and ingenious way to keep the cave from collapsing while the mortar was setting, which must have happened with the Notre Dame Grotto in 1896.

The collapse stories, now from several sources, had been verified. Father Maguire had identified the problem, although he did not know who the problem solver turned out to be, or that it had actually collapsed. His mention in his letter of a problem, and the possibility of a Grotto collapse, indicates he had picked up on something he must have heard, but could not confirm.

The man sitting on the bench in the photograph at the beginning of this chapter is Robert Braunsdorf, the architect. The man standing with his foot on the bench is believed to be John Gill, the contractor.

A Group Work of Art

Joan Romine wrote a book entitled, *COPSHAHOLM, The Oliver Story*, about the building of Copshaholm,[152] the Joseph D. Oliver estate. The house became "a physical link from the stone cottage birthplace of James Oliver. It was named after the village in Scotland from which the family emigrated and means 'Clump of trees on a hill overlooking a river.'"

The stone for the home was gathered in 1895, the exterior was completed and the house roofed that same year. The interior work continued throughout the entire year of 1896. The family moved in on January 1, 1897.

Excerpts from a diary kept by J. D. Oliver's father, the founder of Oliver Chill Plow, are quoted in her book. Copshaholm was also built of stones from the farm fields of St. Joseph County. Joseph's father, James, took it upon himself to comb the countryside in search of stones to be used in his son's new home:

He plunged into the task with the tireless energy and unbounded enthusiasm he had always shown for any of his business projects. Although he was 71, he enthused more over finding a big stone for the house than a small boy would over picking up an arrowhead in the same field.

After locating the stones, James hired teams of horses to dig them out. Often after a huge stone had been hauled from a river bed or farm field and laboriously split, it was found to have some defect and could not be used. It was tedious work. More were rejected because of color, seams or other imperfections than were accepted.

Daily entries in his journal show him hunting stones for Copshaholm, "from March to June of 1895 for the house, and from June to September for the stable." They provide a glimpse of the way a project like the Grotto might have been handled in the spring of 1896, the same year the interior of Copshaholm was being completed. By then, farmers in the area would have been alerted to the value of the rocks in their fields. Many already dug up boulders, rejected for use in Copshaholm in 1895, might have been perfect for use in the Grotto a year later.

Several diary entries give some idea of the magnitude of the task of lifting and transporting such heavy rocks in the days before mechanized heavy duty equipment. Oliver speaks of one day hiring nine teams in all to haul stone.

In some cases, finding 8 and 12 foot stones and resurrecting them from the beds where ice-age glaciers had deposited them centuries before. Men and horses strained to load them. Wagon axles were broken, horses became mired in sand and mud. Occasionally a country bridge broke under the weight, compounding the problem. James Oliver often recorded that five and six horses had to be used on one stone.

Joan Romine also noted in her book the charges made by workmen hired in that era. "Common labor, 15 cents an hour; bricklayers and masons, 35 to 45 cents an hour; carpenters, 20 cents an hour, and stone was sold for one dollar a cord."

Many skilled old country stonemasons would not have been here to build the Grotto if Oliver hadn't brought them to this country from the Polish Province of Germany. These same stonemasons worked in his factory, as farmers worked at Notre Dame, when the weather was too cold to ply their trade.

A noteworthy newspaper article on the subject was written by Jeanne Derbeck for the *South Bend Tribune*, in 1970. It was shared by Leonard Preuss, a descendant of the Luzny brothers who worked on the Grotto. It speaks of "at least three rare examples of an art that is almost lost": Tippecanoe Place, the Oliver Mansions and People's Church. Copshaholm would be another example.

She quotes Elmer Hammond, a brickmason and the son of a stonemason, noting that "the secrets of the old craft of stonemasonry are all but unknown today."

"The skill required was unbelievable. The work shouldn't be confused with cobblestone building. Cobblestones are simply picked up out of a field and placed together where they fit. But stonemasons broke large stones to show the colors and beauty inside. Then they put the irregular shapes together to fit perfectly," Hammond explained. "Working only with hammers and the eye — much like diamond cutters — stonemasons had to know just how to break the stone to get the best color effect and the right shape."

Hammond recalls that, as a small boy, he would go with his father to work and sit by the bonfire to watch the stonemasons. "They would bring in a wagonload of big stones. Those old-timers could walk right up to them and know right where to hit them. Then they fit them together with such precision that the concave half of an old curling iron was used to make the depression in the mortar between the stones. Sometimes they fired the stones first.

"My father and two uncles had a set of hammers ranging from two pounds to 20 pounds. They had a concave head and wedge-end tip. I remember watching my father take a stone as big as a barrel and blast away at it with hammers. He would even put corners and tapers on it," said Hammond.

Special care was needed to build the arches. "A group of men working together to create an arch like that, measuring solely by eye, — it's a real group work of art," he said.[153]

Anyone viewing the Grotto at Notre Dame, all these many years later, would have to agree, it is also a "real group work of art."

Chapter 9

The Dedication of the Grotto

Father Maguire nears the end of his letter of correction concerning the 1896 Grotto with this brief description of a little known event that occurred as the Grotto was nearing its completion.

The "spring" actually did appear and old Father Letourneau felt it was a miracle since it appeared almost at the same spot as the one at Lourdes. But wiser people closed it up so as to prevent wild rumors regarding it.

This incident at the Notre Dame Grotto paralleled a similar occurrence that happened at the Grotto of Lourdes in France in 1858. When Bernadette scratched a hole in the dirt of the floor of the cave at Lourdes, a spring appeared. It became the origin of the Lourdes water that is still sent all over the world.

In August, another entry on the progress of the Grotto was published in the *Annals* confirming the information in Father Maguire's letter regarding the spring which appeared at the Grotto:

Grotto of Lourdes at Notre Dame, Indiana

We are glad to be able to say that the work on the Grotto at Notre Dame is progressing as well as one could expect under the circumstances. . . . The Grotto will be a thing of beauty and a great incentive to devotion to the Mother of God. We claim no miracles in this work, but we do claim that most remarkable coincidences mark the beginning and progress of this shrine. As has been announced already in the Annals, the first favor asked by the one who started the Grotto was granted on the first day of May, 1895. The second favor was a handsome contribution towards building it, and this came on the first day of May, 1896. Finally, while sinking the foundation the builders struck a beautiful spring of clear cold water in the same spot relatively as the one found in the Grotto at Lourdes, France. The mechanics received orders to open the ground and wall the spring with rocks. To do this they were obliged to use a heavy pump which has a capacity of lifting from twenty-five to thirty gallons a minute. They kept this pump working for five hours before they could reduce the water. As fast as the water was pumped out the spring boiled up in place of the vacuum caused by the pump. These circumstances are given simply for what they are worth, without trying to impose on the credulity of anyone; but the facts remain. In the name of the Blessed Virgin we sincerely thank all who have contributed to this work. The Blessed Virgin knows how to reward her children.[154]

Very early pictures of the Grotto[155] show that an ordinary backyard pump for drinking water marked the spot where the natural spring appeared.

The *Scholastic*[156] reported this added bit of information. "A plaster of paris model of the proposed Grotto now stands in the back sacristy of Sacred Heart Church and indicates that an ornate shed was meant for the drinking well."

Society of the Guardian Angels

An earlier *Annals*, which described the progress of the Grotto, stated the proposed completion date:

The work on the foundation of the Grotto has commenced, and we hope to see it finished by the 15th of August next — Feast of the Assumption.[157]

However, by accident or design, the dedication of the 1896 Notre Dame Grotto, originally planned for that date, occurred ten days earlier, on *August 5, 1896, the Feast of Our Lady of the Snows.*

Our Lady of Snows refers to St. Mary Major. This church is so-called because it is the major, the largest, and most illustrious shrine of Our Lady in the eternal city (Rome). . . . It is called Our Lady of the Snows because of the tradition that the original outline for the church was traced in snow, August 5, 358, after the prayer of a Roman patrician, John, and his wife. Childless, they had promised to make Our Lady heiress of their property, and sought in prayer for some intimation of her will.[158]

This was the same day Sorin departed from France for the New World in 1841. Sorin related the occurrence in his *Chronicles*. He wrote that he had "absolutely nothing to do with the choice of the day," and refers to it as a "happy coincidence," an intimation of her maternal protection. Had Sorin been there to witness the 1896 Grotto dedication, undoubtedly he would have proclaimed it another "happy coincidence." Once again, she had chosen for herself that date, as further reassurance of her inspirational guidance to all those "who look up to her" on the Dome and at the Grotto "as their guiding Star."

The Grotto's Dedication

In September of 1896, the last entry in the *Annals* described more fully the occasion of the Grotto's dedication:

Grotto of Lourdes at Notre Dame, Indiana

On August 5th, 1896, the Feast of Our Lady of Snows, a beautiful statue representing the Blessed Virgin as she appeared to Bernadette at Lourdes was set in place in the new Grotto here at Notre Dame. The ceremony of the occasion, though short, partook of a simple grandeur that is not usually seen outside of Catholic countries. In the cool hours of the morning the Religious of the Holy Cross — priests, brothers and nuns — to the number of five hundred or more assembled in the spacious College Chapel to assist at Solemn Mass. All who were present approached the Holy Table and, when the services were over, formed in procession leading across the University lawn and through the picturesque grove in which Our Lady's shrine is situated. The brothers were in front carrying the statue and telling their beads, while the acolytes and priests followed with candles and waving banners. The sisters, chaunting the Litany of Loretto and the Magnificat, walked behind the ministers of the Mass. Those who have never witnessed a procession of this kind cannot know the beauty and the glory of it. Hard indeed would be the heart which would not thrill at the sight. To be sure, we do not refer to the mere specular aspect of a number of men and women marching in picturesque habits through a wooded glen, — though that in itself is something uncommonly striking; we have in mind, rather, the faith of which is hardly any left in our day. No man could gaze on such a scene without feeling in his inmost consciousness — whatever his outward expression might be — that in the Catholic Church faith at least is not dead. And when on this occasion, the statue was finally in place and the religious knelt down before Our Lady's image offering prayers of thanksgiving and supplication, it was clear beyond doubt that here at Notre Dame there exists a faith in the Blessed Virgin's power, before God which is as strong and living as that which existed in the very "Ages of Faith" themselves. It is gratifying to be able to say this much, for it means that blessings are in store for the home of the new Grotto as well as the country round about from which the pilgrimages come. When the statue and the Grotto had been blessed, a short sermon was preached by the Very Rev. William Corby, C.S.C., who gave in brief the history of the Grotto from the moment the first donation was received down to its present state of almost final completeness.[159]

Ongoing News of the Newly Erected Grotto

Shortly after it was dedicated, an entry in the *Scholastic* described the new Grotto:

Constructed entirely of unhewn rocks, great boulders, some of them weighing as much as 2 to 3 tons go to make up the foundation and even near the keystone of the arch the stones are so large as to give the impression of instability.[160]

The *South Bend Tribune* capsuled a subsequent pilgrimage made to the newly erected Grotto of Lourdes at Notre Dame.

The annual pilgrimage from Kalamazoo to Notre Dame took place today. Two trains of 10 coaches each, all loaded with people (5 passengers from Mattawan, 66 from Lawton, 85 from Decatur, 114 from Dowagiac) came over and many of them attended services in the church of Sacred Heart. After services the excursionists visited the University and points of interest about the city.[161]

The *Kalamazoo Augustinian* also detailed this 1896 trip. It described how the first train from Kalamazoo reached Notre Dame at eight o'clock:

At Dowagiac Fr. Joos got aboard with a number of Indians which was an event of the trip. . . . Strangers from

a distance were also on the train, even far off Detroit was well represented. . . . At the Grotto the procession halted and the usual prayers and offering of candles were made. The Grotto was a beautiful surprise. Although much had been promised, more than what was promised was realized. It is a wonderful creation. It was the favorite spot for the pilgrims throughout the day. The spring was tested and more than one favor was received. It was a day of joy, peace, devotion and happiness long to be remembered.[162]

The article ended with this interesting disclosure which indicated that the ordinary backyard pump placed over the spring at the Grotto, shown in the last picture, was immediately put to use:

Many gallons of water from the pump at the spring were carried away.

Although it is the only reference to this practice yet found, more than one local resident has mentioned how their ancestor never left church services without stopping at the Grotto for a drink at the fountain. The backyard pump was later replaced with a tall drinking fountain.

Since its dedication in 1896, many heartfelt descriptions of the newly erected Grotto have been published in the *Scholastic*.

The tall maples in the hollow, near the entrance to the Grotto are shedding their brown leaves and when the sun shines, cast ghostly shadows upon the rocky sides of the Grotto's walls. The place is fitted to inspire serious thought, and if you go there during the day you will find many kneeling in supplication on the rude benches before Mary's statue.[163]

A year later, in August of 1897, further work on the Grotto was mentioned.

The grotto is still unfinished. After it was found some months ago that the water got through it, the mound at the rear was taken away and the back newly cemented, covered with asphalt paper and tarred. Rain cannot penetrate it now, but the rear is still unfinished. The erection of a new mound would be a welcome relief from the desolate blackness that now confronts the visitor.[164]

The conclusion of Father Maguire's letter touches on this subject. He ends his letter with this last sentence:

The grotto was begun and completed in 1896 but each year little touches here and there have made it the beauty spot it is today, a place worthy of our Blessed Mother.

On December 28, 1897, a little over a year after the Grotto was dedicated, Rev. William Corby, C.S.C., the originator of the 1896 Grotto, died at Notre Dame, Indiana.

Five months later, on May 25, 1898, Father Thomas Carroll also died. The generosity of the priest from Oil City, Pennsylvania who financed the building of the Grotto is remembered in the *Scholastic*:

Out of the wealth that his businesslike methods enabled him to acquire, he founded one of the first scholarships at Notre Dame. In doing this he built for himself another monument that time can not destroy. No one knew better than he the need the Catholic young man has for education and no one was more willing than he to help the good work along. The scholarship at Notre Dame is only one of many that he directed to be founded in this country, in Italy and in Ireland.

Only three years ago the back of the Community house was nothing but a bare brown mound with an old willow and one or two poplar trees . . . . "Here in the quiet of the grove so close to the Church of the Sacred Heart was a location suitable in every respect." In a few months the Grotto was completed [1896]. Father Corby selected the site. Corby to Carroll "Let the Grotto be built here and let those that visit it say a prayer that God may grant us both a happy death." The Grotto was built there and now . . . both are dead, within months of each other.[165]

Five years after the completion of the Grotto, on December 28, 1901, at the age of 58, Robert Braunsdorf — the architect who engineered the building of the Notre Dame Grotto — died unexpectedly after a a brief illness. Just weeks before, he was conducting his duties as supervising architect at the new St. Paul's Episcopal Church. A huge piece of rose granite at the site caught his eye. Unknowing, he set it aside to keep for his future grave marker. Six weeks later, it was carved into a beautiful six foot rose granite cross that now marks his grave in the Cedar Grove Cemetery on Notre Dame Avenue adjacent to the University.[166]

It is unlikely the Grotto would ever have been accomplished without Robert Braunsdorf's know-how. That it is still standing after almost 100 years is evidence of his problem solving prowess. Over the years, a number of his descendants have also been associated with the University of Notre Dame.

Plaques at the Grotto

On June 30, 1907 a pilgrimage to the Notre Dame Grotto inspired a plaque placed at the Grotto to commemorate it. This plaque is long gone now, but its former presence there can still be seen on the left side of the Grotto. Its early existence would not have been known or remembered were it not for a Postcard Collectors Convention held in South Bend. Among postcards of Notre Dame, there was an early one of the Grotto postmarked, January 2, 1912. On the other side of it, was a friendly message dated New Years Day, 1912.

For a number of years it was the only plaque at the Grotto other than the donor plaque. There were several illegible lines of script on it. A search through old photographs of the Grotto produced only one photograph showing the plaque. Fortunately it was large enough to decipher the words with a magnifying glass. It read: "In remembrance of the First Pilgrimage from Holy Trinity Parish, Chicago, IL June 30, 1907." Below it was the same message in Polish.

Why the plaque was missing would have to remain a mystery. Perhaps it deteriorated in time, or came loose from the stone and was never remounted. It disappeared about 1920-21 leaving a diamond imprint on the Grotto from that time on.

About the same time, the first "For Favor Granted" plaque appeared at the Grotto, this time to commemorate the date, February 26, 1918. Beneath the date were the initials G.F. and A.M. The armistice was signed and World War I ended on November 11, 1918. Perhaps the plaque represented a prayer answered for a young couple planning their future during wartime. Or it may have been placed there by two Notre Dame students upon their safe return. It is unique for three reasons. It was the first plaque, other than the donor plaque, placed on the Grotto; it has two sets of initials on it; and thirty-three years went by before a second "For Favor Granted" plaque appeared on the Grotto.

THE GROTTO, NOTRE DAME UNIVERSITY, NOTRE DAME, IND.

Chapter 10

A Poet Linked to the Grotto

In 1913, a poet associated with Notre Dame, the Grotto, and the trees on campus, appeared on the scene — Joyce Kilmer.

A brochure in the University Archives entitled *University Statue Shrine Stories* contains an interesting reference to Kilmer and the Grotto. In its pages, Father Henry Kemper speaks of a former classmate:

My old Notre Dame classmate, Charley O'Donnell, who later became Poet Laureate of Indiana and president of his alma mater, Notre Dame, was a personal friend of the poet, Joyce Kilmer.

They say the big tree that shades Our Lady's niche," a tree that looks at God all day and lifts her leafy arms to pray," was the inspiration that made the patriot convert, Joyce Kilmer, famous, with his best-known poem. Kilmer volunteered in The Fighting Irish Brigade and was killed in action July 30, 1918 at the age of 32. The original flag of the Irish Brigade, carried through the civil war by General Meagher's boys, was presented to Notre Dame last summer.[167]

On the right side of the Grotto steps leading to the church is a huge stump that must have once been "the big tree that shades Our Lady's niche." If it were true that it had inspired the poem, "Trees," what a lovely story to be associated with the Grotto. Hardly a child goes through his schooling without having come in contact with Kilmer's poem:

Trees

I think that I shall never see
A poem lovely as a tree.
A tree whose hungry mouth is prest
Against the earth's sweet flowing breast;
A tree that looks at God all day
And lifts her leafy arms to pray;
A tree that may in summer wear
A nest of robins in her hair;
Upon whose bosom snow has lain;
Who intimately lives with rain
Poems are made by fools like me
But only God can make a tree.

— Joyce Kilmer

Kilmer was noted for writing the poetry of the people; he mirrored their thoughts. He discovered in the most ordinary things rich and unsuspected meanings.[168]

His biographer, Robert Holliday, speaks of "Trees" and describes Kilmer as a poet:

The exquisite title poem now so universally known, made his reputation more than all the rest he had written put together. That impeccable lyric which made for immediate widespread popularity.

His song was as old as the hills, and as fresh as the morning. Precisely in this, in fact, is his remarkableness, his originality, as a contemporary poet; and in this will be, I think, his abiding quality. "Simple and direct, yet not without subtle magic," wrote Father James J. Daly, S.J., in a review of Trees and Other Poems printed in America, his verse "seems artlessly naive, yet it possesses deep undercurrents of masculine and forceful thought; it is ethical in its seriousness, and yet as playful and light-hearted as sunlight and shadows under summer oaks."

Only the name of James Whitcomb Riley expresses in greater measure the rich gift of speaking with authentic song to the simplest hearts.

In letters sent home during the war in Europe, Kilmer wrote:

"At present, I am a poet trying to be a soldier. To tell the truth, I am not interested in writing nowadays, except in so far as writing is the expression of something beautiful. . . ."[169]

A thesis written about Kilmer in 1927 by a friend of the family, Sister Roberta Bresnan — "Home Life as a Theme in the poetry of Joyce Kilmer" — speaks of Kilmer:

He had a quiet way of being genuine. He loved the simplest things of life because he was himself perhaps the simplest. His poetry expressed the remedy for all this world's woes, in one small word of deep and lasting significance, the word "home." When we designate it as a place, it immediately shifts to a feeling, a person, an object. It may embrace an entire country or it may be confined within the perimeter of four walls.[170]

A description of the campus — the way Joyce may have viewed it when he was there — was penned by a writer in an 1886 newspaper. It confirms that the tradition of praying places among the trees was as much in evidence at Notre Dame then as now.

The grounds around the college are laid out in finely shaded walks. As we pass over the grounds we notice that which always finds a tender spot in the hearts of all Catholics in the great number of oratories and abodes for prayer that are to be found in secluded parts of the grounds, that students on their walks may have an oppor-

tunity of offering to heaven their prayers undisturbed and with only the sky and the trees for witness.[171]

For such a memorable poem to be associated with the Grotto would be an honor worthy of every effort made to verify it.

Researching Joyce Kilmer

There was very little in the University Archives about Joyce Kilmer and only a few mentions of lectures he made on campus. A few letters exchanged with Charles O'Donnell and John W. Cavanaugh, arranging those lectures in 1914, gave no evidence to pinpoint his first visit to Notre Dame prior to that first lecture. Sometime before, or after, that first lecture, O'Donnell and Kilmer must have become friends and correspondents. Father Charles O'Donnell was also a chaplain where Kilmer was stationed during the war in Europe. He corresponded with Kilmer's widow, Aline, until his death.

One publication did have a picture of Kilmer's daughter, a Benedictine nun, and his youngest son, Christopher. They were photographed together during a celebration honoring Kilmer. It might be almost impossible to locate a lay person, but a religious was another matter. Although the chances that his daughter might still be living 57 years later were rather slim, it seemed worth a try.

Within minutes Kilmer's daughter, Sister Michael, was on the line in St. Cloud, Minn. She said she was sorry to report that, to her knowledge, no tree had been recognized as the one that inspired her father's poem. She said her older brother might be able to remember more about it and she offered his telephone number in Vienna, Virginia.

Kenton Kilmer, oldest child of Joyce Kilmer, was most hospitable. He confirmed his sister's impression. He said he also had a letter written by his mother, to another inquirer, explaining the origin of the poem "Trees" as she knew it. He offered to send anything he had that might be of help. Many places, he explained, including Kilmer's alma mater, Rutgers, had trees they felt had inspired Kilmer's poem.

The material he sent indicated that Richmond, NH, Prairie du Chien (Campion), and a Catholic Summer School and Retreat House on the shores of Lake Champlain, were other places said to have trees that may have inspired Kilmer's poem. He included pictures of the family home, its trees, and a copy of the poem handwritten by Kilmer at the time. He then described when and where this much loved poem was written.

He said "Trees" was written at Kilmer's home in Mahwah, New Jersey, on February 2, 1913. It was written in the afternoon in the intervals of some other writing. The desk was in an upstairs room, by a window looking down a wooded hill. It was written in a little notebook in which his father and mother wrote out copies of several of their poems, and, in most cases, added the date of composition. On one page, he said, the first two lines of "Trees" were written, with the date, February 2, 1913, and on another page, further on in the book, was the full text of the poem. It was dedicated to Kilmer's wife's mother, Mrs. Henry Mills Alden, who was endeared to all her family.

Father Schidel, a Holy Cross priest on campus, said he, too, had heard the same story over the years. He asked Father Charles Carey, a nephew of Father Charles O'Donnell — the poet Laureate and Kilmer's good friend — if his uncle had ever mentioned Joyce and the Grotto.

Father Carey said he did remember one comment his uncle made about walking around the lake and Grotto lawn with Kilmer. He said his uncle told him he and Kilmer had stopped to admire what they both felt was a perfect tree, the one sheltering Our Lady and the Grotto perhaps? This could have occurred before the 1913 poem was written or, more likely, afterwards, in discussing it.

A book about the campus written by a Holy Cross priest, Father Sigmund Jankowski, who built the St. Stanislaus Grotto in South Bend, mentioned how Joyce Kilmer visited their English class and recited his famous poem. This priest began his studies at Notre Dame in the fall of 1913, eight months after it was written and just weeks after it was published. He described his remembrance of him in his book:

. . . It was one of my happy graces to have Father [Charles] O'Donnell as a teacher in English. Into our class-room one day, he invited his fellow-poet, Joyce Kilmer, the author of "Trees." He himself recited his immortal lines with a commanding artistic touch. He was a mild-mannered man whose eyes betrayed a wealth of inspiring thoughts, and also a definite spark of courage, enabling him later to give his life for his country in World War I. . . .[172]

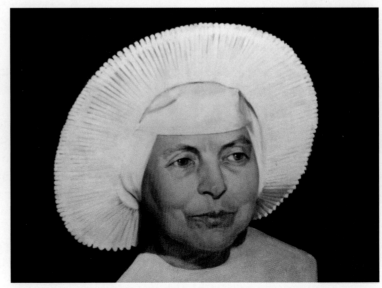

Sister Madeleva, former President of Saint Mary's College, and a poet, was also a friend of Joyce Kilmer from her early days as a nun. Sister Madeleva took a summer class in creative writing from Fr. Charles O'Donnell at St. Mary's and through him she met Kilmer. In her autobiography, *My First Seventy Years,* she speaks of her friendship with them:

More than once Joyce Kilmer came with Father O'Donnell to visit. Their minds were quick with poems waiting to be written.

The importunities of war pressed. Both men volunteered for service. Both went overseas. Joyce was killed in action on July 30, 1918, near Ourcq in France and buried beside a stream that bears the same name. Father blessed his grave before coming home.[173]

There was no grade transcript of Sister Madeleva's creative writing class with Father O'Donnell and her letters and papers gave no clues to her first meeting with Kilmer on the St. Mary's campus. However, one of her poems about candle-light could have been written for the Grotto. This portion of it would be an inspiration to all who visit there.

Candle-Light

Day has its sun,
And night the stars.
But God has candle-light.
Upon the world's great candle-stick He sets
The little taper of yourself to ashine,
That . . .
Your immortality may flame and burn
Across His infinite immensity forever.

Sister M. Madeleva, C.S.C.[174]

A Letter from Kenton Kilmer

Kilmer was quoted as saying: "I can honestly offer "Trees" and "Main Street" to Our Lady and ask her to present them as the faithful work of a poor unskilled craftsman, to her son."[175] The priest who wrote the brochure about Kilmer and the Notre Dame Grotto was also a friend of Father O'Donnell. Perhaps, he had repeated something he remembered him saying about Kilmer and used the "they say" because he couldn't confirm it.

Father Schidel said that Belloc, a fellow poet of Joyce, spoke of "poetry being the distillation of the mind." He offered the theory that Joyce may have written the poem in the bedroom of his home, but he might have been affected by trees he had seen in many localities, and his thoughts may have "jelled" into a poem upon looking out his window at the trees in his yard. In other words, we know where the poem was written, but probably only God knows where and when it was inspired.

A reply from Kenton, in which he responds to Father Schidel's observation, concluded the Kilmer research admirably:

Mother and I agreed, when we talked about it, that Dad never meant his poem to apply to one particular tree, or to the trees of any special region. Just any trees or all trees that might be rained on or snowed on, and that would be suitable nesting places for robins. I guess they'd have to have upward-reaching branches, too, for the line about 'lifting leafy arms to pray.' Rule out weeping willows.

. . . I think Father Schidel's opinion is just right and in complete accord with

what my mother and I agreed on. Dad meant trees in general, was surely thinking of the trees he was looking at, and probably of trees he had seen in the past, such as the famous one on the Rutgers campus. But what he was thinking and saying applies equally to trees he didn't see until later, or trees he never would see. Dad would surely be pleased with Father Schidel's citation of the Belloc quotation, for its aptness to the subject, because Dad was a fervent admirer of Belloc's poetry.

. . . It is plain from comments in my father's letters, . . . that Dad's devotion to Christ was always joined with the love of His Mother. I am sure that a grove of trees dedicated to the Blessed Virgin could have inspired him to write such a poem as 'Trees,' if the poem had not already been written.[176]

Kilmer was on campus in the fall of 1913, the year he wrote and published "Trees" (February 2, 1913). However, there was no evidence to prove that he had visited the campus and the Grotto prior to the time he wrote it, although it was very possible.

Short of an affirmative answer, it was a most satisfying conclusion to a study of Kilmer and his association with the University and the Notre Dame Grotto.

Joyce Kilmer's "Trees," and Tom Stritch's view of the Notre Dame campus from his book, *My Notre Dame*, express, so well, the warmth and welcome received from trees:

Few American colleges can rival its layout, none its trees. Of all the things to look at around Notre Dame I think I like the trees the best. . . . I seldom look at that island without thinking how lovely its redbud trees look from the Grotto lawn in the spring.[177]

Another appreciator of trees, Father Cornelius Hagerty, an avid canoeist, made this interesting observation about their special appeal to lovers of nature: "Trees stand still and let you look at them and are there at all seasons."[178]

Their words evoke a mental image of Joyce Kilmer circling St. Mary's Lake with Father O'Donnell, pausing in the shade of the Grotto lawn, and admiring that "perfect tree" shading Our Lady's niche.

The essence of Kilmer and his poem "Trees," written by Rev. Thomas J. O'Donnell, C.S.C. '41, appeared in a 1963 *Scholastic*.

The canopy of trees, digging their roots into the unhewn rock, is the proudest grove on campus. And rightly so. These trees are a garland of green on a crown of rocks. They have lived up to all the beauty of Kilmer's poem . . . as all trees must. But these have done more. They have listened to May songs; they have watched flickering vigil lights; they have stood as silent sentinels while anxious prayers and burdened hearts lifted hopeful eyes to Our Lady. The trees of the Grotto — if they could speak — would speak only in a whisper. . . .[179]

Chapter 11

The Landmark Sycamore — Guardian of the Grotto

Another tree on the Grotto lawn speaks in a whisper the legend it has to tell. A brief mention of it turned up on an index card in the *Scholastic* card catalog file. On it were the words: "Legendary Tree Stands in Rear of Corby Hall."[180] It told of a wronged Indian whose spirit had entered into the tree and formed its unusual shape.

The full story would have remained hidden were it not for the discovery of a two page account of it in an unindexed 1926 Dome. Someone had done a masterful job of documenting the legend. The two page story, illustrated with a decorative border and a small but very good picture of the sycamore, was called, "The Legend Of The Sycamore Tree."

It was not an unfamiliar story. The year before he died, Father John J. Cavanaugh, former president of Notre Dame, told the tale one day at Holy Cross House. He referred to it as "that odd-shaped sycamore that stood in back of Corby Hall near the Grotto." He said it was known as The Vengeance Tree because it had the shape of an open hand outstretched in a pleading gesture.

Father Cavanaugh was a great story teller. The fate of the "Missing Empress Eugenie Crown" was another story he told. Although many may have dismissed them as more of Father Cavanaugh's genial Irish wit — the kind of fireside stories a beloved grandfather might spin to amuse his grandchildren — they were such great stories about early Notre Dame, that once heard, they were never forgotten.

Was it campus lore or was there at least a kernel of truth in the legend of the sycamore? It seemed only fair to Father Cavanaugh to check this one out, too, to see if it could also be verified, most especially, because it was on the Grotto lawn, a witness to all the history that had transpired there.

Brother Vitus, oldest religious on campus at 98, had no special recollections about the huge old sycamore tree, other than the fact that it had been an impressive landmark on the campus for as long as he could remember. He said it probably dated back to the founding of the University.

The Age of the Sycamore

The tree's circumference measured an astounding 20 feet 4 inches. Taking a core sample, the only true way to age the tree, was out of the question. It was too old and too special a tree to take any risk in harming it. Instead, measurements and early photographs were sent to the Forestry Department at Purdue University for their assessment.

They affirmed its earliest age to be at least 200 to 220 years old and possibly older. "The unusual shape of the tree reflected the presence and absence of buds and growing points when the tree was very young. It was considered a happenstance of nature."[181] Most sycamores have straight trunks with branches very high up on the tree. The branches on the Notre Dame sycamore are waist high making it a most unique example of this oddity.

To arrive at an approximate 200 year age, 1794 or a bit earlier which would have fit the legend, the tree would have to have grown from 4¹ᐟ²" to 5" in ten years. Literature enclosed with their letter confirmed it. The proximity to water and the excellent campus care it received would account for the unusual growth.

A *Scholastic* article describing the "The Walk To The Stile" provided more evidential information about the sycamore. Daniel Vincent Casey, detailed, in eloquent prose, "The Stile" (an arrangement of steps for getting over a fence or wall, while forming a barrier to the passage of sheep or cattle) and the walk which led to St. Mary's Academy. Hidden away in this article was a reference to the sycamore. He speaks of the ancient level of the lake:

Forty years ago, when that splendid old sycamore yonder was a hill-side weakling, all this basin was under water, and St. Vincent's was, in very truth 'the Island'.[182]

The article was written in 1896. The splendid old sycamore had to be the landmark tree, and 40 years ago would have been 1856. A "hill-side weakling," as compared to "that splendid old sycamore yonder," would mean it could have been up to fifty years old at the time, which would place its age somewhere near the late 1700s or early 1800s. It was more than old enough to have been on the grounds before Sorin's arrival.

The problem between the whites and the Indians intensified throughout the Old Northwest in the late 1790s and early 1800s:

Over the next decade hostilities escalated. Wiser chiefs not only sought to keep liquor from their warriors, but blamed the Americans for their corruption. The decisive American victory at Tippecanoe in 1811 did not diminish Potawatomi hostility. Frustrated by the steady loss of Indian land, many young Potawatomis no longer followed their traditional village chiefs, who continued to cooperate with the Americans. They were well stocked with trade whiskey, and angered over the sight of white men establishing farms in an area they believed their own.

Young warriors continued to ambush and kill white settlers and the whites retaliated by burning Indian villages.[183]

There were also negotiations by the government for Indian land during the hostile period when the unfortunate incident that produced the Indian legend might have taken place:

The situation was complicated by the fact that squatters had invaded Indian lands and now demanded immediate removal. Several resulting clashes between whites and Indians seemed to confirm predictions of imminent bloodshed if something was not done soon.[184]

In 1830, Congress passed the Indian Removal Act which allowed the government to move Indians beyond the Mississippi River to make room for the settlers who were streaming westward.

Timothy Howard's *History of St. Joseph County Indiana* described those early Indian days in a tearful account of the Indian removal on September 4, 1838, at Menominee village at Twin lakes, five miles southwest of Plymouth, one of the "rendezvous for these foundlings of the forests."

He mentions that 67 years later, on February 3, 1905, a bill[185] was proposed to authorize the erection of a monument to preserve the memory of the Potawatomi and Miami Indians, to mark the dawn of civilization in northern Indiana and rebuild the first house of Christian worship in the entire great northwest, east of the Pacific Coast (Badin's Indian chapel at Menominee village).

Representative Daniel McDonald concluded his stirring 1905 address with these words:

The Potawatomi Indians will not be forgotten. Their memory has been preserved . . . in the rivers, lakes and various localities bearing their names. Aubenaube and Kewanna, and Tiosa, in Fulton county, and the beautiful Tippecanoe, with its rippling waters of blue; and the picturesque Manitou, and the lovely Maxinkuckee, the St. Joseph, and especially the famous Wabash.

All these names will perpetuate for all time to come the memory of the Potawatomi Indians, the first owners and inhabitants of all the beautiful country north of the Wabash river and south of the great lakes.

> The Indians all have passed away,
> That noble race and brave,
> Their light canoes have vanished
> From off the crested wave.
> Amid the forest where they roamed
> There rings no hunter's shout —
> But their name is on your waters —
> You can not wash it out.
>
> — Lydia H. Sigourney[186]

Though most of the Indians were sent to Kansas, there were a few exceptions made for the Pokagon band of Potawatomi Indians who had become Christians during earlier times when Jesuit priests first came as missionaries. Even after 1838, there were still Potawatomi Indians in the vicinity. Sorin mentions that 200 Indians were in the area when he arrived in 1842.[187]

Although the Potawatomis had ceded all tribal lands in Michigan, [1837] many Indians held individual reservations, and other tribesmen still wandered through the Saint Joseph Valley."[188]

Interesting Descriptions of Early Notre Dame in Indian Times

Numerous interesting excerpts from a variety of sources in the University Archives, verify that Indians — and Indian Chiefs — were very much a part of the Notre Dame campus in the early days of its history.

The beautiful Lake [St. Mary's], being only a mile from LaSalle's portage and in the midst of a rich hunting ground, was the central meeting place for the entire region. Here the Indians came to meet the traders, and here the missionaries came, bringing with them the light of God.[189]

An old ledger containing early obituaries recorded this death notice, entered on the 28th of March, 1847, for William Richardville (1846-1847).

This young man, the son of an Indian Chief, of the Miami Tribe was our first student who died. He died of consumption in the old building where the present Infirmary stands in the actual corridor between the students office and the minims wash room. He was buried in the present Parish Graveyard [Cedar Grove Cemetery].[190]

The *Scholastic* reported: "On July 4, 1848 at commencement exercises, a premium was awarded Thomas La Fontaine, Indian son of the Chief of the Miamis."[191]

Father Sorin described the University of Notre Dame in the 1860s as having the appearance of a most agreeable and romantic little village.[192] When he was considering the question as to when the new Our Lady of the Sacred Heart Church should be dedicated, he painted another romantic picture of it and includes "his dear Indians."

What a consolation will it not be to see the dedication of a temple in honor of our Blessed Mother on the spot where we well remember having seen with our own eyes the wigwams and the fires of the Potawatomis![193]

Howard's *History Of St. Joseph County Indiana*[194] also paints this picture of what the Notre Dame campus was like when Indians were still a part of it in 1845.

To the right of you, to the left of you, in front of you, and behind you, reigned the primeval forest. There were not thirty acres of clearance in the whole section of land belonging to the college.

In 1876 he recalled these earlier times:

When several of the students were sons of civilized Indian Chiefs or other distinguished braves among the remnants of the tribes yet left in northern Indiana and southern Michigan, even finer sport was found in the weekly excursions, by foot and carryalls and other hired vehicles and winter sleigh rides. Bears, wolves, deer, turkey, coons, opossums, catamounts and prairie hens were found in the pathless woods and prairies, while the lakes and streams were covered with wild geese and other aquatic game. The boys found a bear in a bee tree, trying to rob the honey. The Indian boys soon smoked out the bear, and then made short work of him, much to the amazement of their white companions. They managed also to get the honey which the unfortunate bear had been after.

With the Indians and the bears, such exciting excursions came to an end, but the charms of the weekly tramps continue even to this day. They are, however, of necessity now confined to the grounds of the University and chiefly by the margins of the charming lakes.

Perhaps part of the necessity of confining those excursions to the grounds of the University is explained by this unfortunate hunting accident and the heroic deed associated with it. It occurred on October 7, 1878, six weeks after Father Sorin's 1878 Grotto was dedicated.

We have this week a melancholy duty to perform in announcing the death of Mr. George W. Sampson, who had just entered on his third year as a student at Notre Dame. His death was caused by the accidental discharge of a fowling piece while he was absent with a hunting party. Mr. Sampson was passionately fond of this amusement, and on Monday last, the first extra holiday of the year, he left the College in high spirits with a few other young men to enjoy a day's shooting in the country and at the same time to try a magnificent new breech-loader which had been presented to him during vacation by his father. While on his way back he met his untimely end. Rev. Father O'Sullivan of Laporte who was on the opposite bank of the St. Joseph River at the time the accident occurred, immediately plunged in and swam across — though risking his own life thereby — and was present to soothe the unfortunate man's last moments with the consolations of religion. . . . The incident is one of the saddest ever chronicled in the annals of Notre Dame. A young man of bright promise and of the happiest disposition, gentle and amiable towards all, — to know young Sampson was to be his friend, and we have every reason to hope that the favorable judgment which all who knew him on earth were so ready to pronounce on him has been ratified above. May he rest in peace![195]

If the sons of Indian Chiefs were students on campus in those early days, were there also Indian Chiefs living on or near the campus who could have passed on the legend to the early religious on campus?

An 1859 guide to the campus indicates that a few Indians who left Kansas and returned to Indiana were cared for by the University.

Here we cross the highway [US 31] leading from South Bend to Niles and find ourselves on the other side of the boundary line separating the college grounds [Notre Dame] from those of St. Mary's Academy. The gate of the Academy is attended by a lone Indian, one of the few remaining in the region. His cottage stands before you as a porter's lodge on the public road. Kindness and charity bestowed this situation, when old age and infirmity were upon him.[196]

Another reference to this practice provides a glimpse of the times and the plight of the displaced Indians:

Among the Indians in the northwestern part of the county was a petty chief named Sagganee, who, when the Indians were removed to the west, went to Kansas with some of them, but soon returned saying that he could not live there because there was no sugar tree. He was a devout Catholic and would never eat anything without first crossing himself. In his later days he was cared for at the Catholic University of Notre Dame, at South Bend, where he passed away, and where his remains lie buried. He is said to have been a great brave in his day and to have fought in the battle of Tippecanoe in 1812.[197]

Local records verify that Chief Sagganee was present in the area and might have been the "Gate House" Indian who lived on campus. He was a chief, an old man in 1859 and fought in the Tippecanoe Battle in 1812, which would definitely put him in the right time frame to be the Indian Chief in the legend.

Two other Indian burials at Notre Dame were also recorded. One Indian named Alexis was buried in 1896. The second one mentioned, Chippa,[198] was also a chief and a possible candidate for the legend:

Brother Frances Xavier buried in Cedar Grove Cemetery, Notre Dame, Chippa, an Indian reputed to be nearly 150 years old. He was one of the few aboriginals remaining in this part of the country and formerly belonged to the tribe of Miamis who lived in the neighborhood of Ft. Wayne.[199]

Although all these Indians were reported to be buried on campus, there were index cards in the burial records only on Chippa and Alexis who died in the 1890s. Nothing could be found at St. Mary's or Notre Dame on the burial of the Indian gatekeeper or Chief Sagganee. However, early burial records at Cedar Grove Cemetery were destroyed in a fire, which might explain their absence.

In 1932, the *South Bend Tribune* described the reinternment of Indian remains in Cedar Grove Cemetery under the heading: "Mystery Cloaks Indian Burial Grounds." Beside a picture of the marker, on a huge boulder placed over the common grave at Cedar Grove, is this explanation:

Perhaps a tribal chieftain and his warriors are lying beneath this smooth green mound in Cedar Grove Cemetery at Notre Dame. No one could discover the names of these Potawatomis when they were removed from the tiny Indian cemetery at the top of Angela hill in 1928. Their first resting place was hidden in a thicket and marked with a plain iron cross. All identification has been lost in the mystery and silence so peculiar to the race. The graves were transferred to permit widening of Angela boulevard. On the marker are the words:

POTAWATOMI INDIANS —
REMAINS TRANSFERRED TO
CEDAR GROVE CEMETERY FROM
AN INDIAN BURIAL GROUND
ABOUT ONE MILE WEST —
SEPTEMBER 22, 1928.[200]

In the late 1980s, Indian medicine men presided over a big ceremony at Cedar Grove Cemetery (said to be 150 people, with drums). Two skeletons of their ancestors rescued from the museum of the Western Michigan College were buried in the mound. The sexton, Tim Mosier, who was there at the time, said their visit was very quietly accomplished to avoid any publicity and was over before anyone else knew about it.

On February 6, 1875, the *Scholastic* reported a fourth burial of an Indian Chief, another likely candidate for the legend, "Mr. John Piashway, a one time Chief of the Miamis, was buried here last Wednesday."[201]

Piashway lived in the area where Peashway street is now, directly across from the present golf course at Notre Dame. He was the son of Chief Richardville, also Chief of the Miamis, and married the daughter of another chief, Chief Steven Benneck, who died in 1853 at 75 years of age. His wife's father lived with them on their land across from Notre Dame.

There was no doubt about it, Indians were very much in evidence at Notre Dame from before Badin's time until the Indian removal, and even long afterward. Which means any one of the aforementioned Indian Chiefs who lived in close proximity to the campus could have been the Indian Chief who told the story that became the legend.

The time has now come for the reader to decide whether the story behind the fabled sycamore, on the Grotto lawn, is fact or fiction, history or legend. So here's the story and here's what has been learned about it.

The Brother Who Passed on the Story

Brother Frederick Kraling was a glazier at Notre Dame. He was known to etch important dates on a pane of glass. Evidence of this habit can still be seen today in a windowpane at the old St. Joseph Farm. Brother Frederick was washing a window at the farm when he heard of the big fire on campus. He scratched a memo on the pane that remains clear today: "23 of April 1879, College on Fire."

Between 1879 and 1886 it was announced in the *Scholastic* that Brother Frederick "and his faithful assistants were kept busy painting, graining and otherwise decorating the new building," the Minim's Hall, and Washington Hall. His artistic work in St. Edward's Hall is also described: "The walls of the study-hall are of a most pleasing shade of green which is both beautiful and pleasing to the eye. The walls are painted in oil, and stippled so as to represent pressed leather." The corridors of the Infirmary, as well as the small parlor in the Main Building, were "handsomely frescoed by Bro. Frederick." He also painted, "in new and artistic designs, the hall of the Culinary Department." His multi-talented craftsmanship and his attention to detail is affirmed in this piece that appeared in the June 14, 18 *Scholastic*:

Among the contributions lately placed in the Cabinet of Curiosities are mounted models of cathedrals of

Cologne, Strasberg, and St. Peters at Rome. These are a gift from Bro. Frederick who skillfully constructed the models and the glass cases which surround them.

He also directed the first gilding of the Dome: "Brother Frederick and a capable assistant have been actively engaged for the past weeks in the work of gilding the grand dome of the main building."[202]

The University Archives has the windowpane upon which Brother Frederick recorded the dates and cost of the gildings up until his death. The top of the transcript reads:

Notations on gilding of the Dome as etched by Brother Frederick in the windowpane in the old boiler room, behind the administration building on the site where the natatorium was later erected.

The last date Brother Frederick recorded was in 1904. He died on January 4, 1917, three years before the 1920 gilding. There were several items of particular interest in the transcript of those etchings, which are evidence of his meticulous care in recording history.

He lists the cost in detail (850.50 for the 1886 gilding) and the dates, July 3 and September 9, it was completed. He also adds this mention: 22nd Sept. '86, *Hail Storm.* In the last recorded entry in 1904, Brother Frederick

includes "Gold scrapings net 162.42," and adds a note of humor: "P.S. John had charge of sizing, Steave [sic] of the gold and Jack of the winch and whiskey.[203]

Several months after the discovery of the two page story in the 1926 Dome, another earlier version came to light in paging through a 1917 *Scholastic*. This earlier version included the author's name. Neither of these two versions were indexed.

This slightly longer version of the legend was written by William E. Farrell, a Professor of History at Notre Dame, who knew the Brother who told the story. He explains his reason for writing, "The Legend Of The Sycamore":

The death last week of Brother Frederick[204] of this community, will be learned with sincere regret and kindly memory by those who enjoyed an intimate acquaintance with him and who understood and appreciated his rare personality. For years, he was a familiar figure on our campus, where he could be seen frequently in animated conversation with one or another of those who found him congenial. Few men about Notre Dame possessed such a store of historical incident and legend associated with the grounds and environs of the University. He had read much and had talked frequently with the brave pioneers who had preceded him in the community, about the interesting places for miles around. He was equally familiar with the written sources and the oral Indian legends pertaining to these places.

Before age and ill health had made inroads on body and mind, he was remarkably gifted with clear memory and poetic insight. It was my privilege to know Brother Frederick well and I recall with "fragrant retrospec-

tion" the incidents and legends related by him several years ago in our occasional talks or on long walks through pleasant places. One legend, I shall endeavor, as he often requested, to tell.

The Legend Of The Sycamore

A little to the west and to the rear of Corby Hall stands an old, impressive-looking sycamore tree. If one is at all observant of nature's manifold beauties, those that appeal to the sense of grandeur, as well as to the sense of delicacy, this noble tree, especially in the season of foliage, cannot but arrest attention. Its majestic proportions are in themselves enough to command admiration: it towers above its fellows, and gazing calmly down upon them, seems like a tall, white-haired seer, who quietly regards the youthful lives about him and gravely recalls the memories and associations of his own springtime of life. From its sturdy trunk, huge limbs shoot at symmetrical angles in every direction, ever widening as they rear higher. The grandeur and symmetry of it all is truly striking.

The physical beauty of the tree is, however, incidental only to the chief interest that is attached to it. If you examine the outlines carefully, you will detect an almost exact formation of the human hand projecting from the ground and lifted as if in appeal, the trunk forming the wrist and the five limbs into which the trunk divides, forming the fingers.

For some years after the founding of Notre Dame, it was not uncommon to see an Indian moving about the grounds, revisiting old haunts and enjoying the natural beauty which then, as now, was very great. One old chief, in particular, was observed coming here several times. He seemed most interested in two places; one along the shore of the lake, where, usually in the evening, he would stand with arms folded, silently contemplating the waters with their peace and beauty at sunset; the other was near the sycamore, then in its youth. He would linger at this spot for a long time with head bowed or with eyes raised to heaven, as if in silent prayer. One of the brothers who had observed this several times became interested and inquired from the Indian why he spent so much time near this tree. The Indian did not speak for a few seconds. His face was calm, yet revealed his suppressed grief. Then he lifted his hand impatiently as if to wave the matter aside, but when the brother spoke again in a tone of sympathy, the old chief told his story.

In the earlier days, when raids between the white men and the Indians were frequent, one white settler, who

had lost a friend he cherished greatly, swore eternal enmity against every Red-skin. On one occasion this man, while hunting, was passing through what are now the grounds of Notre Dame, when he caught sight of an Indian, fishing peacefully on the shore of the lake. The Indian was unarmed and suspected nothing. He was a Christian convert, a man of peace and had always sought friendship with the white man. At the sight of the Indian, however, the Indian-hater could not restrain his feelings. He crept up softly toward the shore of the lake and, springing suddenly from the bushes, drove his hunting knife into the back of the fisherman. The Indian with a yell, started up and ran eastward from the lake, but when he reached the spot where now stands the great sycamore, he fell exhausted. Here his assaulter reached him again, and in spite the Indian's supplications and protestations of innocence, attacked him a second time.

The Indian in agony cried out, saying: "What have I done that you should kill me in this way?"

But the white man, answered, "You are an Indian, and Indians have killed my dearest friend."

The Indian, then on the point of death, exclaimed: "I am innocent of the blood of any man. I appeal to God for vengeance." With these words on his lips, the Indian died.

Some time after this occurrence, a little tree of strange shape sprang up where the Indian's blood had trickled into the earth. Later the chief, who knew the circumstances of the Indian's death, on passing that way was struck by the peculiar shape of the tree, a miniature of its present form. Its signification then dawned upon him. Here was the hand and wrist of his dear friend extended to heaven. As the sapling grew it still retained its strange shape and the hand remains to this day lifted in appeal to God as a warning to all who might put to death an innocent man.

As with most stories of this kind, it may have had its origin in some fact and was then embellished by the Indian imagination.[205] *Such is the tale told by the old chief to the brother, and the brother, who loved such beautiful things as legends, passed the story on to us. Call it a tale of fancy, invented by an over-vivid imagination; call it an unbelievable dream; but the huge old sycamore, remains to this day on the Grotto lawn, a relic of the romantic days of Notre Dame, a record of a day long since passed, and as such, its story will continue to live with us.*[206]

The Indian chief's words in the legend aptly describe those hostile times during the late 1790s and the early 1800s when the legend was born and the sycamore is most likely to have taken root.

As the story goes, the innocent Redskin being unable to reap human vengeance for his death, entered in spirit into the tree, and stretched its branches to heaven in supplication for God's justice. Tradition holds that the event in this legend actually happened though it cannot be confirmed from surviving records.

An Archival Treasure

The only aspect of the Indian Legend left unexplored was the reason why the tree was called The Vengeance Tree. The vengefulness of the white man toward an innocent Indian, and the Indians toward innocent white settlers and each other, is difficult to grasp. The savagery of bloodthirsty vengeance was considered almost inborn in the Indian culture.

This aspect of the Indian Legend seemed to warrant a more thorough examination, if the information could be found. One last timely piece of history emerged to complete a picture of those early Indian times — the transcribed journal of a German missionary priest — who visited the Ste.-Marie-des-Lacs mission before Father Sorin's arrival. It was discovered just in time to become a most unique postscript to add to Notre Dame's Indian era and the Legend of the Sycamore on the Grotto lawn.

This German missionary's narrative provides an eye-witness account of the effect Christianity had on the Indians and the events that transpired during his stay. It also included an early settler's explanation of the Indian's attitude toward vengeance. It was published in 1845, but was written in the summer of 1840 or 1841.

It begins with a very detailed description of the log chapel and the Indians camped by the lake, seen through the eyes of a visiting missionary priest very impressed with his surroundings.

The Missionary Lodging

I am writing these lines to you in a log cabin on the elevated bank of a small, quiet lake in northern Indiana, on the southwestern border of Michigan, close to the St. Joseph River . . . .

A small, quiet lake . . . like a magic mirror throws back to the observer the vault of heaven above it and the friendly environment around it . . . .

[On its] banks some noble friends built a log cabin several years ago, in which I now dwell.

. . .

The lake in front of me is situated in the cold even in the greatest heat, in mind-freezing North America; the fire behind me has been raked by a semi-savage Canadian, and the bell-ringing comes from the necks of horses belonging to a group of Indians of the Potawatomi tribe who have put up their temporary camp at the lake; the log cabin itself in which I am putting together this letter to you is the mission house of St. Mary of the Lake (Ste.-Marie-du-Lac).

So that you can get an idea of an American mission house, I will let you see first the lodging of the missionary. It is a simple room in which you will look in vain for mural paintings or wallpaper, stucco work and frescos. The four walls of the room consist of roughly cut logs; one wall is formed by a enormous fireplace. The two windows, which face each other, have no mechanism to allow them to open, but accidents have provided openings in the glass through which the air can come in and out. The curtains — even the most wretched hut in North America, such as the one of the missionary, has to have "Curtains" — do look shabby, but the bed and its covers and curtains are even shabbier; yet they look pretty cheerful in this poverty. There is a canopy, like the kind of wooden four-poster covers our grandparents used to have, to keep outbreaks of the elements of earth and water away from the sleeping apostle of the Indians, because the boards of the roof are not joined together closely enough to have sufficient security against the weather.

In order to keep the missionary from losing his courage in this American forest abbey, the poor cabin is adorned inside with the sign of triumph of the One Who is the Way, the Truth and the Life, who didn't even have a place where He could rest his head.

If you were standing next to me in person, you would already have cast your eyes on the surprising abundance of books, which you surely wouldn't expect to find with a "Blackrobe" in such a wasteland among the Indians.

Not only Missals and books of Psalms, Bibles in several languages and church fathers, but also the old spiritual heroes from Athens and Rome, as well as the new ones from England and France — not only put up here, but also, as you could convince yourself by a closer leaf through, frequently used. You can't expect German books here, because the former occupants of this cabin emerged from French schools at a time when even in Germany the German language was neglected and despised.

The House Chapel

Go up with me now to the upper part of the mission house. The stairs are not very comfortable, — the way to heaven is onerous. So — one more wooden step and you are in the chapel.

The garret has been changed into a very friendly oratory, where at present the divine service is celebrated also, because the old chapel on the ground couldn't escape the frailty of old age and its repair has been postponed for lack of means.

Now look around the temporary chapel until I have changed for the divine service, because the regular priest of this house, a Frenchman born in Canada, is traveling and asked me to celebrate in his place.

There on that side of the attic chapel where the altar table is set up for the offering, the wall is covered tastefully with freshly washed linen, on which fresh green cedar twigs from the trees of the primeval forest at the lake have been arranged ingeniously; through the striking white of the linen it distinguishes itself as the almost sublime work of an artistic weaver.

The Madonna picture, engraved copperplate, simple but good, and very big, symbolizes the humility of the mother of our redeemer, and looks down, fair and lovely, from the linen-forest wall covering, and makes you feel quite religious. A wooden cross is standing on the simple altar, which faith in the Crucified brought over the wide ocean, between two simple candlesticks which have been sent over by good-hearted people from Europe. The flowers of the nearby prairie in the not very graceful pots between the candlesticks go well with the whole scene.

If you have looked at the religious part of the chapel, turn around and see how the sturdy children of nature from the north of America, natives of the Potawatomi nation, sit on their tree stumps and silently wait until the divine service starts.

It is a miracle how these rough seats could have been brought up the frail stairs, an even bigger one is how the thin wood floor can support these wood blocks with Indians sitting on them.

Admire the sturdy physique of these "Savages" with their long, jet-black hair, protruding cheek bones on upward-tapering oval skulls, and deep, dark, expressive eyes, which you can come across in Europe only in very soulful people.

Some among these Indians have piercing, frightening facial features, which would frighten at first sight, if we weren't convinced that these people have already accepted Christianity, have thrown away their axe and scalping knife, and use bow and arrow only for hunting game to make their living.

You see how many of the children of the forest present have in their hands prayer books printed in their language, with which they constantly follow the priest in his ceremony at the altar, as their faces light up with inspiring faith in the Savior of the world. Don't miss how I, the poor servant, am honored and loved by them because of the great Master, and asked for frequent blessings. How does the expression NOSE (Father) sound, with which they address their priest? It is so indescribably winning! They, formerly animal-like, live now in the greatest modesty with the scantiest clothes on their body and a woolen blanket as their outer garment, happier and more content than most of the rich in the most progressive cities in Europe, who try to think about the work of faith with the rational intellect.

Those men have to be praised very highly, who have struggled with the greatest troubles in this house I have introduced to you, to carry out their plans to cultivate these wild people.

Mr. [Father] De Seille, the son of very highly regarded parents in Belgium, is resting from all his struggles and sufferings in the old chapel ground near this mission house. In the house where he so often broke the bread of eternal life for the Potawatomis, and fed them with the food of the angels, nobody was present at his death who could have provided the last rites to him. Before he passed away he crawled with the greatest effort to the altar in the small chapel and refreshed his soul for the last time with the consecrated bread.

[Father] Petit, formerly the famous lawyer and popular speaker at Rennes (Ille-et-Vilaine) in France, after half a year of his presence in the same house, preached in the language of the Potawatomis; and then, as a victim of the purest humanity on an onerous trip which he made with the savages across the Mississippi to St. Louis, a city on that river, he was physically defeated, only to celebrate his resurrection in the hereafter all the more victoriously.

But now it is time that I say Holy Mass; the Indians are waiting for it. They came here from a great distance to celebrate the requiem for their missionary (Petit), who accompanied their tribesmen in their exile [their forced march to Kansas] and died on the way back. [He was 28 years old.] Now I ask you, as soon as I am dressed for the Holy Sacrifice of the Mass, to behave yourself properly; don't look around, and be devout. And if you hear a rising, loud murmur during the main part of the Sacrifice, do not fear.

This is . . . an outpouring of faith in the holy mystery of the religion that penetrates them, to which they are now so loyally devoted that they, since baptism, have stood clear of any grave offense against godly and generally applicable human laws.

A Visit With Mme. Coquillard

The missionary priest goes on to mention a visit to the nearby home of Mme. Coquillard. He describes his admiration for the young adopted Indian he meets there.

During my stay in South Bend I was sitting one morning in the Coquillard family's parlor and talking with the little son of the household when suddenly a handsome, slender, young Indian came in. The strongly built child of the forest came into the room with dignity and moved freely and without inhibition on the expensive carpets of my friend's parlor, as if he was always used to the luxury of refined England. . . . The young Indian was very well dressed: He wore perfectly tight-fitting leggins — that means "leggings" or a kind of two-part trousers worn like long stockings and tied to the hips with string. These leggings were decorated on the outside with a wide border that stuck out a little. Over them a clean shirt hung down to the knees, fastened with a leather belt around his hips like the dust coats of our students. In his belt he had a bowie knife and on his feet he had fine moccasins (Indian shoes) cut from soft deer hide, like tobacco pouches in the shape of feet, sewn together only on the instep. Because of its lightness and softness

this kind of shoe is very beneficial for the silent walk of the quick-footed, cunning savage.

The moccasins of this young Indian were moreover decorated with embroidered leather trimmings, which covered the ankle and almost the whole upper part of the shoes. Such was the squaw's embroidery; nobody would expect such neat needlework from savage Indian women. His well formed head was bare; his shiny black hair was combed from the front to the back and fell down his neck; his glowing jet black eyes were focused on me, the "Father". (With "Nose," Father, as I already mentioned, the converted savages address the missionary.) And as he stepped closer to the Father with graceful posture, he knelt down to receive the blessing of the "Blackrobe" and asked me to accept the present which he presented in the name of the Indian band that had sent him. It was a very big, just recently shot, and already totally cleaned turkey . . . .

He then relates this incident — the sad story of another young Indian — told to him by Mme. Coquillard. In recounting the story to him, she touches on the subject of vengeance and explains the Indian's belief in justice. Mme. Coquillard, who was reputed to be part Indian, was an interpreter for Badin, DeSeile and Sorin. This disturbing incident is reminiscent of the legend of the sycamore tree:

When Madame Coquillard noticed my obvious admiration for the handsome build and fine figure of an Indian young man, she told me that not long ago in the vicinity one such well built young Indian had been killed by his own grandmother. The young man had killed an Indian from a different tribe in a state of great excitement. Shortly after the crime had happened, the murderer regained consciousness and, knowing well that according to pagan Indians' laws of vengeance, his life became forfeit to the family of the murder victim, he fled and disappeared. The vindictiveness in the hearts of the Indians, where the power of Christianity hasn't reached yet, is unbelievable. If they die before they can get hold of their desired victim, they leave the execution of the revenge plan as the holiest tradition for their offspring, which they couldn't carry out because of the lack of opportunity. So unsatisfied feelings for revenge pass on to several generations. Now the family of the murder victim demands from the family of the murderer a reconciliation sacrifice, which cannot consist of anything other than the extradition of the murderer himself or another member of his family related by blood. If a relative of the murderer had surrendered himself, the shame of the murder and on top of that the shame resulting from his weakness of character, because of the penance he failed to do, would have remained on his head, and even his relatives would have looked upon him as an outcast. Considering all this, the grandmother of the murderer knew how to lure her grandson out of his hiding place, and they met in the vicinity of Mr. Coquillard's house.

The grandmother, a strong, vigorous Indian women, now told her grandson, since he had to die, it would be more honorable to be killed by her than to die the death of revenge under the humiliating hands of the enemies who were pursuing him — and saying this, she stuck her knife in the chest of the unsuspecting young man. The grandson quickly breathed his last, and the grandmother's barbaric sense of honor was satisfied. But now nature also claimed its rights towards that woman. As she saw the young man lying on the ground in his blood, she raised such an outcry of lamentation and such howls of mourning that the stones of the valley and the trees of the forests asked to mourn with her. She fell down on the grandson, tearing her hair, pounding her chest, stamping her feet on the ground on which the corpse was lying. This severe pain passed into a frenzy which lasted almost a whole day. The other relatives also came by and helped to complete the dreadful picture of furious agony. A messenger was sent to the family of the murder victim by the family of the grandson — the reconciliation had been accomplished. "This scene of agony," said Mrs. Coquillard, "is always fresh before my eyes; the impression she had on me is indelible. I was suffering badly and couldn't at all get the howls of mourning out of my ears. Thanks be to God, who sent the missionaries to relieve them from such scenes."

The visiting priest explains how Christianity was transforming the Indians attitude toward vengeance:

At this remark, I myself appreciated the divinity of the Christian faith, which is capable of making gentle children and lambs out of brutes and hyenas. Indians, even the most frantic men, give up their vindictiveness, which had been part of them for all times, once they have sworn allegiance to the banner of Christ.

. . .

These wild children of nature with their otherwise sharp and glaring physiognomies had now with the enjoyment of the Lamb nothing but faces of saints. Their black eyes bathed in tears, which rolled down their copper red cheeks in big and heavy pearls; a kind of transfiguration was poured out across their faces, which showed the pagans the power of the faith and showed the faithful the inner sun of grace, which shone out of the hearts of these inhabitants of the forest who had been innocent since their baptism.

A greater humility, a higher decency, a firmer faith and a deeper worship can hardly be found anywhere than in these natives of America in the church at Bertrand, which became apparent to the astonished and ashamed descendants of Europe. This edifying behavior of the Indians also prevented them from being derided and ridiculed by the different-minded residents of Bertrand, when they knelt in front of the priest to receive his blessing if they met him some-where in the village, which they did with a special trust in the "Great Spirit".

A striking example of the influence of the early missionaries in this regard is the description of such an incident related by Badin himself when he first came to St. Marie des Lacs and which he sent by letter, as requested, to the Bishop:

Documents respecting the Pout. of St. Joseph, furnished by the Rev. S. T. Badin, Logan's port 30. Oct. 1832:

The late good Bp. Fen[wick] of Cincin[nati] having desired me in May last, to give to the Ind[ian] Department occasional information of considerable events and other subjects respecting the tribe among whom I reside, I shall begin relating the circumstances incident to a murder which took place last Spring, soon after my return from Cincinnati.

On the 9th day of last June, Topinabee, a man of about 25 years of age, chief of the whole tribe of the Pout., who would not listen to religion, did in a drunken fit kill Nanankoy, a man justly esteem'd in the nation — The murderer surrendered at a council held at Carey on the 11th June and looked with resignation for the punishment with the drawn and glittering knives of the brother and friends of Nanankoy.

A sinister silence followed after some peaceful speeches of Pokagon [an elder Chief of the Potawatomi]. My interpreter [Angelique 'Liquette' Campeau], an old woman of 68 years of age, much respected and beloved by the Indians, after unsuccessful attempts to avert a vengeance, which probably would have provoked many other murders, disarmed the men by generously offering her own life in these words addressed to the sullen and indignant brother of the deceased. "Kill me, I stand here to be killed in lieu of Topinabee."

The brother stunned by this unexpected effort of charity, consented to delay inflicting the deadly blow and having been also brought by the Agent (Col. Stewart), from council to a private conversation he resolved to refer the decision to a certain chief, his near relative and to a pretended prophet on the Wabash who gave a bloody answer. But before coming to the dreaded execution several long talks were held with me where I made them so sensible that the prophet was not the son of God as he pretended to be that they laughed at his impostures and their own

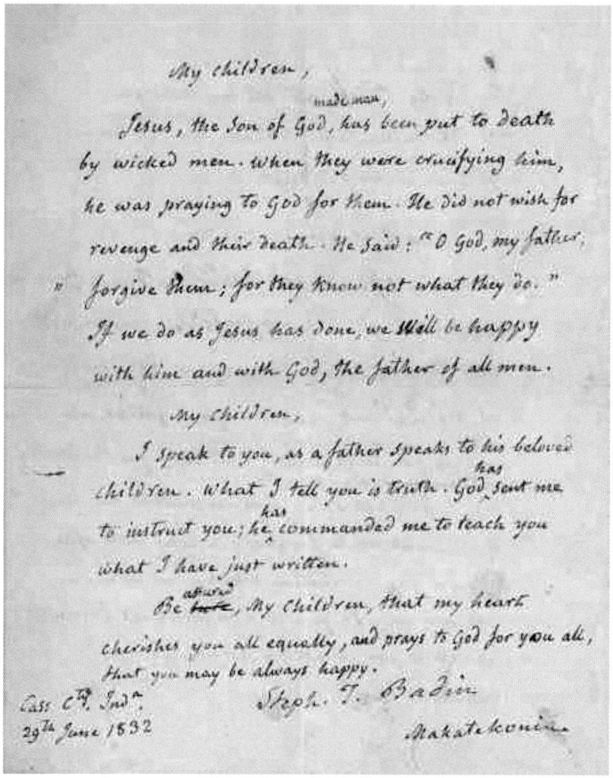

[Handwritten letter reproduction, left column - two images of the original letter by Steph. T. Badin]

credulity. Finally a council was held on the 29th June, to whom I addressed the following letter, and it was agreed that Topinabee would be redeemed by making certain presents to the family of the deceased. All the red with some white brethren contributed to assist the chief in paying the price of redemption. — It may be remarked here that Topinabee had come to me on the 17th June fallen [fell?] on his knees [and] promised me in the presence of God to drink no more whisky and he has been faithful to his promise.

Following is the speech on the evils of whiskey and the futility of killing Topinabee which Badin delivered to those assembled at Carey Mission, Niles MI on June 29, 1832:

To all the Chiefs and all my children of the Poutouatamy nation, this day assembled in council, on St. Joseph River.

My children, Your affectionate father, the French Priest, salutes you all, — My children, you know that French Priests have always been the friends of the Indians. Listen to your father who wishes you to be happy, and tells you the truth, in the name of God.

God has said: "Love one another, and forgive, if you wish me to forgive you, who have often offended me in drinking whisky, and in many other ways. If you forgive not others their offenses to you, I will not forgive you your offenses to me."

My children, Jesus, the Son of God, made man, has been put to death by wicked men. When they were crucifying him, he was praying to God for them. He did not wish for revenge and their death. He said "O God, my father, forgive them; for they know not what they do." If we do as Jesus has done, we will be happy with him and with God, the father of all men.

My children, I speak to you, as a father speaks to his beloved children. What I tell you is truth. God has sent me to instruct you; he has commanded me to teach you what I have just written. Be assured, my children, that my heart cherishes you all equally, and prays to God for you all, that you may be always happy.

Cass Cy. Inda.
29th June 1832

Steph. T. Badin
Makatekonia

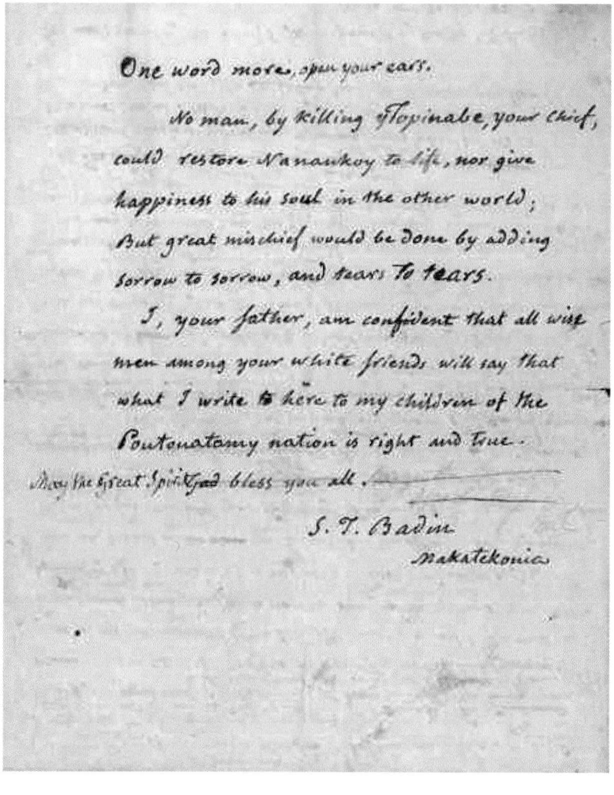

One word more, open your ears.

No man, by killing Topinabe, your chief, could restore Nanankoy to life, nor give happiness to his soul in the other world; But great mischief would be done by adding sorrow to sorrow, and tears to tears.

I, your father, am confident that all wise men among your white friends will say that what I write here to my children of the Poutouatamy nation is right and true.

May the Great Spirit bless you all.

> *S.T. Badin*
> *Makatekonia*[207]

This impressive document, the original of the above letter, is preserved among Father Stephen T. Badin's papers in the University of Notre Dame Archives. It is a testament to the early French missionaries' care and concern for the welfare of the Native American Indians who relied on their revered Blackrobes for Christian counsel.

Father Badin wrote of his interpreter, Angelique, whose actions saved the life of Chief Tobinabee: ". . . I do not know of a priest more industrious, more penitent, more patient, more learned, more genuinely pious then she is in all this country" [Quoted in Buechner, *The Pokagons*, page 302].

An Indian Baptism

The visiting German priest goes on to describe an Indian baptism he performed at St. Mary's Lake during his visit there:

Near the mission house, whose interior I have briefly described for you already, a little hill rises, in the shape of a mountain ridge, which extends in a straight line for several hundred steps, and faces with its precipitous side the lake with which I made you acquainted in the first chapter of this letter.

On this ridge now you see several tents made from rush mats, pitched in the simplest way. In front of them you still see the smoking ashes of their fires, on which the "redskins" prepared their meals in the gypsy way. The men, having said their prayers in the chapel of the wilderness, now stroll around in the temporary camp altogether carefree and unconcerned about the activities of the neighborhood, and puff away on their pipes with wonderful manners. The squaws, the born Cinderellas in the family life of the natives in America, are industrious and active in their traveling household, and clean and tidy up the pieces of their household possessions, which are easily counted. The little savages, for want of a bathtub, get their morning refreshments in the lake, while the older boys are following the horses in puris naturalibus, which, hobbled at the bottom of their front legs, can only hop like frogs, but while doing so take their fill of lush prairie grass in the broad meadow on the banks of the lake. Walk now with me up the hill, where I will baptize an Indian born this morning. I will celebrate the baptism in front of the tent where the mother of the child is. She came yesterday riding à la Turc with the Indian train and is lying now fresh and healthy under the rush roof. She is wrapped tightly into a woolen blanket and of her body only the head with its long black hair and glowing eyes is visible. Her whole situation brings instinctively back to my mind the Egyptian mummies I have seen, even more so since her glance is focused on me without movement. In the tent everything is unusually clean, though nothing remains so that you, as a doctor, will be reminded of the delivery

that took place here only a few hours ago. A plain mat has been spread out for me in front of the tent; the beautiful blue sky is arching above me like a dome made from lapis lazuli; the clear surface of the lake reflects the cheerful splendor of the sky; the manifold greens of the nearby bushes, like the fine cedar, tulip, and oak trees of the forest on the opposite side, decorate the lake, which now is viewed as the font; and the grass slope with its decoration of far-western flowers, which stretches all the way to the lake, serves as the carpet of the imposing house-chapel in God's wonderful temple of nature.

To a small tree next to me in front of the Indian mother's tent I am fastening a Crucifix, sign of eternal salvation and highest "humanity," which I used to carry with me on my trips. So the little tree at St. Mary of the Lake becomes a beautiful symbol of the tree of deliverance and reconciliation, which would solemnly enable the son of the wilderness to participate in it through baptism. The baptismal water is ready; the white child of the redskin rests on the arms of its godfather; a group of Indian faces surrounds me, wildly painted but calm in their expressions; a Canadian person who understands the Potawatomi language is at my side; the baptism is carried out; the savages are praying in their language the prayer of the Lord, the apostolic confession of faith; and the child is named Anthony. St. Anthony is your patron saint and that of several other friends, to whom, as to my loved ones at home, I want to declare in this way my constant remembrance. The child's father's name is "Little Crane"; I will always remember his heartfelt thanks for the admittance of his son into the great association of salvation.[208]

"So the little tree at St. Mary of the Lake becomes a beautiful symbol of the tree of deliverance and reconciliation, which would solemnly enable the son of the wilderness to participate in it through baptism." This line of the German missionary's interesting narrative could have been written about the Legendary Sycamore itself, which would have been but a stone's throw away from the little tree on the hilltop he is describing. In its own way, it has also become a witness to, and a symbol of, the participation of the sons of the wilderness in the history of the founding of the University over one hundred and fifty years ago.

****

There's an interesting parallel to Notre Dame's Sycamore. Sorin also founded St. Edward's University in Austin, Texas, in 1871. He chose the site of its Main Building for its hilltop view and a huge live oak growing there. It was called the "Umbrella Tree" and the "Lone Tree" because it was the only tree on the spot. The live oak is quite an impressive tree situated near the Main Building and just above the location of the Grotto. Directly in front of the tree is a large plaque. On it are the words, "Sorin's Tree." Could Sorin have chosen the hilltop setting and preserved the tree because of the huge sycamore at Notre Dame?

Recently an article appeared in the *South Bend Tribune* featuring a photograph of Michigan's largest sycamore. This particular tree had been core-sampled, a risk that would never be taken with the campus sycamore, already judged the largest and oldest sycamore in St. Joseph County. Michigan's Champion Tree's circumference is listed as 256" and its age has been determined to be 250 to 260 years old. At last, a similar sized tree to compare measurements with to determine the approximate age of the Legendary Sycamore. Huge sycamores of comparable size were taken down at the Culver Military Academy earlier, but an inquiry about them came too late; the stumps had been removed without counting the rings to age them.

Measurements and the ring count of the core-sampled Champion Michigan tree were compared with the one at Notre Dame which is 244" in circumference. Using the formula provided by Purdue, it is likely that the approximate age of Notre Dame's sycamore could be, as it was earlier thought to be, from 200 to 240 years old. Using the conservative 200 year figure would mean it was present on campus in the late 1700s, a time when there was much hostility between the early white settlers and the Indians when the Indian legend was said to have taken root. Which means it could have been a fanciful tale, fiction based on fact, or in the category of an "urban" or "rural" legend attached to the tree.

A special trip to visit the Michigan tree revealed it to be a massive kingly specimen. However, it is without a place to perch nor is it as friendly and inviting as Notre Dame's Landmark Sycamore which seems to beckon people to lounge in its sheltering arms, as the children of Tish and Patrick Holmes — Mary Kate, Christopher, Patrick, Kelly and Kielty — are doing in this photograph

In the summer of 1997, a film company from Chicago spent a whole day filming "Notre Dame's Family Tree" for a special segment aired during the half-time of the first football game played in the newly opened University of Notre Dame stadium.

This venerable old tree, judged to be the oldest and largest sycamore in St. Joseph County, is more than worthy of homage. If the legend draws attention to that fact, it deserves to be associated with the stately old tree on the Grotto lawn. Thus far the story holds up very well.

One thing is certain. The Legendary Sycamore is definitely alive and well, as real now as it was on a summer day in the life of a Black Robe missionary; when Chief Little Crane's son was born and baptized, Anthony, in 1840, at Ste.-Marie-des-Lacs, now the University of Notre Dame.

This majestic old sycamore has been immortalized by countless student pictures taken up in it, and in front of it, from the early part of this century. The wife of a member of the University faculty, James Murphy, now retired, said they have pictures of each of their children taken in the sycamore at various times when they took them to the campus.

Father Schidel, who first suggested checking the *The Domes* for early pictures of the tree, presented a 1931 copy of *The Dome*, and opened it to the only identified photograph of the sycamore. Under it were the words Father Cavanaugh had used to describe it — The Vengeance Tree. He then produced a photo album of his early days on campus and another 1931 snapshot of the sycamore. Three students stood in front of the tree and one was standing up in it. When asked who was in the tree, he grinned and said, "It was me."

During its long life this magnificent Sycamore has seen it all. It has become a witness tree — a silent sentinel standing guard over the campus and the Grotto — watching not only the heartaches and the sorrow, but also the joys, of an endless parade of people passing to and from the Grotto.

And it has endured, as life endures, generation after generation, as one of the last antique lords of the Indian hunting grounds. Only God knows how many years its graceful limbs and lovely foliage have embraced the campus grounds, how many photographs[209] have been taken in front of it, and how many, from little on up, have been cradled in its sturdy branches.

How providential, that two such historic and legendary spots on campus — The Grotto and The Legendary Sycamore — share the same lovely lakeside setting. Perhaps it is best that no positive proof of this story is ever found and it remains the legend that it is. If it were proven beyond a shadow of doubt then it would no longer be a legend. It would be history and not nearly as fascinating a tale to tell.

"Old College"
The oldest building presently on campus, built in 1843 on the
shore of St. Mary's lake.

Chapter 12

The Ghost of a Grotto in the Glen

In Father Maguire's 1953 letter of correction, in which he stated that it was Father Corby who built the 1896 Grotto and not Sorin, he made what turned out to be an erroneous, but fortuitous, statement of his own:

Father Sorin may have expressed a wish for a Grotto and he may have made one somewhere on the grounds but I never saw it or heard of it. If he did construct one he probably built it on the grounds of the Sisters.

Shortly after the discovery of Father Maguire's letter, someone made the statement that there was no Grotto on the Saint Mary's grounds and never had been! Such a positive statement might have been enough to discourage further research on the Notre Dame Grotto at the onset, had it not been for the discovery of an eye witness account of the remains of a Grotto in the glen at Saint Mary's. It was this early clue that led to the discovery of the two previously unknown Grottoes, plus a third one in the glen.

Father Claude Boehm, who is in his early eighties, lives at Holy Cross House on the Notre Dame campus. He was the Chaplain at St. Mary's Convent for thirty years, until his retirement. When he heard of that emphatic denial, he came back with an equally affirmative reply: "Oh, but there was!" He had tripped over the remains of it himself many years before. "It was so overgrown," he said, "you wouldn't have known it was there. It's probably all overgrown again, by now, but you might still be able to find evidence of it."

He then told a charming story of how he had stumbled "head first into it," in the wooded glen between the Church of Loretto and the St. Joseph River, which borders Saint Mary's property.

He explained that in the 1960s the number of Sisters he ministered to was beginning to dwindle with fewer new Sisters coming into the order. To fill his time he used to bird watch in the glen behind the rectory.

One day he accidentally came upon the ruins of an old Grotto. It was overgrown and almost completely hidden by fallen trees. Brush and ground cover had nearly covered the floor of stones. The sides of a rising incline formed the walls of the Grotto and its niche was missing its statue. He said he spent many an afternoon there after he found it, removing the debris and weeds covering it and the area surrounding it.

In the process he discovered in the cavity of a huge tree facing the Grotto, a statue of St. Joseph. He said it was about four feet high. Sometime, during the time he spent working there, the statue mysteriously disappeared. He never saw it again.

Another time he was attacked by a nest of bees and made a hasty retreat to the rectory. The alcohol he put on the bites, he said, "was like dew from heaven."

Probably more than 35 years had passed since he had uncovered the Grotto. Would there be anything left of it? Father Boehm willingly made a map to assist in finding it. Then he decided to go along and point it out in person, raising eyebrows at the nursing station on the way out. He had not been back to Saint Mary's in seven years.

He brushed aside advice not to attempt the steep road to the floor of the glen, and said he wouldn't have any trouble. A staff was fashioned from a fallen limb for him and he slowly descended the hill. At the bottom, he was soon following a rise in the ground bordered by an avenue of huge trees marching their way to the river's edge.

Then the niche appeared, barely visible, over the top of the rise. A slight incline had to be negotiated to reach the floor of the meadow directly facing the empty niche. A huge dead limb crisscrossed the front of the Grotto area narrowly missing the stone niche, the only part still visible and intact. Brush, branches and overgrown ground cover, along with sand washed down from the bank, almost obliterated the scene. Yet, with a little imagination and a brushing away of weeds and dirt, one could see that a very presentable facsimile of a Grotto had once enhanced the meadow it had been placed in.

The blue blossoms of myrtle periwinkle were opening, flooding the greenery with Our Lady's blue. Beside the niche, was a blossoming trillium as if to herald the arrival of long awaited visitors. Photographs were taken to document the Grotto that never was, or at least had been long forgotten.

It was unlikely Father Sorin had built this Grotto as he was known for doing things on a grand scale. The stones appeared to be no larger than could have been carried from the riverbank by two Sisters. Still, there was so little left of it, it was hard to tell. Its setting in the wilderness launched an exploration of its origin.

It became a key piece in researching the story behind the Notre Dame Grotto, because it led to the discovery of Mother Angela's early indoor Grotto built in 1874, and the first outdoor Grotto built at Notre Dame in 1878 by Father Sorin.

A mention of the Grotto in the glen in a chance meeting with a Sister at Saint Mary's revealed someone still living who had worked on it, and the approximate time it was built. "Oh yes, I remember the Grotto in the glen," she said. "It was completed just before I entered the order, probably around 1937." She said she wasn't there when it was built, but she knew a Sister who worked on it and she was living at the convent infirmary.

Sister Miriam Kathryn was able to confirm the approximate 1937 date of the Grotto and she explained the original story behind its beginnings. She said building the Grotto in the glen was the idea of her Mistress of Novices, a project that was begun and completed by them in their recreation time. Thirty to forty novices took turns working on the Grotto. Half worked at the laundry and half on the Grotto. The Sisters gathered the stones, as large as they could carry, from the riverbanks where there had once been a stone retaining wall, now all but washed away by the strong current of the St. Joseph River. Two Sisters would stand on the small bluff and pass the stones to the Sisters below, who then put them in place on the incline walls of the Grotto.

As near as she knew no pictures were ever taken of it. She said she would love to see the Grotto uncovered and used again as it was, for a brief period of time, when the Sisters regularly used the glen for recreational purposes.

However, as time went by, it became more and more isolated, not a good place for the Sisters to go alone or with companions. Eventually, as the college grew, security became a problem and it became off limits for any kind of recreational activities. The statue disappeared from the niche, and gradually, with the passage of time, weather and erosion, the wilderness reclaimed it. The Grotto in the Glen, where violets, myrtle and wild flowers bloom in profusion, is visited of late mainly by chipmunks, squirrels and ground hogs. The cheerful voices and songs of the Sisters are gone forever.

St. Angela's Island

Saint Mary's Cushwa-Leighton College Library became a source for more than books associated with early Notre Dame and St. Mary's history. Bob Hohl, their long time reference librarian, became an encouraging influence in the search for historical information at Saint Mary's, offering insightful suggestions along the way. He was particularly interested in seeing the bulky 1878 maps of Notre Dame and St. Mary's before they were stored away for safekeeping.

On the 1878 map of the St. Mary's campus, he noticed a place in the glen labeled as a pond. It must have triggered something in his memory, because he said, "You know, I've often wondered about something I've read in Eugene O'Neill's Nobel prize winning play, *Long Day's Journey Into Night*.[210] He speaks of his mother and the girl's school she attended in the Midwest. Others who have read it, thought it might have been St. Mary's. An island is also mentioned in connection with the school. Let me know if you run across any information about it."

The 1878 St. Joseph County map had a numbered listing of all the buildings on both campuses. A reference to a St. Angela's Island was on it that had gone unnoticed before. It was in the St. Joseph River, barely visible without a magnifying glass, a short distance off the shoreline. A lane led to it. How large it was, and whether there was a causeway to it, was not discernible.

An 1865 Guide to Notre Dame and St. Mary's mentions the island:

This lovely island like an emerald gem in the bosom of the placid St. Joseph is a favorite place of recreation for the pupils and is popular among the young ladies as a resort for fishing and summer picnics.[211]

St. Angela's Island is Dedicated in 1857

A St. Mary's history book described an interesting event centered on the island one hundred and thirty-eight years ago. It occurred when Father Moreau, the founder of the Holy Cross Order, arrived at Notre Dame from Europe on his first visit to the New World. While visiting the newly established St. Mary's Academy, he dedicated St. Angela's Island and blessed its altar and statue of Mary. It was later referred to as the shrine of Our Lady of Lourdes. A special welcome was planned for him by Mother Angela.

The summer of 1857 filled the community's cup of joy to the brim. It brought a visit from Father Moreau. Long had the father founder desired to see the fruit of his children's labors in foreign lands. It was twenty years since he had founded his congregation . . . .

Business did not exclude pleasure, however, as an account of the blessing of Saint Angela's Island clearly shows. It was the feast of Our Lady's Nativity. . . .

In an earlier book, *On the King's Highway*, Sr. M. Eleanore, C.S.C., records Mother M. Elizabeth's detailed description of the elaborate ceremony she witnessed.

By way of preparation Mother M. Angela borrowed from town several bolts of muslin for decorative purposes. Joseph and a few other men hired for the day hauled brush-

wood to make bonfires at short distances apart on the way to the island. Under a large tree on the island they erected an altar, which the Sisters decorated with candles and wildflowers. On a wire between the trees in front of the altar they hung a large lamp frame made of white down and feathers. On the trees along the path leading to the altar they put small tin holders for candles and nailed pictures under them. The bridge was draped in muslin and was lit by colored lamps.

In the afternoon the Sister sacristan at Notre Dame sent over to the Academy parlor the surplices of the priests. There was an early supper, after which all the Sisters from St. Mary's and from Notre Dame formed in procession with lighted candles. At seven o'clock Father Rector and the clergy having been invited to what they supposed was a little entertainment came from Notre Dame, took chairs, placed them in front of the Academy, and began to smoke and enjoy themselves in the company of Mother M. Angela and her Council. When the bell rang, Mother invited the clergy into the parlor and asked them to put on their surplices. They were somewhat surprised until Mother told them that the Sisters wished to have Father Rector bless the island. At her request the clergy took ranks. She then opened the back door of the Academy to disclose to their astonished gaze the illuminated path which seemed a fairyland of light. Father Moreau stood as if entranced.

The long procession filed through the woods, singing as they went. In half an hour they reached the rustic bridge, where the Sisters halted in ranks through which the clergy passed. Father Moreau blessed the island, giving it the name of St. Angela. Father Sorin and Father Sheil, Provincial of New Orleans, were his assistants. After the blessing Father Rector spoke to us in French, which Father Sheil translated for us. Father Moreau expressed his extreme pleasure over finding in the woods of far-off Indiana such great love for the Mother of God and promised that he would never forget the heavenly scene he witnessed that evening on ground consecrated to Mary Immaculate. He said he had much to say, but the American night birds sang so loud he could not make himself heard. These night birds were the katy-dids and the tree frogs who were shouting their protest against this invasion of light and human sound into their own domain. No matter what katy did or didn't do on other occasions, on that night, at least, she out-talked a whole religious community. Some few persons com-

plained to Father Moreau because Mother M. Angela had burned so many candles; but he reminded them of a certain box of ointment once poured on the Master's feet.[212]

Eugene O'Neill's play, *Long Day's Journey Into Night*, was written in 1940. He received the Nobel prize for it in 1957, after his death. It referred to his mother going to a convent in the Midwest. Although it did not give the name of the school, throughout the whole autobiographical play there were references to his mother and a number of one or two line mentions of a convent in at least ten different places. The last and most lengthy reference on the last page of the play refers to O'Neill's mother:

I told Mother Elizabeth I wanted to be a nun. I explained how sure I was of my vocation, that I had prayed to the Blessed Virgin to make me sure, and to find me worthy. I told Mother I had had a true vision when I was praying in the shrine of Our Lady of Lourdes, on the little island. . . . I said I knew, as surely as I knew I was kneeling there, that the Blessed Virgin had smiled and blessed me with her consent. But Mother Elizabeth told me I must be more sure than that, even, that I must prove it wasn't simply my imagination . . . . I never dreamed Holy Mother would give me such advice! After I left her, I felt all mixed up, so I went to the shrine and prayed to the Blessed Virgin and found peace again because I knew she heard my prayer and would always love me and see no harm ever came to me so long as I never lost my faith in her. . . . That was the winter of my senior year. Then in the spring something happened to me. Yes, I remember. I fell in love with James Tyrone . . . .[213]

Eugene O'Neill's mother, Ellen Quinlan, graduated from St. Mary's and his father, James O'Neill, graduated from Notre Dame. Edward Fischer quotes Marion McCandless on this famous couple in his book:

WHERE LA SALLE PADDLED

As a married couple they later traveled up and down the land together. James O'Neill was one of the great tragedians of his day. His Monte Cristo will always remain a classic of the American stage. But the greatest contribution the O'Neills made to the theater was to give it their son, Eugene, the famous playwright.[214]

Locating St. Angela's Island From the Glen

The description St. Angela's island and its candlelight procession prompted a search of maps of the St. Joseph River to see if the island could still be located, if there was anything left of it. It had been one hundred and thirty-six years since its dedication by Father Moreau.

An aerial view of the St. Mary's campus taken in 1966 and filed at the County/City Building indicated a small island in approximately the same spot as the 1878 map had shown it. It proved, without a doubt, another bit of campus lore. Now Notre Dame and Saint Mary's both had an island.

Time and erosion would account for a change in size. It was not uncommon for an island to appear and disappear over time. The 1966 map also showed a large tree on it. It was probably the same tree mentioned in the description of Father Moreau's visit.

What the glen looked like in its early days, when there were landscaped paths, walks along the river, and flowering shrubs and trees in profusion, could only be imagined. Father Boehm has described the glen, now a wilderness, as a riot of color in the springtime, carpeted with violets and myrtle, daffodils and crocuses, and countless other colorful perennials, planted ages ago. Fragrant lilacs and bright forsythia dot the now wild landscape.

One day, Sister Rosaleen, Saint Mary's College archivist, and a student helper, were going through storage boxes of old photographs in an effort to date them and identify the people in them. They came across a very good matted 8$^{1/2}$ x 11" photograph labeled "St. Angela's Island." At last, no more doubts about it, there it was as clear as any photograph could make it. It is the island photograph in the last episode.

The density of the undergrowth during the summer months made exploring the glen at that time almost impossible. Locating the island from the glen would have to await early spring or fall. The location of the remains of the Grotto was hidden in the undergrowth. It had not been easy to find it. A picture was taken from the grotto, facing toward the buildings on the bluff above the glen, using a turquoise maintenance building as a landmark. When the film was developed, an obvious avenue of trees, otherwise not apparent to the eye, appeared in the photograph. The old map revealed a lane leading to the island in the river. Did that avenue of trees border that long unused lane? Would there be anything left of this once lovely island?

Early spring arrived. It was time to locate the island. Brush and brambles led past a huge uprooted tree. Each step had to be anticipated beforehand to avoid ruts and numerous groundhog holes. Further on, water could be seen in the distance. The riverbank was closer than expected, possibly 200 feet beyond the abandoned Grotto. Eight to ten feet of water-washed sand separated the mainland from a sandbar with six foot high brush sparsely covering it. Its size was difficult to gage because trees along the shoreline hid it from view. From the glen side

of the river, it appeared to be the island, yet there was no dead tree.

Following the riverbank to the north end of the sandbar resulted in the discovery of the island. It was just as it was pictured in Sister Rosaleen's St. Angela Island photograph. The small island was so close to the larger sandbar that it looked as if it might have been attached to it at one time.

It was still wooded, as it was in Sister Rosaleen's photograph. There were a few medium-sized trees and a span of water of perhaps eight feet, which would have required the footbridge noted on the 1878 map. One larger standing tree appeared to be dead. The description of Moreau blessing the island had mentioned the altar being near a large tree. Perhaps this was the same one.

A profusion of crocuses and other plants were sprouting on a slight incline facing the island. Here the Sisters must have pinned up their veils and skirts when they worked in the glen, planting the bulbs, and clearing the underbrush. A climb to the top of a slight incline, which hid the island from view from the college grounds, revealed the avenue of trees. They led directly to the island just as the lane was shown on the 1878 map.

Not only the Grotto in the glen had been located, but also, evidence of all that remained of what must have once been a lovely little island oasis on the Saint Mary's side of the St. Joseph River. The glen and the island must have echoed with young voices and high spirited activity in days gone by. In the 1890s, the river bank had twice been retained with a stone wall to protect the shoreline. Pictures, as late as 1905, show cows being pastured nearby.[215]

Father Charles Carey called the glen at St. Mary's "Perley's glen." He thought its name came from an early family named Perley, who once owned the property. He said they used to go to the glen as young seminarians to avoid the crowds on campus during football games. He painted yet another picture of those early carefree days, this time of male voices echoing through the glen. He said they used to swing from the grapevines over the St. Joseph River. It must have been a perilous sport, considering the swift current in the St. Joseph River.

A'Hoy on the St. Joseph

An interesting article, "A'Hoy! on the St. Joe,"[216] described in detail the beautiful swift flowing St. Joseph River, as it was one hundred and twenty-two years ago. Notre Dame students and professors embarked from St. Angela's Island, on "the often contemplated trip" down the St. Joseph River to Niles, on July 4, 1873.

These our three good and fair galleys, [Notre Dame's early racing boats] the Santa Maria, the Pinta and the Nina darted from the northern point of St. Angela's Island at 10 a.m. They were manned by the merriest crew that ever beheld the swift St. Joseph. The boats were to keep 50 yards apart following one another; the little Nina, with Fathers Lemonnier, Carrier, Zahm and Berdel in the van; the Santa Maria following carrying seven

aboard, Prof. Stace, coxswain, and the Pinta with seven more aboard, nobly bringing up the rear (which she never did before).

The account describes the river as it was in 1873:

Only a few rods from the point of embarkation, a huge boulder firmly driven in the swiftest part of the current suggested momentary fears of ill omen for the rest of the voyage. The Nina swung around it in approved style and in this was skillfully imitated by her two followers. The Dutch Gap, famous in Scholastic lore, was the next distressing peril. The St. Joseph took, once upon a time, into its head to change its bed, and regardless of the property of Mr. Von Dickenhausen, took a short cut across his field which it divided unequally into two parts, making him at the same time the sole undisputed proprietor of an Island. Well the new channel had been cursed by the evil-eyed Von Dickenhausen, so the legend says, and many a reckless adventurer had risked his life in its angry current. The old trees snatched from the stolen field blocked and obstructed the navigator's path, in a manner that made the boldest heart quiver with fear. The Nina, with the priests aboard, slackened speed and bade her followers to be on the watch and put on the brakes also. The peril, as it drew nearer, like fabled tales, grew less; and bolder grew the hearts of the shirking galleys. Little Nina with prow well directed and vigorous dash from the oar, nimbly jumped over the abyss and its whirlpool and in an instant more swam far beyond, just in good sight of her followers which followed her lucky track with the same dexterity and luck.

The river is described as they go along, the old Mill and its rosy looking and talkative miller (where Isaac Walton is now), "the cottages of Bertrand and its venerable old-fashioned bridge, the little church of the earlier St. Mary's Academy, a city once famous and thickly populated, now alas, reduced to a mere name." After several landings to view the beautiful groves on the shore of the river, the Niles dam is sighted and portaged and Niles is reached:

The best speed was now made, all the oars were lustily plied — the wooded bridge was cleared in a twinkling, then the iron bridge. At last the landing was reached, and the travelers got for the last time on terra firma. Half an hour later the boats were placed on board a car of the M. C., and at 5 1/2 P.M. all were back at Notre Dame.

Two years later, the October 1875 *Scholastic*, reported the fate of the noble Pinta. "The Pinta now sleeps the sleep of peace on the bottom of the lake. She preferred death to defeat — and she got it."[217] She must have had lots of company there among the many other items discarded in the lake.

One can only wonder what caused this quiet sanctuary to become, once again, an untamed wilderness.

Chapter 13

Grotto Leaves Lasting Impressions

During the mid 1920s, Rev. Claude Boehm, C.S.C., then a seminarian at Holy Cross Hall, served tables in the South Dining Hall at retreats for laymen during the last weekend in August. On the last day of retreat, a conference conducted at Sacred Heart Church, which ended after dark, was concluded with a huge candlelight procession. It would wind its way from the front door of the church past Corby Hall and along the lake road to the Grotto for benediction. Father Boehm said it was a very impressive sight with as many as a thousand participants and people watching. The early annual May celebrations at the Grotto often included most of the student body.

In a 1932 *Scholastic* article, "Grotto Has Inspired Notre Dame Men For Forty Years," Raymond Waters describes some of those added "little touches" to the Grotto mentioned by Father Maguire in his letter of correction:

"A wooded dell . . . always a cooling and refreshing spot." These are the words a Scholastic *writer used to describe the site upon which is the Grotto, our own shrine to our Lady of Lourdes as she stands in her niche in the arc of stone. Today, in describing the site, the Grotto itself, we have only to add the word . . . "inspiring." To those who find adversity smothering their hopes, who long for the soothing words of a mother far away, the Grotto is always a source of inspiration.*

The Grotto is ever the scenic spot of the campus. In winter, in spring . . . at all times . . . it affords a perfect picture of serenity, of beauty. There is scarcely a student who at some time within his four years here doesn't take a snapshot of this spot, the students in prayer, the evergreens and ivy, . . . and towering above all, in the background, the golden dome.

For years it has been the custom of many to say their evening prayers at this spot. They trudged and groped their way down the terraces in utter darkness. When they reached the spot, the only light, saving that of the moon, was the glow of the candles, ever burning for some intention. It was a dangerous undertaking. This has been remedied during the past summer. Through the kindness of two students at summer school, funds were secured for the recently installed lighting system. Now the terraces leading to the shrine are lighted by lanterns of French design. The image itself stands out in the amber glow of hidden lights, linking the grotto with Lourdes at the Ave Maria hour.[218]

The practice of singing hymns at the Grotto after supper during May was introduced in 1929 by Father O'Hara at the suggestion of a student. One hundred students were present at the opening on May 1, 1929. This practice lapsed after 1948 when the dining hall service changed to a cafeteria system and students did not eat at the same time.[219]

Fr. John O'Hara, A Spiritual Presence

In the 1920s and early 1930s under the direction of Father John F. O'Hara the Grotto became a spiritual rendezvous for the student body and Father O'Hara became a great inspiration to students.

Father Hope in his book, *Notre Dame — One Hundred Years*, describes Father John F. O'Hara, later Cardinal Archbishop O'Hara, as a superb Prefect of Religion, an office he exercised without interruption from 1918 until he was made president in 1934. He explained his duties as Prefect.

The Prefect of Religion is without any disciplinary authority. He cannot suspend or expel students, he cannot punish them. He has no authority in strictly scholastic problems. His work lies in the hearts and minds of the students. He acts as the guide and counselor of their conscience. And the students know this. There is, about his office, all the secrecy and sanctity of the confessional. So the students are more ready to listen to his advice and his encouragement.[220]

Father O'Hara had notes, which later evolved into daily religious bulletins, put under the doors of students to remind them to come to the Grotto to pray. Students called them letters from God. In one of those

bulletins dated, June 1, 1925, Father John O'Hara leaves one of his reminders.

A year ago Ralph Adams Cram [who later designed the South Dining Hall] stated that the Grotto is the best piece of art at Notre Dame. Aside from its artistic value, many a student has found it the most inspiring place on the grounds. If you neglected it during the month of the Blessed Virgin, you still have a week in which to learn its beauties and its inspiration. Drop down there after Holy Communion: call again before you go to bed at night. Stand back far enough to see the dome and statue towering over it; then approach and kneel before the statue. The girlish figure in white built this school. On your knees thank the Blessed Virgin for Notre Dame. The old boys who amount to something want to visit the Grotto when they come back here; you will in your own good time if you learn its secret while you are here.[221]

Rev. Eugene P. Burke, C.S.C. describes the Grotto during those times:

Fairly large groups visited the Grotto in the spring and early summer before retiring for the night. They could be found there in little knots on their way to and from class and frequently in the month of May in the evening as many as a thousand to fifteen hundred gathered at the foot of Our Lady of Lourdes to sing a few hymns and recite the Salve Regina.

Our Lady on the dome has looked down on the activities of the campus and has been an inspiration and source of encouragement to thousands of students and professors who have lifted their eyes heavenward as they passed over the network of pathways on the campus.

The new college building erected in 1865 was crowned with a small dome and statue of the Mother of God, a new autograph of Notre Dame's faith in Mary. Notre Dame, its spirit and life were but the reflection of its devotion to the Lady on the Dome. The same spirit and devotion to the Mother of God which marked its beginning and has over-shadowed it with blessings through all its years.

How far this little candle lighted in the snowy wastes of Lac Ste. Marie over a hundred years ago throws its light.[222]

In an essay in his book *Reflections in the Dome*, Edward Fischer recalls the vase of twelve red roses, placed week after week, at the foot of Cardinal Archbishop John F. O'Hara's marble tomb in Sacred Heart Church — a token of gratitude from the class of 1928.[223]

A former security guard at the Sacred Heart Church tells the story told to him by another long-standing security guard, now retired. Workmen were preparing to place the heavy marble lid on Cardinal Archbishop John O'Hara's vault in the church when concern was expressed that someone's fingers might get pinched in the process. The decision was made to take a break for lunch in hopes that a solution would present itself. When lunch was over and they returned, the foreman had with him a square cake of ice which was split into four small pieces. One piece was placed on each corner and the heavy marble lid was put in place without difficulty. When the ice melted the task was accomplished.

The Fifth Horseman

According to his wife, Teresa, another admirer of Father John O'Hara, during his years as Prefect of Religion was Frederick Snite. She said her husband also spoke of him as a spiritual presence on the campus and a great inspiration to the students.

The family of Frederick Bernard Snite, Jr. donated the Snite Museum. Throughout the greater part of his life, Frederick was known as "The Man in the Iron Lung." His story was told in the December 6, 1946, *Scholastic*:

On football weekends you would see Fred B. Snite in his house-trailer-like vehicle parked on the sidelines. Through a specially built mirror attached to his iron lung, which he brought into the public limelight, he watched the game. Despite his handicap he followed the fortunes of the Fighting Irish, seeing all the Notre Dame home games he could and listening to away games by radio.

Fred Snite . . . the scion of a wealthy Chicago financier . . . graduated from Notre Dame in the spring of 1933. Two years later he was ready to enter his father's business, but to celebrate the event properly, the elder Snite took his family . . . on a world cruise. Snite was to enter the Chicago loan firm upon his return. But things didn't work out that way; fate had smiled in another direction. In China, Fred Snite was suddenly taken ill while on a plane trip to Peiping. . . . Taken to a Peiping hospital after precious time had been lost and after a local physician had misdiagnosed his ailment, Snite was pronounced critically ill with the dreaded poliomyelitis, or infantile paralysis. Fortunately the only 'iron lung' in China was at that time in Peiping. Snite, unable to speak or breathe without artificial aid was placed in the lung, and little hope was held for his recovery.

However, the doctors didn't reckon with Snite's pluck. With splendid disregard for cynical predictions, Snite remained alive and within a few months he was not only talking again, but was speaking Chinese almost as fluently as a native. He never complained about his plight, but accepted it philosophically. In 1937, after his case had been making the headlines for a year, Snite was returned by boat to the United States. The following year he was again watching Notre Dame football . . . from a spot directly behind the goal posts.[224]

The July 5, 1937 original LIFE magazine recorded Snite's arrival in the United States from China in three photographs. Ship's officers in surgeon's masks helped carry the 1,100 lb "Iron Lung" to a special Pullman car waiting on the pier. He arrived in Chicago with his Chinese nurses where he was transferred from Pullman to hospital. His father, who paid $50,000 for his son's trip, said he hoped he would be out of the respirator in seven years. He remained in an "Iron Lung" for the rest of his life.

On a trip to the Grotto of Our Lady of Lourdes in France in 1939, Fred Snite returned with three relics which he gave to the University of Notre Dame: a small piece of wood, a small stone from the Grotto, and a framed letter written by Bernadette to a friend.

Grantland Rice, the sports writer, rose to lyric heights in celebrating Rockne's fighting backfield by proclaiming them the 4 Horseman, victors of the backfield. For his courage in battling his disease and his victory over his disabilities, Fred Snite was dubbed "The 5th Horseman":

Condemned to spend a life of pain in a cumbersome Iron Lung, this Fifth Horseman of Notre Dame showed indomitable courage. His special trailer in which he traveled throughout the nation was a familiar sight at the north ramp of Notre Dame stadium at home games. He was indeed, one of Notre Dame's all-time great competitors.[225]

His own words from, *The Man in the Iron Lung* expressed his philosophy:

"The faith that brought me peace also taught me that this life is a preparation for the next. In other words, I had a job to do like everyone else. I had not been left out." — Frederick Bernard Snite, Jr. in a prepared statement published in the Miami Herald, March 2, 1952.

He did his job well. His story like that of thousands of other handicapped people, is a success story. The public never saw him without a smile on his face, and those of us who were close to him can tell you that an hour rarely passed without a little joke on his lips. If he ever sang the blues, nobody heard him not even those of us who were with him hourly, day after day.

The man in the iron lung was no Superman. The radiant spirit that was to become his did not develop overnight.

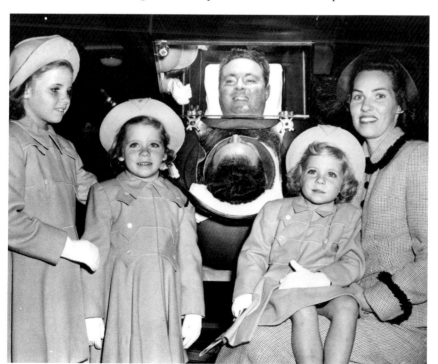

It was the product of a long struggle. The words of one of Frederick's favorite nurses, and a devoted friend, echoed many of his former nurses: "As long as I live, the memory of Mr. Snite's thoughtfulness will never die."

One day Frederick mentioned Lourdes. "If it's God's will that I be cured, I will be. If not, I won't; obviously He has other plans for me. Whatever happens, I figure I have a right to ask for only one thing: the strength to face up to it."

Father Matthew Walsh speaks of Snite's Grotto experience at Lourdes:

"To Frederick at Lourdes," says Father Walsh, came, "the miracle of resignation. Our Lady procured that for him beyond any doubt, and he never hesitated to give her credit for it." Fred had a good faith, of course, before he went to Lourdes. He had already reached a degree of resignation. But, as he used to point out, he never before had had the deep well of peace that was his the day he came up from the waters of Lourdes after the doctor and others tried to persuade him to keep out of the piercingly cold baths (he went in twice).

After that he had the untroubled conviction that he would not be cured. In later years, he had the depth of resignation to tell me more than once that if God gave him the choice of getting well or staying in the lung, he would stay put.

He sent out countless messages of cheer to sufferers all over the world.[226]

There was no room for self-pity or bitterness in his life which, apart from almost complete confinement in the respirator, was surprisingly normal. He married Teresa Larkin in 1939, and they had three daughters. . . He became a symbol of the triumph of the spirit over the body. The image of 'The Boiler Kid' was frequently seen in newspapers, magazines, and newsreels nationwide. He published a newsletter entitled, appropriately, Back Talk, *and his optimism encouraged countless other polio victims. . . . At his funeral in 1954, at the age of 44, he was mourned by many more than the 1500 who came to say farewell to this remarkable, dauntless young man. [Excerpts from information circular "The Fred B. Snite Family," Snite Museum of Art.]*

Teresa Snite, Frederick's wife, graciously supplied information about his Grotto experiences. She said there was no doubt that he had been inspired to go to Lourdes by the Notre Dame Grotto. "In going there," she said, "he felt he had received a miracle of grace rather than a healing, a total acceptance that it was what God wanted him to do, that his respirator was his ticket to heaven."

More Grotto Memories

Under the heading, "White December Finds Grotto In Usual Mood," a wintertime scene at the Grotto in 1939, the year Fred Snite returned from Lourdes, is described in the *Scholastic*:

And now it is December. The trees that shade her in summer, yawn their nakedness into the cold blue sky. Mossy beds of flowers that usually stretch over the rocks to her niche are tangled dry weeds. The cracking coldness of the season numbs the iron kneelers at her feet and causes lighted candles beyond to sputter and jump casting leaping shadows on the Grotto walls. But she is not alone. Even when the heavy snow will bury the weeds and clutch the tree trunks she will not be without visitors.

These Grotto visits are more than tradition at Notre Dame. They are an essential part of her life. Students cannot fail to come to this shrine of Our Lady that was erected so they can stop by at any time to offer her their problems or just to say "hello".[227]

The Dome underscores the above description with this lovely wintertime perception:

It catches the last rays of the setting sun and its snows are the whitest white of winter. Proof of the sincerity of this devotion to Mary can be seen on any inclement evening when there are still hundreds making the trek to the Grotto to make their day complete. Private visits to the Grotto afford an excellent opportunity to pause for a moment during the day, perhaps to light a candle and speak to Mary about one's problems and decisions.[228]

Another added improvement to the Grotto is noted in the *Scholastic*:

On the right side of the Grotto a statue of the Blessed Virgin stands in an elevated niche. This is illuminated at night, the result of the work of Rev. Lawrence V. Broughal, C.S.C., for many years faculty advisor of the Scholastic, *who also had the stairway lights installed.*[229]

In the early 1940s, new artforms in sculptures appeared on the campus. The University inaugurated a beautification project to fill the many empty niches in the buildings on campus with sculptures. Seventeen sculptures were completed by Rev. John Bednar, head of the art department, and Eugene Kormendi, artist in residence and teacher of sculpture. The World War I portico in the east entrance of the Sacred Heart Church was completed in May of 1944 and the Grotto received its own piece of art:

In addition to plans for the erection of the statues, the University's art program will take in other aspects of art on the campus. A three sided drinking fountain sculpture by William John Schickel, former student of Ithaca, N.Y., has been completed. The theme of the work is carried out with relief depictions of Our Lord at the well, Our Lord preaching from the boat, and Our Lord washing the feet of his disciples. Mr. Schickel worked under the direction of Fr. Bednar and Mr. Kormendi.[230]

The three sided sculptured drinking fountain replaced the earlier one which was in the same spot at the Grotto where the natural spring appeared. Many a toddler has since put his foot in the lap of the Lord in boosting himself up to get a drink from the Grotto fountain.

Another poignant letter associated with the Grotto was published in the *Scholastic*. It was written by the mother of Lt. Lawrence A. Barrett, in remembrance of her son. He died in a plane crash in 1941 at the beginning of World War II.[231]

With the coming of the warm weather, students have begun to wend their way back to their halls by way of the Grotto each night after supper. This hymn-singing has long been a tradition of Notre Dame. As the mother of the late Larry Barrett, graduate cum laude with the class of '40, wrote to the students right after his death in an airplane crash:

"How glad I am that Larry had those happy years at Notre Dame. He carried from there his habit of living his faith; if ever a boy used his religion, he did, with all his heart, as he did everything. I have a comforting little belief that on May evenings when the boys are at the Grotto, his dear deep voice rises again . . . 'Macula non est in te' . . . such a host of Her Notre Dame boys are even nearer to Her now, young and fine forever."

The article concluded with a mention of one of those students who wended his way back to his hall by way of the Grotto:

The Prefect of Religion pointed out that one of the greatest athletes of Notre Dame fame, chunky Greg Rice, two-miler superb, was one of the most frequent visitors to the Grotto. Many stories are told of how Greg would wrap himself in a towel to protect himself from the bitter Indiana weather, and would spend a short time each night at the Grotto.

A memorial was placed at the Grotto for another pilot who also lost his life during World War II. He was killed in an airplane crash on July 27, 1943.[232] The embossed wording on the black hand rest of the kneeling railing is hidden, but easily discerned by anyone who stops to read Tom Dooley's letter. The same lettering is also on the circular candle tiers in the candle area. It has been repainted many times which has made it almost indiscernible. It reads: "In memorial to Paul Purcell 1943."

Paul Purcell graduated from Notre Dame University in 1940. He was the only athlete at Notre Dame to receive a special sportsmanship award as a result of his boxing. He must have had a special devotion to the Grotto and the memorial was placed there by his family, in remembrance, to perpetuate that devotion.

Eight years later, during and shortly after the Korean War, two more "Favor Granted" plaques, the last ones, took their places on the weathered rock walls of the Grotto. One appeared on January 28, 1951, bearing the initials, J.L.B., and the other on August 3, 1954, bearing the initials, M.H.M. Like the one placed there in 1918, during World War I, the remaining two plaques mounted on the Grotto also have stories to tell that may never be known.

They will always be something for visitors to wonder about. Since plaques are no longer allowed on the Grotto, they now have a special distinction; they must represent the heartfelt gratitude of all answered prayers.

Chapter 14

The Song of Bernadette Movie

Hollywood made a beautiful inspirational movie about the Lourdes Grotto in France during the second World War. It premiered in 1943. The book it was based on was written by a Jewish man, Franz Werfel, who escaped from the Germans and found shelter in Lourdes. He vowed that if he escaped the war alive, he would sing the song of Bernadette. He kept that vow and her story was published in 1942. From the book, a screenplay was written with the same name: *The Song of Bernadette*. It was an event that would add its own dimension to the story behind the Notre Dame Grotto.

A book entitled *The Glories of the Catholic Church in Art, Architecture and History* by Maurice Francis Egan and *St. Bernadette*, a pictorial book on the Lourdes Grotto in France, written by Leonard Von Matt,[233] covered the beautiful countryside and the site of the Grotto. Von Matt's book had a number of pictures of Bernadette at the time she first saw the apparitions. It also had a close-up photograph of the Our Lady of Lourdes statue in the Grotto in France. When it was compared with the photographs taken of the replica of the statue in Lourdes Hall at Saint Mary's, it showed it to be the same size and likeness done by the original artist, just as it was described by Mother Angela in 1873. Both Mother Angela and Father Sorin must have brought back from Paris an exact copy of the Our Lady of Lourdes statue done by the same sculptor. Discovering Leonard Von Matt's lovely illustrated book about St. Bernadette, Lourdes, and the surrounding countryside, was the next best thing to being there.

The first book was written by Maurice Francis Egan who was brought to Notre Dame from New York by Fr. Walsh to chair the Literature Department. He lived adjacent to the campus on Notre Dame Avenue in a home built for him by the University. Egan loved lilacs. He wrote to all his friends asking them to send him different varieties of the bush to make a hedge around his home. He then christened it, "The Lilacs," a name it still retains today.

It is worthy of note that Maurice Francis Egan's impressive book, *The Glories of the Catholic Church in Art, Architecture and History* was published in 1895, a year before the Notre Dame Grotto was built on campus. Notre Dame University was included but not Sorin's 1878 Grotto. In 1895 the 1896 Grotto was still a dream in Fr. Corby's heart at the time. It became a reality the following year.

In it, Egan explained why he wrote the book in which he describes and pictures famous churches and shrines all over the world. He said he felt that many people could not afford to travel to these places to see them in person and the next best thing might be a book picturing and describing these famous churches and shrines. One of the churches and shrines he depicted was the Church of the Holy Rosary and the Grotto of the Holy Virgin at Lourdes. It begins with his description of this world-famous shrine.

Grotto of the Holy Virgin — Lourdes.

Lourdes is a small village in the south of France, at the common entrance to several deep gorges of the Pyrenees. Near the town is an almost perpendicular cliff known as Massabielle, which means, in the dialect of the country, 'The Old Rocks." In this cliff is a natural grotto about twelve feet high and twelve feet deep, within which is a sort of niche about six feet high, of almost oval shape. It was in this niche that on the 11th of February, 1858, the Virgin Mother of God appeared to the little shepherdess, Bernadette Soubirous, who was gathering sticks along the banks of the neighboring stream. Her form, full of divinest grace, 'was surrounded with an aureole of inconceivable brightness, not like the piercing light of the sun, but rather like a bundle of rays softened by a gentle shade, which irresistibly attracted the gaze, and on which the eyes reposed with ecstatic delight.' She held a chaplet, whose milk-white beads were gliding one by one through her fingers, while she seemed to be listening to the recitation of the rosary throughout the world. Again and again Bernadette went to the spot accompanied at first by a few of her child companions, and afterwards by crowds of people, and each time beheld the same gracious vision, at the sight of which her person was so transfigured that her every movement and gesture had a nobleness and dignity that seemed to onlookers more than human. The glorious apparition sometimes spoke to her, and once, after imparting to her a secret of personal import, regarding which she required secrecy, she commanded her to tell the priests that she wished a chapel built there in her honor. The celestial visitations still continued for a time; a copious spring of water burst forth in the cave at the Virgin's command, though it had always before been perfectly dry, and Bernadette was commanded to drink of the water and to bathe herself with it. At last, on the feast of the Annunciation, in response to a request made by Bernadette on an earlier occasion, that she should reveal in unmistakable terms her identity, the fair Vision raised her arms toward heaven, with the words, 'I am the Immaculate Conception.' Thus did the definition of the apostolic doctrine of the perfect and perpetual purity of

the Mother of God receive a special confirmation from her own sweet lips, and prepare the way for the rich out-pouring of Divine favors which soon followed.

For the fervor with which the villagers received this celestial manifestation soon communicated itself to all parts of the Christian world. A great basilica was built at an enormous cost above the grotto, and other buildings were put up one after another until the whole city has arisen around the sacred spring, whose waters have flowed throughout the world, their channels marked by miracles of bodily and spiritual healing. Shrines in honor of Our Lady of Lourdes have sprung up even in the most distant places, and the wonders worked by Our Lady's intercession under this title have everywhere confuted the enemies of the supernatural.

In the spot where the Blessed Virgin appeared stands a life-size statue conforming to the description given by Bernadette, and at its base still grows the wild rose which the feet of the Holy Virgin touched. The upper church of the basilica is lined with the silken banners of various nations and confraternities and guilds, which have been hung there by visiting pilgrims. . . .

His detailed description of this world-famous church and shrine follows.

Church of the Holy Rosary — Lourdes

The church of the Holy Rosary at Lourdes consists of an upper and a lower church quite distinct and necessitating distinct descriptions. The lower church, usually called the Church of the Grotto, is built just below the apse of the basilica and was blasted out of the solid rock. Thus it may be said that the Almighty himself not only laid the foundations of the Church of the Grotto but even raised its walls; the work of man has been merely to carry away the debris. It has no windows, light being admitted through a cupola, and not a single pillar supports the roof and arch; it reminds one of the subterranean vaulted chapels so common in old cathedrals.

The glory of the basilica, however, is the interior of the upper Gothic church, where all the great celebrations of feasts are held. Simple in its design it owes all its splendor to the beauty of its decorations. There are magnificent silken banners woven in every country and in every clime testifying to the gratitude of thousands of pilgrims, while ensigns of the great powers droop in a semicircle around the sanctuary, the Stars and Stripes being conspicuous in the foreground. The magnificent blaze of color produces an effect which description can hardly exaggerate. The walls of the church and the long corridors of the crypt are covered with marble tablets

commemorating cures and other favors attained through the intercession of Our Lady at her world-famed Grotto.

Among the many lights which are burning before the high altar is one whose flame is never extinguished. It was called the 'lamp of Ireland' because its anonymous donor was a native of the 'ever-faithful isle;' and there it will burn as long as the church stands in that far away valley of the Pyrenees, symbol of a Faith that never dies.

Stranger and more distinctive signs and symbols are those laid down by repentant sinners at the feet of the Virgin, so that the whole world may see that there have lived strong men who have put away those things hurtful to their spiritual life and growth. There is a battered bronze medal, the Victoria Cross for which thousands of England's sons have died; there a grand cordon of the Legion of Honor; there are swords that are now sheathed and left to rust in this court of peace. There, most magnificent and singular of all, is a strangely shaped miniature in a jeweled case closed forever to the world; the face perhaps of some darling sin or unholy desire.

Surely the human heart is here naked in all its weakness, superb in all its strength!

Although there have been a great many pilgrimages at Lourdes — notably the Festival of the Banners in 1872, and the English pilgrimages of 1883 — when all France assembled to implore Mary's intercession for their stricken land, nevertheless there is no special history of the pilgrimages to the Grotto chiefly for the reason that the greatest cures have been wrought in obscurity and quiet and upon those of the humblest origin. God loves to work in silence and in His own good time, acting not when the world is on tiptoe for the event but when the world is asleep or absorbed in trivialities. The population in the mountains and valleys in the neighborhood form the most constant train of visitors, but the pilgrimage is also made by thousands every year from all parts of France, Belgium, Spain and Germany, by many from England, Russia and America, and even by pilgrims from the far east, eager to see the spot touched by the feet of the Virgin and to implore her intercession in their earthly and spiritual needs.

Above the main entrance to the basilica, let into the white stone of the facade, is a large enamel portrait of Pope Pius IX, who proclaimed the dogma of the Immaculate Conception.

It seems fitting that the most ardent champion of Our Lady should have a place of honor in her church, and significant truly that here the peasant girl Bernadette and the pontiff of the universal Church, the genial Pio Nono, are side by side, all earthly distinctions merged and lost in their one title — children of our Blessed Mother.

'Rich men and nobles gave their gold and silver, and delicately-nurtured ladies spent night and day in embroidering banners which cities, and towns and rural parishes unanimously agreed to send with their delegates to Lourdes, to be first laid at Mary's feet, and then suspended like so many trophies from the vaulted roof of the church of Massabielle. Men and woman of every rank and station, and from every part of France, assembled with immense enthusiasm and kept up the festival for several successive days. On Sunday morning High Mass was celebrated on a magnificent altar erected in the vast meadows below the grotto, and the bishops of France pronounced their own benediction and that of the sovereign pontiff upon the immense hosts of pilgrims. It was impossible not to feel as if France herself were actually present there, kneeling penitent and forgiven at the feet of her Creator.'

The Hesburgh Library database listed the earliest book about Bernadette, the English version of the French book, *Our Lady Of Lourdes*, written during her lifetime by Henri Lasserre,[234] her official historian. He wrote about people who witnessed the apparitions and were still alive to be interviewed.

Henri Lasserre's — *Our Lady of Lourdes*

Henri Lasserre's book, *Our Lady of Lourdes*, is a forthright detailed description of all the elements of the apparitions except the personal side of Bernadette's life in the convent, which would not have been available to the author, at that time, because she was still living.

In his book, which was published in English in 1875, the author also tells of his own healing and that of another close friend's son. In his thought-provoking "Dear Reader" letter (quoted in the "Author's Personal Epilogue" in *A Cave of Candles: The Story Behind the Notre Dame Grotto*) he speaks of the extraordinary providential circumstances that led to his becoming Bernadette's official historian. It is an impressive documentation of Bernadette's Grotto experience.

Henri Lasserre concludes his book with this interesting observation:

She lives in the humility of the Lord and is dead to the vanities of this lower world. This book, which we have written and which speaks so much of Bernadette, will never be read by Sister Marie-Bernard.

The later book, written by Franz Werfel, which was made into the 1943 *Song of Bernadette* film, was based on Lasserre's book. Both books start with unusual personal prologues which explain how and why the books were written.

Werfel describes Bernadette as "a little creature clear as well water and yet inscrutable." Seaton's dialogue in the film portrays her protector, Dean Peyramale, once disbelieving, who then encouraged her:

Let nothing make you weaken. The Lady knows exactly what she is doing. She knows why she came to you and to none other. She knows why she is giving you this life to live, too. It couldn't be different; it had to be thus.

Lasserre describes Bernadette's last visit to the Grotto:

On the sixteenth of July, the feast of Our Lady of Mount Carmel, Bernadette had heard within her the voice which had for some months been silent, and which now no longer summoned her to the Rocks of Massabielle, then closed and guarded, but to the right of the bank of the Gave into those meadows where the multitude used to assemble to pray, safe from prosecutions and the vexatious proceedings of the Police. It was about eight o'clock in the evening. Scarcely had the child knelt down and commenced the recitation of her chaplet, when the Blessed Mother of Jesus Christ appeared to her. The Gave, which separated her from the Grotto, had almost vanished from her sight as soon as the ecstasy came over her. She saw naught before her but the blessed Rock — to which she seemed to be as near as on former occasions — and the Immaculate Virgin, who smiled sweetly upon her as if to confirm all the past and shed light on all the future. Not a word proceeded from her divine lips. At a certain moment She bowed Her head towards the child as if to tell her, "We shall meet again at some very distant period," or to bid her a last farewell. After this She disappeared and re-entered Heaven. This was the eighteenth Apparition and it was the last.

Bernadette's personality is reflected in pictures taken of her as a child during and after the apparitions. She became the first Saint photographed in her lifetime. In Lasserre's summation of Bernadette's visions he paints a profound word portrait of the distinctive personal qualities that endeared Bernadette's to all who knew her or were touched by her story:

The testimony of the young girl offers all the guarantees we can possibly desire. There cannot be the slightest doubt as to her sincerity. Who does not, when coming in contact with her, admire her simplicity, modesty and candor? While everybody is discussing the marvels which have been revealed to her, alone, she remains silent. She never speaks unless when questions are put to her; then she enters into details without the slightest affectation, and with the most touching ingenuousness; and her answers to the numerous questions addressed to her are given without hesitation; are clear, precise, very much to the purpose, and bearing the impress of deep conviction.

Subjected to rough trials, she has never been shaken by threats, and she has declined the most generous offers with noble disinterestedness. Always d'accord avec elle-meme, she has in the different interrogatories to which she has been subjected, constantly adhered to her first statement, neither adding to nor taking away from it. Let us add that it has never been contested. Even those who opposed her, have themselves rendered her this homage.

But granting that Bernadette had no wish to deceive others, is it not possible that she was deceived herself? For instance, did she not fancy she saw and heard what she neither saw nor heard? Was she not the victim of a hallucination? How could we believe this for a moment? This wisdom of her replies reveals in the child a soundness of mind, a calmness of imagination, and a fund of good sense beyond her years. In her the religious feeling has never displayed any over-excited character; it has never been proved that she suffered from any intellectual derangement, oddity or disposition, or morbid affection which might have predisposed her to indulge in creations of imagination. She has had this vision, not once only, but as often as eighteen times; she saw it for the first time suddenly, when nothing could have prepared her for what was to be accomplished later on; and during the Quinzaine, when she expected to see the vision every day, she saw nothing for two days, although she was placed in the same way and in identical circumstances. And then what took place during the time the Apparitions were before her? Bernadette was transformed; her countenance assumed a new expression, her eyes kindled, she saw things which she had never before seen, she heard language which she had never before heard, the sense of which she did not always understand, but the remembrance of which she did not fail to retain. These circumstances joined together, preclude the idea of hallucination. The young girl has therefore really seen and heard a being styling herself the Immaculate Conception, and it being impossible to account for the phenomenon naturally, we have just ground for believing that the Apparition was supernatural.

The testimony of Bernadette — in itself of considerable importance — acquires altogether new strength — we might say its complement — from the marvelous occurrences which have taken place since this event. If a tree should be judged by its fruits, we may affirm that the Apparition, as narrated by the girl, is supernatural and divine, for it has produced supernatural and divine effects. What then happened, dearly beloved Brethren? The Apparition was scarcely heard of, when the news spread with the rapidity of lightning; it was known that Bernadette was to repair to the Grotto for the space of fifteen days, and the whole country was aroused. Crowds of people streamed towards the place of the Apparition; they waited for the solemn hour with religious impatience; and while the girl, beside herself with ravishment, was absorbed by the object of her contemplation, the witnesses of this prodigy, deeply affected and melted to tenderness, were mingled in a common feeling of admiration and prayer.

The Apparitions have ceased; but the concourse of people continues, and pilgrims, arriving from distant countries as well as from the neighboring districts, hasten to the Grotto. They are of all ages, all ranks and all conditions. And by what feeling are these numerous strangers urged to visit the place? Ah! They come to the Grotto in order to pray and to demand favors of one kind or other from the Immaculate Mary. They prove, by their collected behavior, that they are sensible as it were of a divine breath which vivifies this rock, from henceforth forever celebrated. Souls, already Christian, have become strengthened in virtue; men frozen with indifference have been brought back to the practices of religion; obstinate sinners have been reconciled with God, after Our Lady of Lourdes had been invoked in their favor. These marvels of grace, bearing the stamp of universality and duration, can only have God for their author. Consequently, have they not come for the express purpose of confirming the truth of the Apparition?

Near death, Bernadette was asked one more time to describe the Blessed Virgin. She replied, "The lady cannot be drawn or painted or embroidered." In her last moments, Werfel speaks of the nuns at her death having "a sense of being, as it were, midwives of the supernatural birth of a soul into another world."[235]

The *Song of Bernadette* Screenplay

Bob Hohl at the Saint Mary's College library was most interested in the pictorial confirmation of the authentic Lourdes statue Mother Angela had purchased from the French sculptor. He also agreed that the earliest book on Bernadette, by Lasserre, would be the most genuine.

He had been viewing the photographs of the statues in Lourdes Hall when he turned around and faced his computer on the desk beside him. "I just thought of something that might be of interest," he said. He typed something into the computer database, then looked up from the keyboard with a smile: "I thought I'd seen this entry before."

"In our college archives we have the script, with photographs, of the 1943 movie, *The Song Of Bernadette*. It looks like the screenwriter sent it to one of the Sisters at Saint Mary's," he said. "There's no further explanation here, but it can be viewed in the Saint Mary's College Archives on the lower floor. It also indicates that the scriptwriter was born in South Bend."

If he was born in South Bend, would he have known about the Notre Dame Grotto and would that knowledge have factored into his writing the script of *The Song Of Bernadette*?

Sister Rosaleen and Sister Monica at the College Archives were surprised to hear about it. They were both curious about how the writer's *The Song Of Bernadette* screenplay wound up at Saint Mary's. Sister Rosaleen was aware of it, but hadn't paid much attention to it before.

She located it and placed it on nearby table for a closer inspection. There were many glossy photographs of the actors taken on location. The script was inscribed: "To Sister Evangelista: With all good wishes from a South Bend boy." It was signed, George Seaton.

The cover page read, Franz Werfel's, *The Song of Bernadette*. Screenplay by George Seaton. In the lower right hand corner were the words: "Revised Final, March 8, 1943." Not much to go on there.

Upon returning it to Sister Rosaleen, a piece of paper fluttered to the floor. It must have been clinging to the inside cover. It was a handwritten letter to Sister Evangelista from the scriptwriter, George Seaton. Someone had cut off the address portion at the top, unwittingly taking with it part of the words on the reverse side of it. This is what it said:

I wish I were one of those terribly clever people who, when they write their autobiographies, always say, when I was fifteen months old I distinctly remember my Aunt Fanny saying to me, etc. If I had such a prodigious memory I could honestly say that I remembered you — for I gather from my sister Ruth that you occasionally visited our home in South Bend when I . . . [the next two or three lines are missing].

Still I feel as if I'd known you all my life because I've heard my sister mention you so many, many times.

I can't tell you how proud I am to know that you asked for a script of "Bernadette" — I do hope you enjoy reading it as much as I enjoyed writing it.

Respectfully yours,

George Seaton.

Who was George Seaton and could it be proven that he had been born in South Bend? There had to be some connection between his sister and Sister Evangelista, but what was it?

Who Was Who, Film Goers Companion, and *Film Encyclopedia* all had information about George Seaton and all of it was impressive. He was a screenwriter, director and producer whose 40 year Hollywood career included winning two Oscars. He was three times president of the Motion Picture Academy of Arts and Sciences; president of the Screen Writers Guild; and vice president of the Screen Directors Guild; and also served as vice president of the Motion Picture Relief Fund.

He won an Academy Award for the screenplay, Miracle On 34th Street, in 1947 and again for his adaptation of Clifford Odet's play, The Country Girl, in 1952, which he also directed and which brought an Oscar for best performance by an actress to Grace Kelly. Among countless other movies, including, The Song Of Bernadette, he wrote and directed Airport, the biggest money making movie for Universal Pictures until Jaws. In addition to a number of other awards, he was also the recipient of the Jean Hersholt humanitarian award and was a trustee of Colonial Williamsburg.[236]

The Song of Bernadette lost the Academy Award for best picture to Casablanca, which was pretty tough competition. However, Jennifer Jones won an Academy Award for best actress. It was her first movie. The film also got Academy Awards for Best Cinema Photography, Best Interior Decoration, and Best Score. George Seaton's script was also nominated for best screenplay.

Seaton's *Miracle On 34th Street* and Capra's *It's A Wonderful Life* share the distinction of being classic movies that are rerun every Christmas. *The Song of Bernadette* is also acquiring that same distinction. Capra and Seaton are gone now, but they spent their lives on something that would live after them.

The very fact that such a noted Hollywood personage was born in South Bend, and nobody seemed to know about it, was enough to suggest another side search. It seemed a simple fact to prove. Unfortunately, it was easier said then done.

Dr. George Plain, head of the Health Department, very kindly checked all his records for that name and birth date. They had no birth certificate in that name. On the other end, no one at Saint Mary's who knew Sister Evangelista had ever heard her mention his name, his sister's name, or the movie itself.

They could only recall that she had friends in Hollywood. The father of two sisters in her class was a Hollywood producer and he regularly sent films for their Friday movie nights at the college. There was no connection between these two men. There were also no records of a Ruth Seaton being a student where Sister Evangelista taught school.

The date of his death, July 28, 1979, seemed to be the only clue to learning more about him. Could he have changed his name as many people in the film business had done? A suggestion was made that, if he was well known, his obituary might have been in the *New York Times*. The NYT index gave the date it appeared. The St. Joseph County Public Library provided a copy of the obituary on microfilm.

His obituary confirmed the name change. He moved from South Bend to Detroit as a child. As a young man he auditioned for Jesse Bonstelle's drama school. She hired him instead for her stock company at $15 a week. The next line provided the answer: "George Stenius, would-be student, became George Seaton, paid actor."

A return call to Dr. George Plain produced the evidence. Ten minutes after receiving the new name he called back with good news. He had found it! The George Stenius birth certificate revealed he was the youngest of three children. It also indicated his father was 40 and his mother 39 when he was born, so his sister Ruth could have been several years older. The birth certificate listed both parents as immigrating from Stockholm, Sweden. Were they Catholic? "It was possible but not likely," he said. However, he did mention that when he lived in Minnesota, they did have a church there called the St. Olaf's Catholic Church.

This information led to the city directory which listed the family as living in South Bend, on William Street, in 1911 and 1912. Records at the convent showed that Sister Evangelista had been a teacher at St. Joseph Academy during those years. Being close by, it was the most likely place his older sister would have gone to school at the time. Although their records did not go back that far, the evidence suggested that Sister Evengelista was her teacher. That's how they met, and they kept in touch when the family moved to Detroit. It was not an uncommon practice for a separated student and teacher.

The All Saints Parish Church, in Beverly Hills, was listed as having conducted George Seaton's funeral service. Their letterhead indicated it was an an Episcopal Church, which answered one question; he was not Catholic. They confirmed the service, but they had no records of family, then or now, to offer. Subsequent inquiries revealed that after his death his wife became mayor of Beverly Hills, CA, but even they had no clues to the whereabouts of any surviving family members.

Interlibrary Loan at the St. Joseph County Public Library checked their countrywide computer database to see if any books had been written about this man. Within a week, a book they ordered arrived from Brigham Young University Library in Utah. Only it wasn't a book. It was a roll of microfilm.

An Oral History on Seaton

At the top of the screen was the heading, *New York Times Oral History Program*:[237] The last thing expected, and the perfect way to obtain information about his background.

It was dated 1977. He died in 1979. It contained not only the answer to how it wound up in the Saint Mary's College archives, but also an interesting detailed background on the filming of the *Song of Bernadette* movie.

His interviewer, David Cherichetti, did a masterful job of asking the right questions. The only one left unanswered was his possible link to the Notre Dame Grotto in connection with *The Song Of Bernadette* movie.

George Seaton's father was a rather famous chef. He followed Oscar at the Waldorf many years before George was born. At the time Seaton was born, in South Bend, Indiana, his father was running the Oliver Hotel. His mother's father was also a very famous critic in Stockholm. When he was about two years old they moved to Detroit. This would explain why he didn't remember Sister Evangelista.

George Seaton became "one of the most consistently successful writer-directors in the history of Hollywood." He got his start in Detroit acting in stock companies and on radio where *he was the original Lone Ranger*. Quite a distinction for a "South Bend Boy," and apparently nothing has ever been written locally about him.

Stenius was a very hard name to pronounce. He was writing pulp fiction at the time and got a rejection notice under the name of Stenius, so he tore off the title page and sent the story in with "George Seaton" on it.

He chose the name George Seaton because he had gone to see Philip Barry's, *Holiday*, and the family name in the play was Seton. He also had a belt buckle with the initials GS, so he didn't want to change his initials. With the new name, his story was accepted. He felt it was a talisman and kept the name. He put the "a" in the name Seton because he said he didn't want to be a complete thief.

Shortly afterward, he went to Hollywood under personal contract to Bill Perlberg. He was getting tired of making mostly comedies. After yet another one, he told Perlberg, "I'll do it under one condition, that if you ever get something serious to do, I hope I get a crack at it." Perlberg gave him his word. Many years and many comedies went by before he was to get his chance.

Even his sister Ruth factored into his Hollywood experience. His sister was teaching English to foreign-born students in public schools in Detroit. She had a great knack for it. When Ingrid Bergman came to this country his sister became her coach, taught her English, and "she's been with her ever since. Anytime Ingrid does a play or a film, my sister is with her, not just for the language, but for the interpretation of the part."

Ingrid Bergman's biography, *Ingrid Bergman, My Story*,[238] speaks of Ruth Roberts. Ingrid tells about her first arrival in the United States from Sweden. "It was strange that within those first few weeks I'd met the women who were to become three of the main pillars of my life: Kay Brown, Irene Selznick, and Ruth Roberts." Of those three women, Ruth Roberts' name comes up most often. In the index, forty some entries are noted of personal letters sent to Ruth by Ingrid.

His sister Ruth, who would have been about eleven years old when they left South Bend, must have kept in touch with her favorite teacher, Sister Evangelista, throughout her life, as she later did with Ingrid Bergman.

In hearing of Ruth's and George's Hollywood activities, Sister Evangelista must have learned of the movie, *The Song Of Bernadette*, being filmed and requested a copy of the script for the Saint Mary's College Library. Ruth then passed the request on to her brother and he went all out with it. The script was handsomely bound in leather, inscribed in gold on the cover, and contained not only a personal inscription, but also a personal handwritten letter from George Seaton.

Gradually, the oral history interview moved into the background of the filming of *The Song Of Bernadette*, and the Lourdes Grotto experience. George describes how Bill Perlberg acted upon his promise to allow him to script a more serious film. He said a book by Franz Werfel came along called *The Song Of Bernadette*.

He read it and raced into Perlberg's office. He told him that this was what he wanted to do and that he was sure it could be a successful film. Perlberg read it and agreed and he went in to Zanuck. When they bought the property Bill Perlberg told Zanuck he wanted Seaton to write it. Zanuck said, "You're out of your mind. He's nothing but a gag writer. He's done all these musicals. We'll have to get someone like Ben Hecht." Seaton said he felt blessed because Perlberg told Zanuck, "Unless George does it, I will not produce it. I promised him and I'm going to stick by my word." They wanted Perlberg to produce it, so Zanuck agreed.

Filming *The Song of Bernadette*

Seaton and Werfel were both living in Beverly Hills at the time the movie was filmed. Seaton had long talks with him before he started to write. He said he felt Werfel had great confidence in him and that it was a happy association. When he did a sequence, he would go over and read it to him. He spoke very little German and Werfel's English wasn't very good, but he said they managed to get along rather well.

This totally Catholic story was written by Werfel who was Jewish. The screen play was written by George Seaton who was Swedish and non-Catholic. A campus newsletter made this interesting observation in 1958: "The best books on Lourdes have been written by non-Catholics."

Although George Seaton did not explain his own reasons for wanting to do the script, other than the chance way it came about, he did tell this poignant story related to him by Werfel himself. He said Werfel told him that when he was escaping from Germany through the woods in France, he had the manuscript of another novel with him which he had just finished. He knew if they ever got caught and the Germans found his manuscript, they would know who he was and he would be shot. So, one night he dug a hole in the ground in the forest and burned his manuscript page by page. When the town of Lourdes took him in, he vowed if he lived he would sing *The Song of Bernadette*. When he was safely out of danger, he wrote the book.

Seaton explained that since Werfel was reporting true events within the past nine decades, he could not draw upon his imagination, but followed rather closely the carefully investigated account of Saint Bernadette, in Henri Lasserre's, *Our Lady Of Lourdes*, which was also written in fulfillment of a vow. Seaton said it was a wonderful experience to work with this man.

He also related how he fought to have the movie filmed objectively, strictly from Bernadette's point of view:

Anytime you put a camera anyplace, it has to be somebody's point of view. By placing the camera behind Bernadette, with Bernadette in the foreground and the virgin in the niche, it becomes somebody else's point of view. Somebody seeing both the Virgin and Bernadette at the same time. And you cannot say that anybody saw the Virgin except Bernadette. It might have been a delusion on her part or it might have been real, but I told them "we have to keep it this way all through the picture. You can't take the position that she does see it because your picture goes right out the window."

Seaton said Zanuck argued this point with him for a long time. But he won the argument and Zanuck finally agreed. "So you never see a shot of Bernadette in the foreground. It's always her eyes and what she sees; but did she see it, or didn't she see it? That's another thing."

When the interviewer asked Seaton if in his own mind he thought she saw the Virgin, Seaton told him he'd have to take the fifth on that. He said after the picture was finished he looked at it and told Zanuck that the critics would tear them apart, because although they leave it up to the audience, they also show all those bits of evidence. He told Zanuck that what the picture needed was a foreword to take the steam out of the critics. Zanuck and Perlberg agreed and Seaton said he wrote a foreword and credited it to a fifteenth century monk. It said: "To those who believe in God, no explanation is necessary to those who do not believe in God, no explanation is possible."

When the interviewer comments, "But it was really you?" Seaton replies, "Well, it worked."

When asked about locations Seaton said:

The director flew his own plane and it was something you only did once with him. We'd be looking locally for a grotto and he'd be flying at 5,000 feet and he'd look down and say, "That looks possible," and he'd go rrrrrrrump and your stomach would be left up at 5,000 feet. He said finally they decided to create a grotto on the back lot. He said they also built the whole village, the Bernadette set, which stayed up for years and they changed it to this and they changed it to that, and now it's Century City.

Seaton explained that Jennifer Jones was chosen to play Bernadette because it was the first thing she had ever done and the part needed someone who had an earthy peasant quality about her. He also explained that the Virgin wasn't matted in, that she was actually standing in the niche. He said it was very tastefully done. When the cameraman got close, it wasn't sharp, he diffused it. It had a wonderful ethereal quality so that very few knew who played the Virgin. It was Linda Darnell.

****

As noted earlier, it is said no deed done in Our Lady's honor goes unrewarded. After Seaton wrote *The Song Of Bernadette*, his career blossomed. He went on to many successful films including academy award winning *Miracle On 34th Street* and *Country Girl*.

He said *Miracle On 34th Street* was one of the joys of his life. He wrote the original screenplay. He took the same attitude as with *The Song Of Bernadette*: "You don't say that he is Santa Claus, you just present the facts and let the audience make up its own mind."

He also mentioned the effect *Miracle On 34th Street* had on Macy's and Gimbels:

The interesting thing about it was that in the film Santa Claus sends customers to other stores. Well, ever since then, they have had at Macy's a Kristeen Kringle who is a comparative shopper. And if she says they haven't got it at Macy's she'll tell you where to go. Gimbels have also done it. They've become more friendly and cooperative, whereas, before the movie they were very competitive. Neiman Marcus in Dallas did the same thing.

In 1994 a news release announced the color remake of 1947 *Miracle on 34th Street* movie for the coming Christmas season. It was warmly reviewed and a definite compliment to George Seaton that his movie has not only survived as a black and white classic seen every Christmas on television, but has now been remade in color.

And this new version, coincidentally displayed the talents of another "South Bend Boy." Doug Kraner, a production designer on the film, who had a hand in the colorful and exquisite Christmastime decorations, is a native of South Bend. This film also has the distinction of being the only movie known to offer a guarantee of your money back if you don't like it. Twentieth Century Fox obviously had great faith in the premise of Seaton's 1947 version of faith, hope and goodness — "that Christmas isn't just Christmas, it's a frame of mind. It's having the faith to go on believing when common sense tells you not to."

In 1999 Seaton's *Miracle On 34th Street* also became the subject of Macy's "Old fashioned Christmas" window displays for the Holidays. Every window was filled with the original, animated, characters depicting memorable scenes from the 1947 movie classic. It was described as 800 hours of perpetual motion, designed to give pleasure to holiday shoppers throughout the Christmas season. Undoubtedly, if Seaton were alive to see it, such a beautiful window display celebrating his movie classic would just be more proof that miracles are still happening *On 34th Street*.

Seaton having left South Bend for Detroit at the age of two at first seemed to rule out any possibility of a connection between the Bernadette script and the Notre Dame Grotto. That is until this last concluding surprise turned up in Seaton's oral history.

He was speaking of his older brother, Arthur:

My brother graduated from the University of Notre Dame. As Dr. Arthur Stenius he was head of the Audio Visual Department at Wayne State University in Detroit for ten years until his death in 1955. During that time he made many advancements in film and was considered a pioneer in the audio-visual field.

It was at least a link between Seaton's Bernadette script and the Notre Dame Grotto. Whether or not it factored into his doing the script, it seems probable he would have known about it. He was seventeen when his brother graduated from Notre Dame and still living at home. Undoubtedly, he was there for that occasion, and probably other times as well, and viewed the special places on campus, possibly even during football weekends. It is unlikely he would have missed seeing the Grotto. There may also have been a subliminal memory of it during the writing of the Bernadette script of which even he was unaware.

Pondering all these significant coincidences and timely postscripts associated with Seaton's movie classics, and seemingly destined to be included in this documentation, has brought another to mind. This one, associated with Seaton's *Song of Bernadette* movie, appeared on campus in the form of a poignant letter.

It arrived in response to a request for Grotto Stories to commemorate the 1996 centenary of the Grotto. This touching story of the writer's vision, her own experience with the "Lady dressed in Light" at the Notre Dame Grotto, and the photograph she included with her letter, are now in the University of Notre Dame Archives, preserved in a special file for all the original Grotto Stories sent in at the time, and for those that are still arriving.

Her letter and photograph also appeared in *Grotto Stories: From the Heart of Notre Dame* compiled and published by Mary Pat Dowing in 1996. It's a story tailor-made for this chapter because the writer not only shared a moving experience of her own vision of "Our Lady" associated with the Notre Dame Grotto but she also shares the name of the actress who played the part of Bernadette in The Song of Bernadette film. It's a story that speaks for itself:

No story to enlighten; no miracle to be told. Yet a picture embedded into my mind and soul and heart. That picture became a photo. That photo became my personal icon.

In Henri J. M. Nouwen's book Behold the beauty of the Lord: Praying with Icons, *he says, "During a hard period of my life in which verbal prayer had become nearly impossible and during which mental and emotional fatigue had made me the easy victim of feelings of despair and fear, this icon became the beginning of my healing. As I sat for long hours in front of Rublev's Trinity, I noticed how gradually my gaze became prayer. This silent prayer slowly made my inner restlessness melt away and lifted me up into the circle of love, a circle that couldn't be broken by the powers of the world. Even as I moved away from the icon and became involved in the many tasks of everyday life, I felt as if I did not have to leave the holy place I had found and could dwell there wherever I went. I knew that the house of love I had entered has no boundaries and embraces everyone who wants to dwell there."*

Now, 13 years since graduating from ND, far from the Grotto, I pull out my photo of the statue of Mary, look at it, and it brings me back to the Grotto, to within, to beyond, to a place no longer defined — my icon. I gave the photo as gifts to most of my fellow Badinites. What to do or say when someone needs comfort? Send the photo. The Grotto became alive with color and passion because once I shared with others my love for Notre Dame. "In the world you will have trouble. But be brave: I have conquered the world." JN Bible

— Jennifer Jones, Class of 1982, Seattle, Washington.

As mentioned earlier, Jennifer Jones is also the name of the actress who won an Academy Award for her performance in *The Song of Bernadette*, the 1943 movie based on the experiences of Bernadette Soubirous at the Lourdes Grotto in France. It was her first movie.

The Song of Bernadette is now finding a new and appreciative audience, as a black and white classic, often replayed on television. The Miracle of Lourdes lives on in the hearts of those who believe in it.

Many newlyweds visit the Grotto to pray and have pictures taken.
Bridal bouquets and flowers are often placed at Mary's feet and in
and around Bernadette's statue.

Chapter 15

Two Black Stones From Lourdes

In 1958 a special year long celebration of the Centennial of the Lourdes Grotto in France was held on campus. It was celebrated from Lourdes Day, February 11, 1958, through February 11, 1959. An estimated 4000 students attended the celebration. Many ceremonies were held at the Grotto and improvements were made there during that year.

Robert L. Hamilton '34 undertook the paving of the grounds [formerly crushed stone] leading to this favorite shrine of Notre Dame Men.[239]

It is believed that the current "Senior's Last Visit to Sacred Heart and the Grotto" stems from a tradition that evolved during that year long celebration. Father Mike Heppen remembers the seniors' last visit to the Grotto during the month of May when he graduated in 1959. The observance appears to have declined in the 1970s. In early 1981, Father John Fitzgerald, C.S.C., and Steven Warner of Campus Ministry revived the tradition. It has now become "A celebration of four years of friendship in song, readings, and poetry" with sacred music of the Notre Dame Glee Club and Folk Choir, starting at Sacred Heart and ending at the Grotto.

Each year the bulletin announcing the Seniors' Last Visit has been illustrated with a sketch of a campus religious landmark drawn by a graduating senior. This attractive sketch of the Grotto used on the '95 bulletin was done by Kathryn Mapes Turner '95.

Another interesting piece of information about the Grotto was passed on by a Holy Cross Sister from California during a display of the colorful artwork of Sister Paraclita,[240] the only Native American Indian in the Sisters of the Holy Cross order. She was visiting the mother house during the summer and was also viewing her work in the convent community room. The subject of the Notre Dame Grotto and all the interesting history associated with it came up in a casual conversation.

"Two black stones from Lourdes are also there," she said. She explained that because they were not easily noticed, it was not common knowledge. Some people knew about them, and some did not, though they may have been familiar with the Grotto for many years. It was something passed on, when someone viewing the Grotto saw the stones being touched or kissed by others and inquired about it. Probably hundreds of people had walked by them, she said, and never knew they were there.

A special trip to the Grotto to locate these two stones produced the same effect. Seeing someone touching them prompted the same curious question. "Is there something special about those stones?"

Who had put them there and when? One was very small, a two inch fragment of stone, which must have been there since it was built. The other stone was black, the size of a Hershey chocolate bar. It looked as if it had been quickly patched in. The cement was much lighter than the rest of the mortar.

The University Archives and the Indiana Province Archives had no photographs of the Grotto picturing the black stones.

Father Edward O'Connor, who conducts the Rosary at the Grotto nightly, said he didn't know about the small one, but he knew the larger black stone was placed there by Father Phillip Schaerf. He was pastor of the Sacred Heart Church from 1957-60, and later head of the Confraternity of Lourdes which dispenses the Lourdes water from France.

He had no idea when he might have placed it there or how it came about, but he was sure there had been no ceremony involved. Either Father Schaerf had cemented it in himself, or with the help of a workman, unbeknown to anyone else.

The Saint Bernadette Reliquary

The Indiana Province Archives provided more information about Father Schaerf. In 1957, he made a trip to Nevers, France, to obtain a relic of Saint Bernadette from Mother General Ann Marie Crebassol of the Sisters of Charity. It was blessed by Pope XII and carried in a procession to the Grotto celebrations. It was then said to have been put in a gold box and placed on the altar in the Lourdes Chapel in the church.

The Lourdes altar was removed from in front of the Gregori painting of the Grotto scene during one of the renovations. The relic was placed in a reliquary in the Sacred Heart Museum. There was nothing in the church, or the museum, that resembled a gold box. Then an article about it, in the *Notre Dame Alumnus* magazine, carried this reference to the St. Bernadette Relic and its distinctive reliquary inspired by the Golden Dome:

A beautiful reliquary was presented to the Lourdes Confraternity from the Rome Club by Jerry Ashley '33 president of the Alumni Club in the Eternal City. A relic (1st class) of St. Bernadette will be placed in the reliquary which in turn will be placed on the altar of Our Lady of Lourdes in Sacred Heart Church on the Notre Dame campus.[241]

However, it was not a simple gold box, but a very ornate and beautiful golden reliquary in the shape of the golden dome of Notre Dame, set upon a pedestal, with Our Lady on top. It is on display, in the center glass case where the chalices are kept, in the Sacristy Museum of the Basilica of the Sacred Heart.

Father Schaerf, on the occasion of Notre Dame's celebration of the One Hundredth Centenary of the Lourdes Grotto in France, spoke of its spiritual miracles in delivering a sermon about Lourdes at the Annual Alumni Mass at Sacred Heart Church a year later, in June 8, 1958:

You know the story of Lourdes and the one word that astounds the world: Miracles, something that cannot be explained by the laws of nature. Everyone knows of the physical cures, but the thousands of unwritten cures of the uncured: The miracles of resignation, these are the baffling paradoxes. The miracles of the conversion of the heart are astounding to those without faith. But it's an old story, it's the story summarized in an eternal mysterious 'Fiat.'

For over a hundred years, thousands have repeated that Fiat at Lourdes, and gone away strong in their weakness. Men like Franz Werfel, the Jew, sang a song about Bernadette the 'little one.' Fulton Oursler called it the Happy Grotto of Happy Failures. Ruth Cranston, the Protestant, called it the Road Back Home. Notre Dame men have understood and lived this 'Fiat' like Fred Snite and Van Wallace, who understood and lived the paradoxical words of Bernadette 'my occupation is to be ill.' . . . Your presence here today . . . emphasizes that simplicity of faith, that purity of heart and humility of spirit without which all learning may become a snare, a delusion, a pathway to outer darkness. . . . Continue to make your 'Fiat' to Our Lady: Notre Dame, that you may have a deeper understanding of the words engraved on the seal of your University of Our Lady: Vita, dulcedo, Spes. . . . Our life, Our sweetness and our hope. Our Lady . . . a symbol of Notre Dame.[242]

110 Year Lourdes Celebration at Notre Dame

Many pictures of this 1958 Centennial of the Lourdes Grotto in France, celebrated on the campus, were evident, but none showed the black stone in place at that time. Then the discovery of an old 1968 *Our Sunday Visitor*[243] — with a cover picture of the Grotto and an article detailing the 110 year celebration of the Lourdes Grotto held at Notre Dame in 1968 — showed clearly the large black stone. It looked like it had been freshly cemented into the

Grotto. Father Schaerf, in ill health, had left his post as pastor of the Sacred Heart Parish in 1960. He left the order and his work with the Confraternity in 1968. Could the black stone have been a farewell gesture?

A thorough search through the *Domes* and the *Scholastics*, just to be sure, finally produced a 1958 picture which provided proof of the first appearance of the black stone at the Grotto. It was placed there in 1958, rather than in 1968 as the picture on the cover of the old *Our Sunday Visitor* had suggested. As Father O'Connor had indicated, Father Schaerf must have put it there, without fanfare, in secret, sometime after the ceremonies. This might explain why nothing was written about it at the time and why it didn't show up in any pictures taken during the formal celebration.

One page in the Sacred Heart Church Archives produced the answer to one more unsolved item of interest. A copy of an article from a 1958 *Scholastic* concerning the black stone was filed away in the last folder checked. It was not indexed in the *Scholastic* catalog file. It is unlikely it would have been found

any other way. Along with the article, was a photograph of a student leaning on the Grotto wall with his head bowed in prayer and his hand on the black stone:

From the time the Notre Dame Grotto was dedicated, the most common expression of Notre Dame men's devotion to Mary has been in their regular visits to the Grotto. The similarity of our own Grotto to the Lourdes Grotto has been captured in fine detail here at Notre Dame. In fact, there is even a stone from the Lourdes shrine in our own Grotto; it was brought back to Notre Dame by Father Maguire, who had visited Lourdes.[244]

The missing piece Father Edward O'Connor had been unable to supply — where the black stone Fr. Schaerf

placed at the Grotto had come from — had been found. It was an article that also revealed an interesting coincidence. The Father Maguire responsible for obtaining the black stone was the same Father Joseph Maguire who had written the letter correcting the misconceptions about the history of the Grotto. It is unlikely any of this research would have been attempted without it. Now, everything about the larger black stone began to fall into place.

The Notre Dame Public Relations publicity drop file on the Grotto produced information about the smaller Lourdes stone, which is directly above the larger one. It is barely visible to most people because it is small and the shade of the mortar appears to be the same as the Grotto. An article in their file sent to *The New World*,[245] a Chicago Diocesan magazine, solved that mystery too:

Directly beneath the elevated statue of Our Lady is a relic from the Lourdes Grotto. It is a small piece of rock from the niche in which the Blessed Virgin appeared. This relic was brought to the University by Rev. John F. DeGroote and was installed in 1939.

A check of the Indiana Province Archives revealed that Father DeGroote make a grand tour of Europe, including Lourdes, in 1939. Twenty years later, in 1958, Father Joseph Maguire also made a grand tour of Europe, with a two day stopover in Lourdes, for his 50th anniversary. Both of them must have had the same thought in mind. This information supplied the story behind the two black stones from Lourdes now at the Grotto.

Father Schaerf was pastor of the Sacred Heart Church from 1957 to 1960. Father Maguire would have been in his 80s. It would be reasonable to assume, that due to his age, he would have been unable to arrange to place the black stone at the Grotto himself and turned it over the Father Schaerf to accomplish. Father Maguire died in his 90s in 1964. Those who lived with him in his retirement years remember seeing him, well up in years, skating on the lake in the wintertime.

It is understandable that those who have visited Lourdes in France would want to bring back a tangible remembrance of their visit there. Stones have a special fascination. From little on up many people are attracted to stones and shells, probably because each is unique, like people, no two are exactly alike.

A last trip to the site of the Grotto in the Glen at Saint Mary's to take additional pictures on a sunnier day produced one of these interesting mementos. A small eye-catching dark rock protruded from the rubble covered bank of dirt, sloping away from the side of the narrow lane, along the hill leading to the top of the bluff. It was about the size of a fist, smoky black and covered with dirt, but the sunlight caught a little glitter in it. One side was smooth and flat. It looked like it would make a good paperweight. A good soak in a pan of soapy water, overnight, transformed it. Once dried, and viewed under a lamp, tiny sparks of light gleamed every way it was turned. It turned out to be a hunk of black hematite, normally a Michigan mineral, a bit out of place in this area. It became a special remembrance of that springtime excursion into the glen in search of the island and the long forgotten grotto.

Black stones in ages past have had a very special spiritual significance. Finding it fit in nicely with this later study of the two black stones from Lourdes that have become an integral part of the Notre Dame Grotto. The Grotto itself has that same unique appeal. The unhewn rocks used throughout, some boulders weighing as much as 2 or 3 tons, lend that touch of warmth and irregularity found in nature to its wooded knoll. There is something about it that is very pleasing to the eye and the soul.

The Symbolism of Stone

Carl Jung, in his *Man And His Symbols*,[246] makes these very interesting references to the symbolism of the stone in religion:

Biblical references to the "stone" are numerous. "Christ is the stone that the builders rejected which became head of the corner." (Luke XX:17). Christ is also called the spiritual rock from which the water of life springs." (I Cor. X:4). Many religions use a stone to signify God or to mark a place of worship. The holiest sanctuary of the Islamic world is the Ka'abe, the black stone in Mecca to which all pious Moslems hope to make their pilgrimage.

From the Bible: "Like living stones, let yourselves be built into a spiritual house . . ." 1 Peter 2:5.

Very few people would not be able to relate to this Jung comment:

Many people cannot refrain from picking up stones of a slightly unusual color or shape and keeping them, [as shells are picked up at the seashore], without knowing why they do. It is as if the stone held a mystery in it that fascinates them. Men have collected stones since the beginning of time and have apparently assumed that certain ones were the containers of the the spirit of the life-force with all its mystery.

The ancient Germans, for instance, believed that the spirits of the dead continued to live in their tombstones. The custom of placing stones on graves may spring partly from the symbolic idea that something eternal of the dead person remains which can be most fittingly represented by a stone.

In some cultures, when visiting a cemetery a stone is placed on the grave in the belief that the dead loved one will know you have been there.

The significance of the black stone at the Grotto, and the attraction it has for those who regularly visit the Grotto, was also explained in Jung's book:

The stone symbolized something permanent that can never be lost or dissolved, something eternal that some have compared to the mystical experience of God within one's own soul. It symbolizes what is perhaps the simplest and deepest experience, the experience of something eternal that man can have in those moments when he feels immortal and unalterable.

The Grotto at Notre Dame must inspire just such feelings in many people who visit there. As Tom Dooley described it, there is "something else" there, a special feeling, that is a different personal experience for each person drawn there by the spirit of the place.

On several other occasions, people have asked about it. Many times since learning of the larger black stone, and having told others about it, the wish that more people were aware of it has been especially strong.

One day, in visiting the Grotto and being drawn to the black stone, a glint of gold sparkled in the sunshine. Like an answered prayer, there appeared over the large black stone the first plaque on the Grotto in almost 40 years.

A small one inch by four inch plaque. On it, were the simple words, *Stone From Lourdes France.* It had not been there two weeks before. Someone else must have wondered about it too, and decided that it should be marked for others.

For many years additional plaques have not been allowed at the Grotto. How it was accomplished only God knows, but seeing it there is bound to be a happy surprise to many other visitors to the Grotto who were not aware of it before. Rest assured, these fingers will never touch the Lourdes stone again without thinking of, and blessing, the person who arranged for it to be there.

Chapter 16

Tom Dooley and More Grotto Impressions

No story about the Grotto would be complete without the personal expression of a former student whose memory will always be associated with the Notre Dame Grotto. Possibly the most celebrated Grotto experience in Notre Dame history was expressed by Dr. Tom Dooley, in the form of a letter sent to Father Ted Hesburgh shortly before his death in 1961. It was placed at the kneeling rail of the Grotto by Father Hesburgh to inspire future generations.

More than one visitor to the Grotto has discerned his religious vocation there. And at least one student, after reading Tom Dooley's letter, decided to become a third-world doctor. Over the years, it has been an inspiration to many who pause to read it. An exact copy of Dooley's letter is quoted in the appendix.

Dr. Thomas A. Dooley, '48 died on the evening of January 18 in a New York hospital. Five days before his death he was visited by Father Hesburgh, who relayed his request for prayers back to the Notre Dame campus. "The Splendid American" died just as the Notre Dame student body had completed three days of prayer in his behalf. A Solemn Mass of Requiem was celebrated for him January 20 in Sacred Heart Church.

In December Father Hesburgh had received a letter from Hong Kong, where Tom Dooley had been hospitalized for a recurrence of cancer that had attacked his spine. An eloquent expression of the faith that had overcome his terrible suffering and prompted his labors in Southeast Asia, a moving tribute to his beloved Notre Dame, the letter was distributed by Associated Press and printed throughout the world after Dooley's death."

Later, a duplicate of the letter,[247] engraved on stainless steel and enclosed in a box with a Plexiglas top, was attached permanently to the kneeling rail of the Grotto.

Tom Dooley was born on January 17, 1927, and died the day after his 34th birthday, on January 18, 1961, just six weeks after his December 2, 1960, letter was written from Hong Kong. In it, he speaks of the comfort of prayer. In part:

. . . Because I can pray, I can communicate. How do people endure anything on earth if they cannot have God?

I realize the external symbols that surround one when he prays are not important. . . . It is the Something else there that counts.

But just now. . . and just so many times, how I long for the Grotto. Away from the Grotto Dooley just prays. But at the Grotto, especially now when there must be snow everywhere and the lake is ice glass and that triangular fountain on the left is frozen solid and all the priests are bundled in their too-large too-long old black coats and the students wear snow boots. . . . if I could go to the Grotto now then I think I could sing inside. I could be full of faith and poetry and loveliness and know more beauty, tenderness and compassion. . . .

In 1959, a year and six months before his letter was sent to Fr. Hesburgh, Tom Dooley wrote another poignant letter in which he mentioned the Grotto. He wrote it in reply to a letter sent to him by a man in Elkhart who had gone to premed school with him. Tom apologized for his delay in replying and mentioned that he answered 600-2000 letters a month. He concluded the letter, from the Village of Muong Sing, with this reference to the Notre Dame Grotto:

Oh, to be able to get on my knees in the Grotto of Our Lady just now! I know that God is everywhere. He's everywhere here. We see him daily in 100 wretched who come to the clinic. We see him in the mountains. We see him in the monsoon rainfall on the thatched roof. We know Him when he outstretches His arm in the thunder. But to be in the grotto at Notre Dame; there I find propinquity. There I have nearness that no rationalization can replace.

Village of Muong Sing
Kingdom of Laos
May 25, 1959[248]

Three years after his death, Father Thomas O'Donnell wrote about Tom Dooley's poignant letter at the Grotto in the *Notre Dame Scholastic*:

Sickness is a great thought provoker. When a person knows his disease or affliction is terminal he reaches back and grasps the great moments that helped him in the past and perhaps can help him now. This was the way with Tom Dooley. With aching fingers he spoke his heart on a typewriter. It does the soul good and warms our hearts to pause in our haste and remember the unhastening hours and the sun that dials its seasons on the aging stone of the Grotto.[249]

Tom Dooley's letter was placed at the Grotto four months after his death. Father Hesburgh assigned the project to Rev. Robert Lochner, C.S.C., who engineered the actual placement of the letter. A close examination of Dooley's letter, and the box in which it is contained, shows the care taken in planning it. The container is not only durable, it has weathered the thirty five years it had been there with no sign of leakage.

A call to Father Bob Lochner in Cocoa Beach, Florida, to inquire about it brought another Grotto story to add to a growing collection. A most affable man, he was friendly and outgoing, and especially interested in the Grotto. He said he felt honored that Father Hesburgh had asked him to research a way to put it permanently at the Grotto. It made him feel close to the Blessed Virgin, and more a part of it.

He explained that the letter was engraved on stainless steel because at that time they were doing the same thing with diplomas, which were then mounted on a block of wood. Through the Notre Dame Hammes Bookstore, he made an arrangement for the letter to be replicated in the same manner. It was framed in the black box, with a Plexiglas top, to protect it. Father Lochner said the Grotto was his favorite spot on campus. He checks the letter every time he visits Notre Dame and is pleased to find that it is still in excellent shape.

He said his next visit to the campus would be on his golden jubilee in 1996. When he learned the Grotto would be one hundred years old the same year, he said he would look forward to saying Mass there to commemorate the occasion. It was an interesting coincidence he hadn't been aware of before.

When Dreams Come True

Father Lochner continued to visit Tom Dooley's mother after his death and often admired the pastel of Dooley in her living room. On one of his visits, feeling her time was near, she told him she wanted him to have the painting that was reproduced on the dust cover of Dooley's book, *The Night They Burned the Mountain*. The pastel painting, a head and shoulders depiction of Dooley with his arm around a child, bears the artist's name, Elizabeth Daniels Baldwin. Father Lochner passed the painting on to his nephew, Richard Lochner, a Notre Dame alumnus and retired Marine Colonel, who also has a copy of the book autographed by Tom Dooley.

His nephew has his own fond attachment to the Grotto and the University of Notre Dame. He realized the dream of his life — to retire close to his alma mater — by acquiring a home at the entrance to Notre Dame. He said the house was the answer to a prayer and seemed to be waiting for him to discover it. He called it Lochner House. It has become known as "The House with Three Flags." The flags of the United States, the Marines and Notre Dame are positioned on his front lawn. They are lighted throughout the night. "The Marines do two things," he said. "We seize the high ground, and we plant flags." He accomplished the dream of his life, to retire near Notre Dame, so he planted his flags at the front entrance of the campus. Even his address is Notre Dame Avenue.

The house also has a special significance. The man who built it, a retired Notre Dame professor, planned to build a Grotto in the basement. When Dick Lochner bought the house, it contained a missing 15' x 15' corner room, on the first floor of the house, that was walled off and floorless. It formed the cathedral ceiling needed to accommodate the height of the Grotto. The Grotto was started, but never completed by the original owner. This may account for the many rocks now used in its landscape.

Col. Lochner met his future wife after the war and they were married by his Uncle in Cleveland, Ohio, his hometown. Immediately after the ceremony, they packed their car and headed for the Morris Inn at Notre Dame. Before they had unpacked their bags, he said he took his new wife to see the Grotto — she had never been to Notre Dame — where he lit a candle and offered a prayer of thanksgiving that their lives had been joined together.

Dick Lochner also plans to pass on Dooley's painting and his book to Notre Dame to be placed in their collection of Dooley Memorabilia.

In 1962 a replica of the Grotto at Notre Dame was erected by Rev. Sigmund Jankowski, C.S.C., Pastor of St. Stanislaus Church in South Bend for 22 years. It has become known as the St. Stan's Grotto. As with the Notre Dame Grotto, the contractor, William Buckles, the only one willing to tackle the challenge, was non-Catholic. Father Jankowski, an Alumnus of Notre Dame, had fulfilled the dream of his life, but it took many years to accomplish it. He wrote a book about his love of Notre Dame and the Grotto. He called it *When Dreams Come True*.[250]

In 1976, Rudy Ruettiger graduated from Notre Dame. In doing so, he also fulfilled the dream of his life. After a long struggle and countless setbacks, he graduated from Notre Dame and played in a Notre Dame football game. His time on the field was only 67 seconds, but he had accomplished his aim.

During his time at Holy Cross Junior College, while he was trying to get into Notre Dame, he *"spent much of the night praying at the Grotto on campus."* He said it was a great source of inspiration and solace to him while he awaited the chance to go to Notre Dame. It wasn't until Ruettiger completed the two-year program at Holy Cross, graduating *cum laude*, that he was accepted at Notre Dame.

Seventeen years after his graduation, he had a second dream fulfilled. His story and his struggle were filmed in an inspirational movie which included scenes at the Grotto. They began filming on the campus in the fall of 1992 and the movie premiered in South Bend on October 6, 1993.

"It's a story of courage," said Pizzo the screenwriter. *"The most courageous thing an individual can do is to go against expectations, go against the identity and definition given by others — whether it is family or*

Christine Astin, Sean Astin, and Rudy greeting Ara Parseghian
at the premiere party in the Hesburgh Library penthouse

community — and take that huge leap based on no hard evidence but only an inner faith."[251]

Another item of interest, associated with Hollywood and the Grotto, occurred during the filming of a much earlier motion picture — the 1931 Lew Ayres movie, *The Spirit of Notre Dame* — the only other movie actually filmed on campus. It was mentioned in an obscure brochure in the University Archives:

When the Universal Film Co. was preparing the Knute Rockne movie The Spirit Of Notre Dame, (Lew Ayres, 1931) a sound recorder near Our Lady's Grotto caught the uproar of a deafening sky artillery. This gave the Hollywood operators many feet of unexcelled thunder which they insert in various films as the occasion requires. Thus movie fans never know how near they are to Notre Dame, the Grotto and Our Lady.[252]

The Nightly Rosary

In 1981, Father Joseph Champlin, spoke of returning to his alma mater and the two days he spent at a conference on "that magnificently beautiful campus." He tells of the morning he walked over to the Grotto:

There I prayed the rosary, recalled moments decades earlier, watched persons stop for a visit and wondered how many million, not thousands, had paused for a similar plea to our Lady since the shrine's erection at the turn of this century.

The stone vault of the cave was blackened from the smoke of past and present votive candles — over 1,000 were flickering on the morning of my stay at the shrine. A single flower here, a bouquet there speak silently about individual testimonies of affection for our Lady.

Nor is devotion to God's mother at the Grotto merely a carry over from the past with no appeal for the young. During my 7:30 a.m. visit a great cross-section of people passed by and paused for prayer. They included a retired Holy Cross religious brother, workmen in overalls, well dressed secretaries, professors with briefcases and several University girls who after their jog around the two small lakes knelt for a long period of time before our Lady. The last visitors symbolized for me the other 8,000 students at Notre Dame of whom many, probably most, and perhaps all have regularly or occasionally honored Mary by their presence at the Grotto.

He also mentioned "the handsome marble lectern and altar at one side of the cave and the sign reminding visitors that rosary devotions are conducted every night at 6:45."[253]

It was Father Tom McDonagh who started the rosary at the Grotto although nobody remembers when. He conducted the rosary there twice a year in May and October for a number of years. Nor does anyone remember when Brother John Lavelle started the 6:45 nightly rosary. However, Father Champlin's article indicates that it was a practice in 1981 and probably even before that time.

Father Edward O'Connor conducts the nightly 6:45 rosary currently, and has for a number of years.

Fr. Hesburgh on one of his many visits to the Grotto.

When Father Hesburgh retired in 1987 students planted a tree for him at one of his favorite places on campus, the Grotto. A tree for Father Joyce is also there along with several other trees on the Grotto lawn given as memorial gifts. This practice started in the late 1970s or early 1980s. Father Hesburgh's tree was given "with upmost admiration" by the Class of 1990. It is a distinctive tree for a man of distinction. Like the legendary sycamore on the Grotto lawn, it has an unusual shape and name. Because of its unique, contorted, corkscrew branches, it has been dubbed the "Harry Lauder Walking Stick Tree." It was named after a well known actor who died in 1950. He always performed on stage carrying a crooked walking stick. His Memorial Tree is pictured on the right side of the path in the photograph at the beginning of this chapter.

Memorial gifts have also been given for the permanent redwood benches placed throughout the campus. The benches began appearing in the 1990s, during preparations for the 1992 Sesquicentennial. The plaques mounted on the benches at the Grotto represent memorial gifts given in memory of loved ones who had a special fondness for the Grotto and its peaceful setting.

The Caretakers of the Grotto

Many caretakers have tended the Grotto over the past one hundred years. During the early 1980s, Franklin McMahon introduced the figure of Brother Roderic Grix, one of those many caretakers, in a painting he did of the Grotto.

Brother Rod began taking care of the Grotto in his twilight years when he was no longer able, due to a stroke, to carry on the constant repair work he did on campus. The Grotto painting which hung on a wall at the foot of his bed was admired by everyone who visited him. He always took pleasure in pointing to himself in it.

He said he had been tending the Grotto one day completely oblivious of the person who was painting it. He was about to leave after finishing his work when the artist asked his name and said he had painted him into the picture. He told him he would be getting prints made of the painting and he'd send him a copy.

He thought no more about it until one day he was surprised to find a large package had arrived for him. True to his word, McMahon had shipped him a 21" x 25" copy of the painting. It was beautifully framed and matted in green. Brother Roderic was in the middle of it, in his green and black lumberjack shirt, cleaning the wax off the candle holders. He never knew the painter, Franklin McMahon, was a well known artist who had also sketched many buildings on campus. His Grotto painting became a source of inspiration to many people in the years it hung at the foot of his bed. Brother Roderic died in the mid 1980s. His lovely watercolor of the Grotto now decorates the living room wall of a dear friend, Mary Grix, who loves it as dearly as he did.

In the one hundred years the Grotto has enriched the campus, there must have been an endless parade of unsung caretakers. Sweeping away the gathering leaves in the fall, cleaning the wax from the candle holders, replenishing its candles and lovingly caring for it.

Brother Roderic was only one of those many caretakers. After his stroke, his work at the Grotto was taken over by Brother Protase Bauer who tended the Grotto with his own special brand of devotion. He would bring the large glass candle containers back to Holy Cross House when the candles burned out. He had a large industrial bucket with sand in it, in which he had placed a light bulb on an extension cord. He used this method to melt the left over wax in the containers. He would then transfer the melted wax to a freshly washed candle holder and place a new wick in it. In this way, he recycled the used candle containers that, before that time, were thrown away. Later, he added an extra touch to them by having someone paint violets on the glass containers. Brother Protase was a quiet, kindly little man always friendly and solicitous to everyone he encountered.

He had a fondness for bright, sunny daffodils. When he found them in the woods in excess, he would divide them and plant them somewhere else to bring cheer to anyone passing by on the campus

Another Brother who spent hours at the Grotto was Brother Cosmas Guttly. Corby Hall, adjacent to the

Grotto area, was home to him for many years. A large screened-in porch overlooks a small court yard of greenery. It also overlooks the Grotto lawn, its park benches scattered among the trees. A constant parade of people pass by going to and coming from the Grotto.

Brother Cosmas was often seen tidying up the Grotto, resting, talking to people, and tending the flower beds there and around Corby Hall. Alice Osberger, a secretary on campus, was walking toward the Grotto on a lunch break one day when she saw Brother Cosmas hunched over a flower bed near Corby Hall. She thought he was ill and went to help him. She said when she got closer to him she realized that he was weeding it.

He also helped in the the church and sacristy. For years this quaint, frail little man, with the round wire-rimmed glasses and skirted black cassock, was a familiar sight to many as he quietly served the priests during Mass at Sacred Heart Church. He was revered by priests and lay people alike as a very holy man.

In between church services, and his other work, he was always at the Grotto. One day a week he would go to Holy Cross House, the retirement home for priests on the campus. There he would help his "good buddy," Brother Edward, attend the infirm priests who said their daily Mass in the long corridor of sit-down altars for use by priests in wheelchairs. Then he would return to the Sacred Heart Church in time for the 5 o'clock service.

Brother Cosmas came from Switzerland. He was a businessman before he became a Brother in mid life, after the death of his wife and child in childbirth. He was gifted in many ways. His daily devotion to the Grotto and its surroundings, was captured in a unique, unidentified, full page photograph of him in the back of the 1990 *Dome*. He was sitting alone on a secluded park bench, dressed in his black cassock, head bowed, meditating or praying a little distance from the Grotto.

With his back to the camera he could not have known the picture was being taken. Only those who knew Brother Cosmas well would have known it was him. Very soon after the picture was taken he was confined, by his infirmities, to Holy Cross House. He died there two months after his 99th birthday.

Herbie De Mike, an employee of the University, has taken care of the Grotto now for a number of years.

If your guest should be non-Catholic,
to make her feel at ease
introduce her to the Grotto first:
That's probably where you'll go first anyway.

Notre Dame Religious Bulletin
October 14, 1941

Chapter 17

A Fire Sparks Renewed Interest in the Grotto

This story would also not be complete without a description of the almost disastrous fire at the Grotto in the predawn hours of September 23, 1985, when the Grotto was loaded with lighted candles, said to be some 1500, during a Michigan State game, which Notre Dame won 27-10. Though a sad occasion, the attention focused on the Grotto initiated many expressions of heartfelt feelings about it.

This firsthand account of the fire came from Brother Borromeo Malley, who was fire chief at the time. He has been associated with the Notre Dame campus for 60 years and is now retired and living at Holy Cross House on campus.

He was sitting in the Clinic lobby at Holy Cross House. He said he was getting ready to leave, when he noticed the road was congested with cars from an accident in front of Moreau Seminary. He had decided to wait until it cleared. Then he grinned, mischievously, and added, "The only thing I have to do in this life is die, and I can do it just as well here as out there." A conversation about the Grotto fire flowed from that happenstance meeting.

Brother Borromeo, straightforward and friendly, had a terrific memory for details. This is the story he related about the Grotto fire which he compared to a refinery or oil fire:

It was one hell of a fire; heavy black smoke belched from the opening of the Grotto. The heat was so intense that when water came in contact with the stone, it caused spalling, which happens when the stones become overheated and chip or fall off in blocks. Large pieces lay on the ground in front of the Grotto.

Candles grouped on the floor of the Grotto, for lack of holder space, had ignited their plastic containers causing a fire. The candle racks had been pushed back, over other burning candles, to make room for more on the floor and the ones below had ignited those above them."

As Brother Borromeo put it, "It looked like one big mess of molten molasses."

The fire left battle scars on the Grotto but did not bring it down. Only a limited number of candles are allowed to burn there now, and glass containers have replaced the plastic ones. The singed

ivy and blackened trees, on the front and above the Grotto, have already grown back; and the statue, although smudged with smoke, miraculously escaped unharmed. Since the smoke damage to the stones required professional cleaning, the fire turned out to be a providential improvement. It was speedily refurbished and repaired leaving only a slightly changed appearance. The darkened interior stones, freshly cleaned of almost 90 years of candle smoke, are kept that way now by a professional cleaning on a regular basis.

It was a timely encounter; Brother Borromeo died less than a year later. Father George Schidel related this typical Brother Borromeo comment in describing his last hours on earth. He was having breakfast with him that morning. They were discussing the fatal airliner crash in Japan, that had just been reported on the news, when Brother Borromeo made the comment: "Well, the next trip I'm going to take is going to be my last!" and he pointed toward heaven.

A few hours later, on Tuesday, April 26, 1994, in the midst of a conversation, Brother Borromeo was taken from this world by a sudden heart attack. He was 81. The previous Friday he was his usual friendly, outgoing self, full of vigor. His "I can die just as well here, as out there," spoken in the clinic waiting room at Holy Cross House the day he described the fire at the Grotto, came to mind. He collapsed and died in the same room.

The expansion and updating of the Notre Dame fire department was due largely to his efforts. Brother Borromeo Malley, who retired after 50 years of service, was honored as the longest surviving fire chief in the United States in 1992.

© David C. Berta

Fire at Grotto Reveals its Importance to Many

Excerpts from an article written by a student, Mike Wilkins, shortly after the Grotto fire, catch the essence of the Spirit of Notre Dame, the Grotto, and the effect it has had upon its many visitors. He has also expressed, with heartfelt feeling, the point of view of those many students for whom the Grotto was primarily intended.

His article appeared in the *Observer* on October 4, 1985, under the title: "Fire at Grotto reveals its importance to many." Mike wrote it ten days after the fire as a personal expression of his feelings about the Grotto and its close call. I am sure it also touched the hearts of many students new to the Grotto experience and what it represents on campus.

I walked down to the Grotto the other night and was very pleased to find it virtually back to normal. That place has come to mean an awful lot to me in the four-plus years I've been here, and looking at its charred shell last week was quite hard to take.

When I first came to Notre Dame, I didn't even know the Grotto existed. I stumbled on it by accident one day as I was walking around St. Mary's Lake. I was immediately impressed with its beauty and the peaceful feeling it seemed to create in everyone who stopped to pray.

Within a month or two, the Grotto had become a pretty regular part of my life. I didn't go there every day, but when I needed a little lift or just a break from the pressures of freshman year, the Grotto was always the first place to go.

I can remember breaking up with my girlfriend from home that year. The night I realized things were finally over I walked down to the Grotto and had a good cry. Being there did not make my problems go away, but it sure made me feel a lot more at peace with what had happened.

Not too long after that, I had wandered down for a late night prayer and there was a girl sitting on a bench crying. After much hesitation, I sat down next to her and asked her what was wrong and if she'd like to talk about it. I have no idea what made me do it. Since I had been in the same position myself, it just seemed to be the right thing to do. My Hawaiian roommate at the time called it the Aloha Spirit. I do not know what it was, but I know there was something

about being so close to God that made me want to help that girl, even though she was a total stranger.

Sophomore year I spent some of the worst moments of my life at the Grotto. One of my best friends was killed in an automobile accident and I was bitter and angry. I lit candles, knelt on the kneelers, sat on the benches, wandered around the grassy area between the Grotto and the lakes — all the while questioning God. I went there frequently after my friend died, mad at God every time.

Yet even through my anger, I felt that when I was at the Grotto, God was near me and He was trying to make me understand what had happened. . . .

Last year, the Grotto became more than just a convenient link to God, but a link to my days at Notre Dame as well. Just before graduation, when the seniors made their last trip to the Grotto, I carried a candle from Sacred Heart Church to the Grotto. I can still remember exactly where I placed my candle. . . . That spot remains a link between me and my memories of the previous four years. It has made the Grotto . . . a symbol of Notre Dame and all this place has come to mean to me. . . .

I guess if anything good could possibly have come from last week's fire it is that I now appreciate the Grotto more and realize more fully the unique role it plays in my life and the lives of many others around campus. . . .[254]

Three weeks after the Grotto Fire, on October 15, 1985, Tom Dooley's humanitarian efforts were recognized on campus with a statue, donated by the Alumni Association. Dr. Tom Dooley became famous in the 1950s as the "jungle doctor of Laos." It was placed just west of the Grotto on the path leading to the legendary sycamore.

By the time Dooley died in 1961, he had saved literally thousands of Southeast Asians. The statue shows Dooley posed with two Laotian children. . . . The Grotto was a favorite meditating place for Dooley during his years at Notre Dame. . . . Placing the statue near the Grotto is fitting, Father Daniel Jenky said, because of how Dooley cherished the place and affirmed this in his letter to Hesburgh.[255]

In the summer of 1996, during the celebration of its centennial, the Grotto's surroundings were newly landscaped. Dooley's letter at the kneeling rail was moved beside his statue and the area was landscaped with decorative plantings. Later a Memorial Bench was placed beside it. On it was this heartfelt tribute honoring another Navy doctor who loved the Grotto and died young.

Memory of
Daniel C. Gaughan, M.D. '88
Keeper of the Grotto, Assistant Sacristan
Lt. Commander, Flight Surgeon, U.S.N.R.
Here he lies in the land of legends;
his heart of gold came home to rest.
FAMILY and FRIENDS

A New Focus on the Grotto

Timothy Howard penned this ageless tribute to the University dedicated to Our Lady of the Lake over a hundred years ago. It is as true today as it was then: "Whoever leaves Notre Dame hopes to see it again."[256]

The same could be said of the Grotto. It occupies one of the most quiet, secluded sites on campus. Its purpose has been realized because she is seldom alone. Students and visitors pause, throughout the night and day, to pray and perhaps light a candle.

An article in the *Observer* printed on February 13, 1986, five months after the fire, brought renewed attention to this lovely campus shrine when the threat of loss was focused upon it.

In a portion of that impressive article, Kathy Martin the feature staff writer, speaks of the student experience:

Scarcely a student passes through the challenges, dilemmas, and triumphs of four college years here without taking refuge at one time or another in the peaceful silence of a moment of reflection before hundreds of glowing candles which are special prayers to the Virgin Mary. It is part of the Notre Dame experience and tradition.

The writer quotes the Rector of Sacred Heart Church:

Father Daniel R. Jenky, Rector of Sacred Heart Church, described the Grotto today as a place where "even non-church-goers feel they can go to be quiet and pray." He said that the atmosphere is "unselfconscious and unpretentious, where normal, active people can share faith without it being a big deal." Father Jenky noted the reaction of a visiting Canadian priest to the enormous numbers of students who came to the Grotto to pray, "At Notre Dame, there is still the atmosphere that gives people permission to pray without looking like they're doing anything weird."

Kathy Martin also quotes former Notre Dame President, Father Theodore Hesburgh, who usually visits the Grotto every day when he is on campus:

"I really believe that Our Lady watches over this place. I feel I ought to stop in and say thanks, and also pray that she keeps watching over it." he said. "I usually get down there in the wee hours of the morning when I leave the

office," he continued. "There is almost always someone down there, rain, sleet, or snow . . . . Every university has a place where students hang out for their social life, libraries where they study, and playing fields where they play sports, but how many have a praying place?"

The Grotto has earned Father Hesburgh's own personal accolade: "I've been to shrines dedicated to Our Lady all over the world. Mary may visit them, but she lives here at Notre Dame."

"Although there are thirty chapels in the dorms and elsewhere on the campus," Kathy Martin says, "the popular place to pray is the Grotto."

Freshman, Kathleen Flynn said the Grotto makes her feel a part of Notre Dame: "I can stop on my way home from the 'brar'. It makes me feel complete. It's not hokey-religious, just quiet and personal."

A companion portion of that same Observer article was compiled by Doug Anderson, under the heading, "What does the Grotto mean to you?" Fr. Ron Wasowski speaks of its open outdoor setting:

It's not quite the same as the church, which is enclosed; this is outdoors. It's a place where people know prayer and devotion are welcome, where you can stop in very briefly and go on. I think it's very special because of that.

This sanctuary among the trees is filled with the memories of a host of fellow travelers journeying through life. John Bruening's comment emphasizes this impression.

On a cold winter night, it's one of the few places you can go to be by yourself, yet never feel alone.[257]

It has been said that the sweetest words in the English language are mother, heaven, and home — Mary represents them all. The inspiration of her faith burns ever brightly in the candles at her Grotto, so that all people in need might come directly to her, like a child to its mother.

Father John E. Fitzgerald penned these words about that special feeling that radiates from the Grotto and touches the heart:

It's quiet and shady there. Just what there is about the place can't be described because it's different for everyone. Nobody knows how many candles have been burned or prayers answered there. From the great Golden Dome of her University Our Lady reigns as our Queen. Yet at the Grotto she seems to have stepped down a little closer to us that she might emphasize the other side of her personal relationship with us — that of Our Mother.[258]

The beauty of nature surrounding the Grotto, the candleglow, the comforting listening presence to turn to, bring solace in all our troubles. Another writer described the inspiration of the newly erected Grotto as he saw it in 1899:

In order to appreciate the beauty of St. Mary's Lake and the Grotto, go when the sun is hung in the horizon's haze; then the spires of St. Mary's Academy are rounded and mellowed and the lake bosom is lit with dancing wave bands of opal and turquoise and orange, and the graceful trees near the grotto let their leaves pulsate in the quivering light.[259]

Almost 100 years after the writer above painted in words his vision of a sunset at the Grotto, Fr. Wm. Blum, C.S.C. was blessed with this memorable photograph he took of a glorious sunrise over Our Lady of the Lake and her Grotto. Visualizing the sunglow on the Grotto "when the sun is hung in the horizon's haze" and the sky is ribboned with a rainbow of colors is a very special remembrance — once experienced never to be forgotten.

On that historic Feast Day of Our Lady of Snows, after the statue and the Grotto were blessed and Father Corby had given a brief sermon, the five hundred assembled for its dedication departed, many returning throughout the twilight hours. A remembrance of that day was recorded in an 1896 Scholastic. It seems only fitting to include it.

. . . white with the snow of moonlight, the thin mist above the mirrored planets on the lake was like the

Madonna's veil. When all left only Our Lady of Lourdes stood there in the moonlight and the crickets chirped steadily in the long dewy grass.[260]

A multitude of people have paused in reflection and prayer at this peaceful shrine since that day. Others, yet unborn, will follow in their footsteps, as so many are doing today. May that river of blessed humanity continue to flow; beneath the Dome; through the Basilica; past the Grotto; along the lakes; through the ages, for endless generations to come . . . .

BLESSINGS FROM HEAVEN BE UPON ALL THOSE WHO NOW TAKE CARE OF THIS GROTTO AND UPON THE PEOPLE, YOUNG AND OLD, WHO COME HERE TO OUR BLESSED MOTHER AND DEVOUTLY PRAY TO HER.[261]

Christmas Eve at the Grotto
by Dennis White / Courtesy South Bend Tribune

The Keystone

There is a wedge-shaped stone at the top of the arch of the Grotto that holds the other stones in place — it's called a keystone — something on which all the things associated with it depend. In a similar way, one single event in my life — something on which all my research depended — inspired me to write: *A Cave of Candles: The Story Behind the Notre Dame Grotto.*

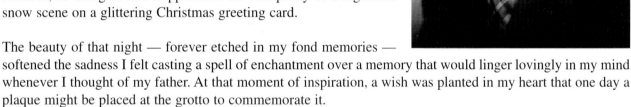

In 1961-62, my father, William Buckles (pictured at right), a semi-retired masonry contractor, was engaged by Rev. Sigmund Jankowski, C.S.C., pastor of the St. Stanislaus Church in South Bend, to build a replica of the Notre Dame Grotto for his parish church of 22 years. My father died at the age of 68 of a sudden coronary occlusion within a year of its completion. It was the last thing he worked on before his death.

Less than two months after his funeral, my brother, who also worked on the grotto, took me to see it. We were both still feeling the effects of our loss. I did not know what a grotto was nor had I ever seen one before. It was a crisp February evening; friendly snowflakes were frosting the evergreens, falling gently, like feathers drifting down. The semi-darkness was bathed in luminous moonlight. Upon my first glimpse of the grotto, I felt that fleeting moment to be frozen in time-lessness, as though I had stepped into the tranquility of a nighttime snow scene on a glittering Christmas greeting card.

The beauty of that night — forever etched in my fond memories —
softened the sadness I felt casting a spell of enchantment over a memory that would linger lovingly in my mind whenever I thought of my father. At that moment of inspiration, a wish was planted in my heart that one day a plaque might be placed at the grotto to commemorate it.

Seven years later, through an extraordinary chance encounter with a stranger, I met Father Jankowski and a large plaque was placed at the grotto commemorating all those who took part in it. Within days of its placement there, Father Jan suffered a debilitating heart attack. From the St. Joseph Hospital, where he had once been chaplain, he was sent to Holy Cross House, the retirement home for priests on the Notre Dame campus. I visited him there weekly until his death three years later on October 7, 1975, Feast Day of Our Lady of the Rosary.

The warmth of our shared friendship endured even beyond Father Jan's death, cementing an ongoing 23 year friendship with both the retired priests and brothers at Notre Dame and the retired Sisters at Saint Mary's campus — friendships that continue to this day.

Suffice to say, the wish planted in 1964 and granted in 1972 — the plaque at the grotto at St. Stanislaus Church — inspired a second wish to know more about the story behind the Notre Dame Grotto.

However, it took many more years, 27 to be exact, from my first glimpse of it, for the stage to be set for that second wish to be granted — in the form of this documentation completed on the eve of its 100th Anniversary.

— Dorothy V. Corson
August 5, 1995

Note: The above personal experience was excerpted from a story entitled, "Always Have a Dream," which I presented to Father Jan on May 7, 1972 to commemorate our placing the plaque at St. Stan's Grotto. When he died in 1975, I wrote a second story entitled, "Friendship is a Chain of Gold," covering his remaining three years spent in retirement at Holy Cross House.[262]

During my research, I discovered Father Jankowski's name in the 1922 *Dome* yearbook. I did not know he graduated *Maxima Cum Laude*, with highest honors. The words under his picture described, so well, the Father Jan I knew: "'Jan' has simply smiled his way into the hearts of his associates. 'If you want to be smiled at, smile!' says he, and somehow or other his policy has produced results."

Finding that description of him years after his death reminded me of a little worn wooden plaque of his that he gave to me as a keepsake before he died. "Stay young at heart," he said as he handed it to me. On it were the words: "If you meet a man without a smile, give him one of yours."

This research has been recorded in remembrance of all those, past and present, who have put their hands and their hearts into the building and perpetuation of the Notre Dame Grotto. It is their presence in spirit, and the homage of countless visitors, that has hallowed its humble rocks and weathered stone. May a fragrance of their loving inspiration and that of every wayfarer who has ever gazed at this humble wayside shrine in wonder and prayer linger forever at the Notre Dame Grotto.

Author's Personal Epilogue

Somewhere I've read "History has a way of delivering the right person, to the right place, at the right time." I have found this to be true on many occasions in my own life and in the lives of the people in the Notre Dame stories I have researched for this book. In this instance, three people of note come to mind: Fr. Edward Sorin, Bernadette Soubirous and Henry Lasserre, Bernadette's historian. They all had an unshakeable faith in what they believed to be their mission in life. Each had a purpose—a dream to fulfill.

Henry Lasserre, in his timeless book, *Our Lady of Lourdes*, described his failing eyesight, his Lourdes water cure, and the Protestant who urged him to try the cure when he continually resisted the thought of it. Two other people in his life at the time, unknowingly, also played a role in pointing him in that direction. His description of the people who influenced his life and the events that followed are another example of the right person being in the right place at the right time to change the course of history.

Through the unusual circumstances of his cure, he was given access to the Lourdes Parish Archives and the Nevers Convent for the purpose of documenting Bernadette's story. He had the records in his hands for four years and kept finding excuses not to begin working on this project. Feeling guilty about it one day he went to confession and the priest told him (knowing nothing about his abilities or credentials), "You must begin at once." He promised he would after he completed some other item on his agenda. The stranger priest, as if from a voice on high, said, "No, now! I command you!"

He said he began that very afternoon going through the papers which had been given to him by the parish priest. Other providential interferences intervened momentarily and he was drawn to yet a third person who factored into his Bernadette experience and planted him upon the path that would make him Bernadette's official historian.

Lasserre profiles the achievements of these three men he considered witnesses and instruments of the miracle accomplished at Lourdes, France, for Bernadette's future historian:

Twenty years later the three men who factored into this phenomenal experience, a Polish count, a Protestant, and a holy man became, themselves, renown in their separate worlds. The Polish Count forsook a worldly life and entered into Holy Orders becoming a Roman Prelate and Archbishop of Salamine, then Cardinal of the Holy Church. The Protestant became Minister of Foreign Affairs and President of the Council in France. The last instrument, the pious old man of Tours who, by the anointing of Lasserre's eyes and his prayers before the Holy Face, 'obtained his deliverance from a threatened relapse, to him was assigned a seat of honor far higher than the other two. Hardly had he slept in the peace of the just, than the voice of the people cried aloud: A Saint has gone to heaven!' His house was turned into a sanctuary and he became the Holy Man of Tours.

This same Holy Man of Tours, earlier, came to Father Sorin's rescue when problems arose with his boat passage to his New World mission which ultimately became the University of Notre Dame.

In a fascinating second book entitled *Miracles at Lourdes*, written in 1884, after his book about Bernadette, Lasserre explains in a letter to his readers his beliefs about how all these wonderful things—in his life and others— came about. It so impressed me that I felt it should be shared in this book about Bernadette and Our Lady's Notre Dame Story. It is as relevant today as it was then. In part:

Henri Lasserre's "Dear Reader" Letter

Dear Reader, have you sometimes reflected on the part played by our Angel Guardian in the various circumstances of life? With what indefatigable solicitude this mysterious companion follows our steps from the cradle to the grave, from the first wail to the last sigh! . . . He concentrates his efforts toward directing our will to good, enlightening our mind, turning our steps from evil, and pointing out the true path which we see not, on account of the vexatious vicissitudes of life. Sometimes our radiant protector acts directly, giving us sudden inspirations, happy thoughts, urging us to write a letter, to say such or such a word, to take such or such a step, indif-

ferent perhaps in themselves, but which, as he well knows, are to be the first links in a chain of secondary causes which will effect our future lives.

The happy inspiration may come to us through some friendly advice, a borrowed book, an unforeseen meeting, a journey which brings us unexpectedly to a certain place, at a certain hour, to the presence of one who will exert a salutary influence over us. . .

Thus do these pure spirits labor in this world to arrest the progress of evil, to extend the reign of good. They suggest fruitful resolutions, they allure the will, and, when it violently resists, they prepare favorable opportunities; and, by a series of well-ordered events, they conduct the mortals confided to their care.

What particularly characterizes the conduct of the angels, is their concealment of their agency under natural appearances: ordinary occurrences of life, fortuitous events, accidental relations. All that these divine messengers accomplish, appears to be done of itself, so delicately do they touch the chords that lead us. Whilst acting everywhere and in everything, we perceive them not. Spiritual beings, superior to ourselves, they are invisible; we feel not their powerful encircling arms, we behold not their immense favors to us…. They dispose all things in silence and secrecy.

When their work is accomplished, however, it sometimes happens that the harmonious unfolding of successive facts, the astonishing concurrence of many incidents to the same end, the close succession of various circumstances, the extraordinary choice of such or such individuals as instruments, the correspondence of certain dates, — a thousand striking particulars unveil with as much clearness the secret intervention of these angelic ministers, as the regular movements of a well-disciplined army denote the presence of its general, or the plan of a dwelling betrays the hand of the workman and illustrates the skill of the architect.

To recall such truths, little known, perhaps, or forgotten, is not an idle digression. It is a torch to enlighten us on our way! — Henri Lasserre, *Miracles at Lourdes* (John Murphy & Co., 1884), pp. 17-19.

––––––

Jaclyn Villano, like Henri Lasserre, believes in angels and answered prayers and has expressed it in this heartwarming angel experience she recorded for a friend on November 11, 1997, in the Viewpoint Section of *The Observer.*

Jaclyn's Grotto story crossed my path more than a year after *Grotto Stories: From the Heart of Notre Dame* was published. It was my hope that one day it might take its place in a future edition of *Grotto Stories*, little knowing then that my own *A Cave of Candles* manuscript was destined for the Internet and it would find its way out into an even wider world as an illustration of the truths in Henri Lasserre's "Dear Reader" letter penned 122 years ago.

"Angel at the Grotto" was the first article Jaclyn wrote for her new column entitled *Chicken Soup* for *The Observer.* It has become another fond remembrance, among the many, that have made the Notre Dame Grotto "A Cave of Candles." There are three things in life everyone understands; candles, prayers and problems.

Angel at the Grotto

I am a firm believer in angels. I think that God uses them to perform the little miracles that help keep our faith strong. I also believe that when an angel isn't available, God expects us to step in, to be His hands and to act as angels for each other.

One of my friends wholeheartedly agrees with me. We were discussing the issue over a bowl of cereal in the dining hall one night, and that's when she shared with me a story that touched my heart and reminded me of how lucky I am to be at this place called Notre Dame. We talked for a while that night, not just about her story, but about all the other 'little miracles' that we have encountered here at ND that make it the extraordinary place that it is.

I went back to my dorm that night, still pondering our discussion. I realized that with all the controversy that has been sweeping this campus in recent weeks, it has become far too easy for stories like my friend's to go untold. This is my hope that the stories shared in this column will encourage and inspire others in the way that they have done so for me.

My friend's story takes place on a day when everything that could go wrong, did. We've all had days like these, when it seems that the world is out to get us with a vengeance. Like many of the rest of us would, my friend needed a place to go and spend some time making sense out of everything that had been happening. So she headed for the Grotto. On the way there, she asked God to send her someone to talk to and help her through the rough time she was experiencing.

My friend has no idea how long she sat at the Grotto that night. She remembers lighting a candle and kneeling to pray, but she soon became absorbed in her thoughts and lost all sense of time. She didn't even realize she had been crying until a gentle hand touched her shoulder and she heard the words, 'Hey, are you gonna be OK?'

Surprised, my friend looked up. Standing in front of her was a stranger, someone she had never seen before, peering down at her with a look of worry etched across his face. My friend was touched by the gesture of this kind stranger, and his genuine concern for her well-being. She assured him that she would be fine, and he nodded and quietly took a seat next to her. After a few minutes in silence, my friend realized that the stranger was sitting there for her, waiting for her to speak if she so desired, or to just sit in silence and know that she was not alone. My friend turned to the compassionate stranger and they began to talk. She shared with him all that had been upsetting her, as he listened patiently and without judgment.

They became good friends that night. Later, as he walked her back to the dorm, she thanked him and told him that he had answered her prayers. She had asked God for someone to help her through this, and that was exactly what she received. He smiled at her, and told her that he honestly didn't know why he had gone to the Grotto that night. He had been sitting in his room and something just told him that he needed to be there.

Stories like this one are reminders that Notre Dame is a special place, for reasons that have nothing to do with football games, or Tuesday nights at Bridget's, or even education. This campus is made special by people like the kind stranger at the Grotto, who did not hesitate to reach out to someone who was hurting and in need.

Who says that angels don't walk the earth?

The Angel Light beamed upon Jaclyn's friend by her compassionate stranger is just more proof that we all have a special gift that is ours alone to give. That same otherworldly feeling came over me in viewing this one-of-a-kind photograph of sunshine filtering through the trees at St. Mary's Lake near the Grotto. Angel Light came to mind the moment I saw it.

Your gift . . .
Is your own unique quality shared
To make another's life sunny.
Given away, it becomes priceless
Because it can't be bought with money.

DVC

I read Lasserre's second book *Miracles at Lourdes* after my journal of research was completed. I don't recall now what prompted this urge to read everything I could find in the library stacks about Lasserre and his writings, except that I was profoundly affected by his *Our Lady of Lourdes* book and reading it had inspired me to leave no stone unturned in the final completion of my research. I would not have felt my mission had been accomplished if I had left anything written about Lourdes, or by him, unread. And I had already learned the Hesburgh Library was unique in the number of interesting old books hidden away on its shelves. When I picked up his second book and reached his "Dear Reader" letter, I knew why this 1884 book had found its way into my hands and why I was meant to read it.

I began to apply his "Dear Reader" beliefs to the synchronicity and serendipity experiences I encountered throughout my research and the ongoing evolution of its outcome. From the initial search, to the present time, the significance of the ripple affect of these curious coincidences and extraordinary connections seem to be unending.

Early in my research I became known as "The Grotto Lady" by those strangers I contacted on campus who remembered my questions but couldn't remember my name. And it wasn't long before I found myself sharing my own synergy experiences every now and then with campus friends I had met in my comings and goings on campus. Invariably, I would receive one of their experiences with the "unexpected" in response. Often they would be associated with the Grotto and thereby became the basis of the oral Grotto experiences I first began collecting. Now and then, even those friends at the archives and the library I've encountered in my twice weekly visits to the campus would affectionately preface their own excited happy happenstance encounters with "I've got a Dorothy for you" before enthusiastically sharing them.

So I am well aware that my good fortune in piecing together this Grotto puzzle is not a unique experience, and that the wonder of these feelings of delight at the unexpected are so personal that often they are not commonly shared in a fast paced work-a-day world. For this reason, I feel it is important for me to share some of what I have experienced in following these creative impulses and inner promptings that have guided my search for answers.

I am hopeful that a few of my readers will follow this trail of memories to its conclusion and reach Lasserre's "message in a bottle" in this "Author's Personal Epilogue." Then I too will have the opportunity to pass on some of my own experiences with those unexpected "sudden inspirations" and "happy thoughts" that have occurred so often in my own research. And in this way, more illustrations of the truism of his words will be added to those so long hidden away on a library shelf.

———————

Over the years since I first read Laserre's "Dear Reader" letter, many more extraordinary "links in a chain of secondary causes" have occurred which can only be described as little miracles of the Grotto since this book version of my research would not be out in the world without them.

My first example of "History placing the right person, in the right place, at the right time." is the story behind the origin of the title of my manuscript, *A Cave of Candles: The Story Behind Notre Dame's Grotto.*

The reading room in the University of Notre Dame Archives is a quiet place for serious study. A nod, smile or hello are usually the only conversational exchanges between fellow researchers. One day I was leaving near closing time after a full day of research. I had just stepped into the library concourse on my way to the parking lot when I felt a soft tap on my shoulder. It was a researcher I had smiled at in the reading room.

He explained that he was a visiting professor from Illinois. It was his first visit to Notre Dame and he had about an hour before leaving for the airport to catch his plane. He wondered if I could tell him if there was a special place on campus he could see in that much time. "Well my favorite place on campus is the Grotto, and it's close by," I said. To which he replied, "What's a Grotto?" I don't know where it came from but without any conscious thought, I surprised even myself when I replied, "It's a cave of candles."

He thanked me for the suggestion, we exchanged brief pleasantries, and he left with a smile on his face. I left with a pleased smile too. My research on the Grotto was already in progress but I had not yet chosen a title for it. Instinctively, I knew it had to be *A Cave of Candles: The Story Behind Notre Dame's Grotto!* What better way to describe it. Monitors at the library have since told me they are often asked, "Where's the cave of candles?"

I never saw the professor again, nor do I know his name, but if he is out there somewhere and remembers this incident, I would be pleased to hear from him so I can thank him for the inspiration of our brief encounter.

An interesting parallel to the above story happened almost ten years later. My new Legends and Lore stories were ready to go online on Easter Sunday, 2003. It seemed the perfect time to create a new main web page and a new name for the website, one that would incorporate all my research stories in one place. The next morning the complete title came to me in the same effortless way and I knew instinctively that it was also the perfect title: *The Spirit of Notre Dame: Its History, Legends and Lore.*

Later, when I began referring to it in routine emails to the campus, I simplified it by using the acronym SOND. Time passed and one day Something told me to see if it might be a word. When I found this meaning in Dictionary.com, I felt blessed: *\Sond\, Sonde \Sonde\, n. [AS. sand. See Send, v. t.] That which is sent; a message or messenger; hence, also, a visitation of providence.*

To me it was an affirmation that The Spirit of Notre Dame, Our Lady is everywhere on her picturesque campus, but her presence is felt most strongly at her Lourdes Grotto. "Mary's Lights" are always there sending a message in candle-glow reaffirming the power of prayer and the foreseeing care and guidance of Providence.

Many of my fondest memories are of people I've met, by chance, on campus—strangers who became my providential friends. The photograph that illustrates this "Author's Personal Epilogue" is another example.

A reporter from a local newspaper heard about my research on the Indian legend associated with the legendary sycamore on the Grotto lawn and asked to interview me. It was a new experience for me. I really didn't want to do it, but I felt the tree deserved to be better known on campus, so I agreed.

When she arrived, she wanted to take a picture of me in front of the tree. When I declined she explained that she couldn't tell the story without some human interest. Reluctantly, I agreed: "Okay, then I'll do it for the tree." That photograph has now become one of my fondest memories of the tree and me and the many weeks I spent researching the landmark sycamore, the oldest tree on campus.

This personal epilogue would not be complete without this last and most extraordinary illustration of the premise of history having a way of placing the right person in the right place at the right moment in time. If this event had not happened this book would not have become a reality.

Throughout my fifteen years of research on the Grotto, Fr. Hesburgh's occasional letters have become an ongoing source of encouragement. When my *The Spirit of Notre Dame* website went online on Easter Sunday, 2003 he wrote: "I know Our Lady will find her own way of thanking you." When I received his letter, one thought came to mind, "She already has, in more ways than I will ever be able to count." However, I had no idea of the surprises yet to come.

In January, 2005, I received an email from a Notre Dame alumnus asking if the website was in book form. It's a question I've been asked many times since my research went online. When I told him it wasn't, he asked me if I would give him permission to make coil-bound copies of my third person website manuscript for his two siblings and a friend who did not have computers. I told him he was welcome to as long as it was for personal use. He thanked me and told me he would also send a copy to me.

He continued to keep in touch and I soon learned he was a retired printer who lives in Phoenix, Arizona. His son now runs his business and his office girl was going to work on his project between her other jobs. Almost a year went by, and I thought perhaps he didn't realize what a job it would be to page, resize the images and print an Internet document loaded with photographs. I remember thinking, at the time, "If that copy ever arrives on my doorstep, it will be a little miracle of the Grotto for sure."

December 2005, rolled around and I got another email titled, "Book Availability" with a one line message. "Where do I purchase this book, Dorothy." To my surprise, it was from Kathy McGowan, the Trade Book Manager at the Notre Dame Bookstore. Two weeks later a surprise package arrived on my doorstep. In it, not one copy but five beautiful coil-bound color photocopies of my manuscript. I was misty-eyed paging through its illustrated pages. It was such a pleasure to be re-reading my research in the comfort of my Lazy Boy.

Everyone I showed them to wanted copies for themselves. Unfortunately, reproducing color photocopies in any volume was cost prohibitive. However, a little niggling notion surfaced. Was this a sign that I really should make the attempt to publish a printed book of the website? It seemed too overwhelming a task to tackle so I decided, once again, to ask Fr. Hesburgh for his advice and let him know his prediction had come true. Our Lady had found her own way of thanking me through the generosity of my Phoenix email friend, Dan Rich.

I related the above story and my notion to publish my manuscript to Fr. Hesburgh and added that I just didn't feel comfortable telling Our Lady's Notre Dame Story without the permission and approval of the University. He was slowly paging through the color copy, when he looked up and said, "You don't need permission. Do it! Do it!"

Then he turned around in his chair, picked up his Dictaphone microphone and began to dictate a letter while I sat there in disbelief. When he finished, he said, "When you receive this letter, I want you to show it to anyone you need help from and tell them I sent you." He then added, "And you may use it as a preface in your book." I had been waiting for some kind of "go ahead" green light to muster the courage to go out on a limb and try it and it came during my visit with Father Ted on March 7, 2006.

All his advice over the years since my first meeting with him in the early 90s came flooding back. His continued encouragement in occasional letters became an ongoing source of inspiration. "Keep up your good work on the Grotto. It's a story yet to be told." "You'll never know if you don't try." "The help will be there when you need it." And lastly, "Our Lady will find her own way of thanking you." Truer words were never spoken. From that moment on, the pace has been hectic but the green lights along the way have kept me going.

My heartfelt appreciation goes out to Dan Rich for the generous gift of his time, talent and experience. And to my dear friend Ann Korb, a Saint Mary's and Notre Dame alumna who, once again, generously offered to proofread it for me. I don't know what I would have done without her. And to my son, Greg, who taught me everything I know about computers with these comforting words of advice: "Just remember, when things go wrong, don't panic. Whatever you can get yourself into, I can get you out of." He's been my lifeline ever since. I would never have gotten past square one without his ongoing good-natured encouragement.

Dan's beautiful coil-bound color photocopies have been a Godsend. I have carried one with me everywhere I go, to book publishers, book printers and bookstores. The perfect timing of their arrival on my doorstep will always make him the right person, in the right place, at just the right time in my life.

Dan's family is truly a Notre Dame family. His father was an alumnus and head of the Chemical Engineering Department at Notre Dame. His brother is a Notre Dame alumnus and his sister attended Saint Mary's. When she received her copy, she made this comment to me in an email: "As I know Dan has told you, we grew up on the University, with daddy teaching there all our growing-up years. I have many times visited the Grotto and never had a clue as to its history. This is really a treat …. reading your book. Thank you for making it possible."

The thoughts of contemporary writer, M. Scott Peck, M.D., author of *The Road Less Traveled and Beyond*, whose book I also read by chance, parallel those expressed by Lasserre, in his "Dear Letter," 122 years ago:

"I am a spiritual person. I know of God not only because of faith, but also on the basis of evidence, namely my experiences of grace. . . . One of the most useful ways to establish something scientifically is to apply what are called the statistics of improbability. That means that the lower the mathematically calculated, probability, the greater the improbability, and the safer we feel concluding that an event was not the result of chance alone. Thus, we may conclude that something occurred because of a significant reason, even if it may or may not be

explainable. That is why I have commonly spoken about grace in terms of 'a pattern of highly improbable events with a beneficial outcome.' It is also why I have concluded that in such patterns we can see the finger- prints—if not the actual hand—of God."

So true, one may attribute these happy happenstances to the intercession of Our Lady—God answering our prayers—or simply to what one thinks of as the light of understanding inherent in that inner voice guiding us along life's way. It matters not how they are manifested in our lives, the final results, if they lighten our load and enlighten our way, are little everyday miracles that make life worth living—for the sweet surprises of the unexpected that await our faith in following them.

———————

Now that I am nearing the end of my archival adventure, I find myself wondering anew, if the real story I've been writing in telling the story behind Our Lady's Notre Dame Story is really those stories within that story. The wonder of chance encounters and answered prayers that came when they were least expected, have kept me on that trail of memories until there were no more clues to follow.

It was this sentence in an email response from a reader in New York City, sent some time ago, that first prompted these wonderings: "Is your story the history of the Grotto or the magic ... hidden hands ... that show up when something is a real labor of love?"

I'm still pondering that one single sentence. At first "magic" didn't seem the right word to describe those "otherworldly" experiences I have encountered throughout my research. Then I found this dictionary definition of magic: "A mysterious quality of enchantment" which defined, exactly, the delight and heightened awareness I have experienced whenever "help from above" has been there when I needed it the most. So too, was the def- inition of a labor of love: "any work done with eager willingness, either from fondness for the work itself or from affection for the person for whom it is done." All of which, fits so well, those loving creative impulses that have a way of setting wonder-working moments in motion.

My email friend's name is Joyce, someone I have never met in person, but I think of her as Joy because she has brought joy to my life and "Joy is a sign of God's Presence." She was there when I needed someone just like her. Her joy-filled electronic presence and the warmth and spontaneity of her "gift of words" have continued to inspirit the completion of this published book version of Our Lady's Notre Dame Story. I will now rest in peace knowing I have left these timeless "Messages in a Bottle" for others to discover—as I discovered them— when I am no longer on the scene. Deo volente.

BE NOT FORGETFUL TO ENTERTAIN STRANGERS, FOR THEREBY SOME HAVE ENTERTAINED ANGELS UNAWARES. — HEBREWS 13:2

Almost anything in the world can be bought for money – except the warm impulses of the human heart. They have to be given. And they are priceless in their power to purchase happiness for two people, the recipient and the giver. – Ralph Waldo Emerson

Always Have a Dream

In life there is nothing more sweet
Then when a dream and you meet
Then all of life . . .
Becomes a delicious treat.

The wonder of nature's sights and sounds
Will on this spacious earth abound,
When in this world you've finally found,
A dream to build your life around.

DVC

Sweet Afterglow

Just as bewitching and charming
As the sunlit sparkle,
Of a rippling, glittering wayside brook
Is the sweet afterglow
Of a warm and welcoming, I-Like-You look.

DVC

In Memory of:
Rev. John J. Cavanaugh, C.S.C.
Former President, University of the Notre Dame

His warm responsiveness reawakened in me my poetic creative expression after a six year silence. You could not be in his company without experiencing the afterglow of his unique personality. Fr. Ted said his father, upon meeting him for the first time, said he had never met another man like him.

WITH A WINK AND A SMILE

Squire Rushnell wrote a little book called *When God Winks: How the Power of Coincidence Guides Your Life.* A priest friend of mine always said: "Coincidences are God's way of remaining anonymous: That's the way He captivates our imagination and wonder." To me, they will always be like a tap on the shoulder and a whisper in the ear, "I'm here . . . ."

Many of the photographs in this manuscript were generously shared by Robert F. Ringel. We met by chance when we both arrived on campus in 1991. Bob had a question about the statue in the Grotto and Rev. Anthony Lauck, C.S.C. a sculptor on campus, introduced us. Whenever we chanced to meet on campus, I shared my research discoveries with him and he shared his photographs with me. Photographs of the legendary sycamore and the sanctuary lamp in the Basilica were some of the first photographs he passed on to me when I told him the story behind them. This illustrated history of Notre Dame and Saint Mary's would not have been possible without them.

On one visit to the campus, I was researching the life of the baker from Holland who baked those famous Notre Dame buns. I had just put a little snippet of information about him in my Grotto manuscript when our paths crossed on campus and Bob pulled out of his pocket some of his latest fortuitous photographs of the wildlife he had taken on campus to show me.

One was a photograph of a squirrel eating a nut on the top of a community cemetery tombstone. This one was unique for two reasons: Bob had no way of knowing what I had been researching: The name on the tombstone was Bro. Willibrord, C.S.C. the baker of the famous Notre Dame buns. It dovetailed with my research and illustrated my story about him perfectly.

The significance was not lost on either of us, and from that time on Bob always showed me the little GOD WINKS he encountered in photographing the wildlife on campus. Below are several he shared that left us both with a wink and a smile. Hope they do the same for my readers.

Bob is retired now. He and his family have returned to his hometown in Mount Pleasant, Michigan, but many of the pictures he has taken in his 15 years of photographing the campus have been preserved in albums in the University of Notre Dame Archives; on their online Notre Dame Photo Gallery; and on my *The Spirit of Notre Dame* website. Here are just a few of his very special "God Wink" photographs:

The Dove represents the Living God sent down to be with us.

Squirrel on a Tombstone

Baby Robin on a Cozy Perch

Raccoon's Lookout

The First Sign of Spring

A Robin's Home

Dear Reader:

If you have a fond remembrance of the Notre Dame Grotto, or have had someone share theirs with you, I would appreciate hearing about it. Just jot it down in a letter, in your own words, be it serious, humorous, uplifting or inspiring and it will be added to the others in the Grotto Stories Collection which is being preserved in the University of Notre Dame Archives for future generations of Notre Dame fans, friends and alumni to enjoy.

Please include your name, address, telephone number, and email address with your Notre Dame Grotto Remembrance, if you wish, or none, if you'd prefer to remain anonymous.

As a new millennium dawns over St. Mary's Lake on the campus of Notre Dame, I leave you with Father Jan's favorite blessing:

God Love You and Bless You Always . . . Now and Forever.

Every sunrise makes the world new again.

Direct to:
Dorothy Corson
Dorothy.Corson@comcast.net

Exact Text of Tom Dooley's Memorable Grotto Letter

Hong Kong, December 2, 1960

Dear Father Hesburgh,

They've got me down. Flat on my back . . . . . with plaster, sand bags and hot water bottles. It took the last three instruments to do it however. I've contrived a way of pumping the bed up a bit so that, with a long reach, I can get to my typewriter. . . . my mind. . . .my brain. . . . my fingers.

Two things prompt this note to you sir. The first is that whenever my cancer acts up. . . . and it is certainly "acting up" now, I turn inward a bit. Less do I think of my hospitals around the world, or of 94 doctors, fund raising and the like. More do I think of one divine Doctor, and my own personal fund of grace. Is it enough?

It has become pretty definite that the cancer has spread to the lumbar vertebrae, accounting for all the back problems over the last two months. I have monstrous phantoms. . . as all men do. But I try to exorcise them with all the fury of the middle ages. And inside and outside the wind blows.

But when the time comes, like now, then the storm around me does not matter. The winds within me do not matter. Nothing human or earthly can touch me. A wilder storm of peace gathers in my heart. What seems unpossessable I can possess. What seems unfathomable, I fathom. What is unutterable, I utter. Because I can pray. I can communicate. How do people endure anything on earth if they cannot have God?

I realize the external symbols that surround one when he prays are not important. The stark wooden cross on an altar of boxes in Haiphong with a tortured priest . . . the magnificence of the Sacred Heart Bernini a tar. . . . . they are essentially the same. Both are symbols. It is the Something else there that counts.

But just now. . . and just so many times, how I long for the Grotto. Away from the Grotto Dooley just prays. But at the Grotto, especially now when there must be snow everywhere and the lake is ice glass and that triangular fountain on the left is frozen solid and all the priests are bundled in their too-large too-long old black coats and the students wear snow boots. . . . if I could go to the Grotto now then I think I could sing inside. I could be full of faith and poetry and loveliness and know more beauty, tenderness and compassion. This is soggy sentimentalism I know, (old prayers from a hospital bed are just as pleasing to God as more youthful prayers from a Grotto on the lid of night.

But like telling a mother in labor, "It's okay, millions have endured the labor pains and survived happy. . . you will too." It's consoleing [sic] . . . but doesn't lessen the pain. Accordingly, knowing prayers from here are just as good as from the Grotto doesn't lessen my gnawing, yearning passion to be there.

I don't mean to ramble. Yes, I do.

The second reason I write to you just now is that I have in front of me the Notre Dame Alumnus of September 1960. And herein is a story. This is a Chinese hospital run by a Chinese division of the Sisters of Charity. (I think) Though my doctors are British the hospital is as Chinese as Shark's Fin Soup. Every orderly, corpsman, nurse and nun know of my work in Asia, and each has taken it upon themselves to personally "give" to the man they feel has given to their Asia. As a consequence I'm a bit smothered in tender, loving care.

With a triumphant smile this morning one of the nuns brought me some American magazines (which are limp with age and which I must hold horizontal above my head to read. . . . . .) An old National Geographic, two older times, and that unfortunate edition Life . . . and with these, a copy of the Notre Dame Alumnus. How did it ever get here?

So Father Hesburgh, Notre Dame is twice on my mind . . . and always in my heart. That Grotto is the rock to which my life is anchored. Do the students ever appreciate what they have, while they have it? I know I never did. Spent most of my time being angry at the clergy at school . . . 10 PM bed check, absurd for a 19 year old veteran, etc. etc. etc.

Won't take any more of your time, did just want to communicate for a moment, and again offer my thanks to my beloved Notre Dame. Though I lack a certain buoyancy in my bones just now, I lack none in my spirit. I must return to the states very soon, and I hope to sneak into that Grotto. . . . before the snow has melted.

My best wishes to the students, regards to the faculty, and respects to you.

Notre Dame Chronological Chart

1685 — St. Joseph Mission founded. First Catholic Mission established in northern Indiana by the early Jesuit missionaries. Abandoned in 1759, when the English defeated the French.

1800 — Legendary Sycamore takes root sometime between 1775 and 1825.

1821 — Ottawa, Chippewa and Potawatomi Indians sign Treaty of Chicago in 1821 ceding their rights to the Northeast quarter of land in St. Joseph County including South Bend, Mishawaka, Notre Dame and St. Mary's.

1830 — St. Joseph Mission reorganized by Rev. Theodore Badin, first priest ordained in the United States.

1831 — State of Indiana allocates a strip of land, 100 feet wide, plus one section (1 mile square) of good land contiguous to it for each mile of the same for a road. Sections, or the procceds thereof to be applied to the road. The road was opened at the end of 1832. The first public land sales were made late that same year.

1832 — Father Badin buys 524 acres in St. Joseph County from the Commissioner of Roads and establishes the first orphan home and school for Indians in Indiana. The first church at Notre Dame, a log chapel known as the 'Indian Chapel,' was erected on this land by Badin.

1833 — The "Asylum" was not approved until February 2, 1833, because a cabin was not built at Notre Dame. Two Sisters went to Pokagon Village for the winter of 1833-34. When a cabin and farmhouse were built the Sisters came to Notre Dame for the short-lived orphanage and school. It did not function for more than a year.

1835 — Father Badin leaves, conveys title to land, now known as Notre Dame, to Bishop Brute. Land reverts to mission, Deseille and Petit replace Badin.

1838 — Most of local Potawatomi Indians removed by the military in 1838. Father Petit accompanies them on their forced march to Kansas. Dies on his way back.

1842 — Father Edward Sorin and six Brothers arrive. As many as two hundred Indians still in the area. Sorin changes the name of the mission, formerly known as Ste Marie des Lacs, to Notre Dame du Lac, his first act of devotion to Our Lady on the site of the future University.

1843 — Corner-stone of main college building (now called the Old College) is laid. Many Indians assist in erecting the edifice.

1844 — First chapel on St. Mary's Island, in St. Mary's Lake, also dedicated to Our Lady of the Lake. Visitors paddle to the chapel in canoes from the shore of the lake. A charter for the college was granted to the University by the Indiana legislature on January 15, 1844.

1848 — Construction begins on first church at Notre Dame to be named Sacred Heart of Jesus.

1854 — Pope Pius IX, proclaims dogma of the Immaculate Conception. Five months later the Academy of St. Mary of the Immaculate Conception, which later became known as St. Mary's, is established.

1857 — Father Moreau, founder of the Holy Cross order, arrives from France. Visits St. Mary's. Dedicates St. Angela's Island and blesses its altar and statue of Mary. In later years it is referred to as the shrine of Our Lady of Lourdes on the island.

1858 — Bernadette, a French peasant girl, sees her first apparition on February 11 at the Lourdes Grotto.

1859 — Chapel of Loretto, facsimile of the original "House of the Incarnation," completed at St. Mary's. It is still there today.

1861 — Replica of Portiuncula Chapel of Our Lady of the Angels at Assisi erected on the "island" at Notre Dame. Throngs of pilgrims visit it to gain plenary indulgences. First replica of a shrine placed at University by Sorin to encourage pilgrimages.

1863 — General Sherman's children attend Notre Dame and St. Mary's during the war years. Mrs. Sherman lives in South Bend while her children are in school.

1865 — *Ave Maria*, a national magazine to promote devotion to Our Lady, is launched by Father Sorin in collaboration with the Sisters of the Holy Cross

1866 — Napoleon, Emperor of France, gives gifts of gold to Notre Dame to commemorate the completion of the first main building. Among them, a valuable crown, gift of Empress Eugenie.

1867 — Sometime around 1866 or 1867, Mother Angela receives permission from Father Sorin and the Bishop to establish the seat of the Association of Our Lady of Sacred Heart at St. Mary's and collect funds for their proposed church to be named Our Lady of the Sacred Heart.

1869 — A decision is made to build a new church at Notre Dame. Father Sorin gives the task to Father Alexis Granger. Father Granger proposes "seat" of the Association be transferred from St. Mary's to Notre Dame and their new church be named Our Lady of Sacred Heart suggesting Notre Dame would be better able to handle the needs of large pilgrimages to Our Lady. Mother Angela, upon Father Sorin's request complies, turns over name and funds to Father Granger and puts off the building St. Mary's church upon the assurance of Father Sorin's help in building it later. Through the Association of Our Lady of Sacred Heart ,which was publicized in the *Ave Maria* magazine, funds to build the church were very effectively solicited.

1871-1872 — St. Mary's builds an addition later named Lourdes Hall. A temporary chapel is built on the top floor.

1872 — Lourdes water with its history of healing is introduced to the United States and cures are publicized in the *Ave Maria*. From the time the first water arrives at Notre Dame until the new church is finished, contributions from grateful users of Lourdes water are used to finance Notre Dame's Our Lady of Sacred Heart Church.

1873 — Father Sorin and Mother Angela make separate pilgrimages to Lourdes. Mother Angela ships to St. Mary's authentic replicas of Our Lady and Bernadette statues at Lourdes. Father Sorin also sends a Lourdes statue of Our Lady to the Minims for their study hall at Notre Dame.

1874 — Mother Angela builds a replica of the Lourdes Grotto in the new addition at St. Mary's, installs the Our Lady and Bernadette statues, and the new addition becomes Lourdes Hall. Sorin presides over many special occasions there.

About this same time, Father Lemonnier, Sorin's nephew and then President of Notre Dame, dies. Sorin honors his deathbed wish by promising to make the chapel in the north end of the sanctuary, the Chapel of Our Lady of Lourdes. Donations arrive continuously for this purpose; however, the chapels are not completed for another 12 years.

1875 — Replica of the beautiful sanctuary lamp at Lourdes is placed in the Sacred Heart Church.

The steamer, L'Amerique bound for France, with Father Sorin and Eliza Starr, St. Mary's art teacher, on board, breaks its shaft and is stranded in mid ocean. Daring rescue is accomplished.

1878 — Sorin dedicates the first Lourdes Grotto (described as a tower-like niche) at Notre Dame. Visitors to the campus add it to their pilgrimages.

1879 — Notre Dame's second main building is destroyed by fire. Debris is dumped behind the presbytery, the future site of the present Grotto.

St. Mary's indoor Lourdes Grotto, said to be the closest replica in U.S., is removed. Only the Lourdes statues remain in a small alcove on the same floor.

1883 — Dome is completed. A month later the statue of Our Lady is hoisted to the top.

1884 — Crown and crescent are added to Our Lady's statue and illuminated.

1886 — Statue and Dome are gilded in gold. Less than a month later two valuable crowns are stolen from the Sacred Heart Church. Empress Eugenie's crown is hidden away for safekeeping.

1888 — Gregori's Grotto painting of the Apparition of Our Lady of Lourdes, behind the Lourdes altar in the Sacred Heart Church, is completed.

1889 — The Our Lady Chapel, which was to have been Our Lady of Lourdes Chapel, a memorial to Lemonnier, is complete with the arrival of its Madonna statue.

1893 — Father Edward Sorin dies. Upon his death, his devotion to the Our Lady of Lourdes Grotto is passed on to Father William Corby former Notre Dame president.

1896 — Father Corby decides to build a more authentic replica of the grotto at Lourdes after a favor granted at Lourdes, France. He proposes his idea to Father Thomas Carroll, a former Holy Cross Priest, known for his generous gifts to worthy causes. Father Carroll pays all of it.

1898 — The Notre Dame Grotto becomes so popular that the Chapel of Portiuncula, which is badly in need of repair, is torn down and other shrines are removed.

1917 — "The Legend of the Sycamore" is passed on to history professor William E. Farrell by Brother Frederick Kraling, who urges him to record it for future generations.

1918 — Joyce Kilmer, author of "Trees," is killed in the first World War. His friendship with Poet Laureate Notre Dame President Charles O'Donnell, his love of Our Lady, the Grotto, and the trees on campus, link his memory and his poem to the Notre Dame Grotto.

1937 — Fred Snite, a Notre Dame graduate, returns to the United States in an iron lung, a victim of infantile paralysis in China. His appearance in his iron lung, via a special trailer, at all home football games and his devotion to Our Lady of Lourdes also ties his memory to the Notre Dame Grotto.

1939 — The first small stone relic from Lourdes, brought back from France by Father DeGroote, is cemented in the Grotto.

1940 — Eugene O'Neill's stage play, *Long Day's Journey Into Night* unearths evidence of St. Mary's long forgotten St. Angela's Island and its Our Lady of Lourdes shrine.

1947 — Author's autographed movie script of *The Song Of Bernadette*, written by acclaimed Hollywood writer and director, George Seaton, is presented to Saint Mary's College.

1958 — Notre Dame commemorates the 100th Centennial of the Lourdes Grotto in France in a year long celebration. A second larger black stone, also a relic from Lourdes, is brought from France by Father Maguire and cemented in the Notre Dame Grotto

1961 — Notre Dame graduate, Dr. Tom Dooley, humanitarian, and "jungle doctor of the Laos," dies January 18, 1961, at age of 34. Upon his death, a replica of his last letter to Father Hesburgh, praising the Grotto, is placed at the kneeling rail. Its presence inspires renewed devotion to Our Lady.

1962 — St. Stan's Grotto, a replica of the one at Notre Dame, built at St. Stanislaus Church in South Bend, is erected by Father Jankowski for his parish of 22 years.

1985 — Notre Dame Grotto is badly damaged by a fire caused by the burning of too many candles during a football game.

1993 — Movie, *Rudy*, depicting the Grotto is premiered in South Bend. It's the first movie about Notre Dame to be premiered in South Bend since *Knute Rockne All American*.

1996 — Notre Dame Grotto celebrates its 100th Anniversary and earns Father Hesburgh's own personal accolade: "I've been to shrines dedicated to Our Lady all over the world. Mary may visit them but she lives here."

Compiled for "A Cave of Candles: The Story Behind Notre Dame's Grotto" by Dorothy Corson

Photo Credits

Many of these photographs were taken by contemporary photographers who graciously gave us permission to use them to illustrate this story. If you wish to use any of these photographs, please contact the photographer.

Front Cover
- A Cave of Candles — © Ed Ballotts / Courtesy *South Bend Tribune*

Back Cover
- Summer Grotto — by L. K. Dunn, Courtesy Notre Dame Photography

Preface
- Rev. Theodore M. Hesburgh, President Emeritus, University of Notre Dame

Title Page
- Homecoming – © by Robert F. Ringel, Courtesy Dr. Kevin A. Danahey, OD

Note to the Reader
- Pink Tulips Grotto Scene — © David C. Berta
- Purple Flowers — Courtesy Dorothy Corson

Contents
- Summer Grotto — by L. K. Dunn, Courtesy Notre Dame Photography

Trail
- Main Building in the Snow — © Robert F. Ringel
- Oldest 1896 Grotto in Sepia — Courtesy University of Notre Dame Archives
- Wooded Dell — © Bro. Martinus Bombardier C.S.C., Midwest Province
- McDonald Studio Sketch — Courtesy Congregation of Holy Cross Indiana Province Archives Center
- Oldest Photograph of 1896 Grotto Dedication (Minims) — Courtesy *South Bend Tribune*, copy from University of Notre Dame Archives

Chapter 1
-Kids at the Grotto — 1913
- Our Lady on the Dome in the Fall — © Robert F. Ringel
- Winter Log Chapel by the Lake — © Robert F. Ringel
- St. Mary's Lake in the Wintertime — © Robert F. Ringel
- St. Mary's Island in St. Mary's Lake (Columba Hall) — © Robert F. Ringel
- Community Cemetery in the Summertime — © Robert F. Ringel
- Replica of St.Severa, martyred as a young girl — © Robert F. Ringel
- Old College, oldest building on campus — © Robert F. Ringel
- Bernadette the Shepherdess — Watercolor by Hoffbauer from *Lourdes: Yesterday, To-day and To-morrow* by Daniel Barbé
- Engraving of Lourdes Church — *A Month at Lourdes* by Hugh Caraher
- Portiuncula Chapel — Courtesy University of Notre Dame Archives
- The Pieta by Ivan Mestrovic — © Robert F. Ringel
- *Ave Maria* 1866, Frontispiece and Title Page — Courtesy University of Notre Dame Archives
- First Church & 1866 Main Building — Courtesy University of Notre Dame Archives
- Present Main Building — © Robert F. Ringel

Chapter 2
- Basilica of the Sacred Heart, cornerstone laid 1871 — © Robert F. Ringel
- Interior of Sacred Heart Basilica — © Robert F. Ringel
- Rosary Church and Grotto — *Les Grandes Guerisons DeLourdes* by D. Boõssarie
- Statues in Lourdes Hall at St. Mary's — by Dorothy V. Corson
- Close-up of Blessed Virgin statue in Lourdes Hall — by Dorothy V. Corson
- Rev. Auguste Lemonnier, C.S.C. — Courtesy University of Notre Dame Archives
- Lady Chapel Ceiling — © Robert F.Ringel
- Sanctuary Lamp (replica of one at Lourdes) — © Robert F. Ringel
- Lourdes Stained Glass Window — © Robert F. Ringel
- Chapel of Loretto — Courtesy Saint Mary's College Archives
- Star of pure silver above Statue of Blessed Virgin in Chapel of Loretto
- Sorin's Rescue at Sea — Courtesy University of Notre Dame Archives
- Notre Dame as Seen from St. Mary's Lake — © Robert F. Ringel

Chapter 3
- Sorin's 1878 Lourdes Grotto — Courtesy University of Notre Dame Archives
- Sorin's Grotto before Chapels — Courtesy University of Notre Dame Archvies
- The Riverbank in the Glen at St. Mary's in 1905 — *YesterYear in South Bend*
- Painting of Mother Angela, C.S.C. — Courtesy Saint Mary's College Archives
- Sorin in cape as young man — Courtesy University of Notre Dame Archives
- Post Office Hitching Rings — © Robert F. Ringel
- Close-up of Hitching Rings — © Robert F. Ringel
- Sorin Statue, Main Building — © Robert F. Ringel

Chapter 4
- Night crown and crescent — *The Dome*, 1915
- Sacred Heart's Clock Tower — © Robert F. Ringel
- 1879 Main Building Fire — Courtesy University of Notre Dame Archives
- Main Building Restoration — © Robert F. Ringel
- Sorin's Spirit and Determination — Courtesy Congregation of Holy Cross, Indiana Province Archives Center
- Snow Dome — © Robert F. Ringel
- Main Building with Snow — © Robert F. Ringel
- Student Waving from Dome — © Robert F. Ringel
- Close-up of Dome exterior and statue — © Robert F. Ringel
- Dome atrium and Gregori painting — © Robert F. Ringel
- Close-up of inner Dome and painting — © Robert F. Ringel
- Close-up of Our Lady Statue — © Bill Mowle
- Crescent Moon and Serpent — © Robert F. Ringel

Chapter 5
- The Missing Empress Eugenie Crown — *Empress Eugenie and her Circle* by Antonine Barthez
- B. V. Crown / *A Spire of Faith* © Steve Moriarty — Courtesy University of Notre Dame Archives
- Empress Eugenie — From *Recollections of Empress Eugenie* — by Pierre Marie Augustin Silon
- Basilica Interior and Lady Chapel — © Robert F. Ringel

- Lourdes Painting in Basilica in color — © Robert F. Ringel
- Madonna in the Lady Chapel — © Robert Ringel
- Napoleon Crucifix / *Spire of Faith* © Steve Moriarty — Courtesy Notre Dame Alumni Association
- Barrier at Lourdes — Watercolor by Hoffbauer from *Lourdes: Yesterday, To-day and To- morrow* by Daniel Barbé
- Celebration at Lourdes — — Watercolor by Hoffbauer from Lourdes
- Bernadette / *St. Bernadette* — by Leonard Von Matt, Courtesy Regnery Publishing
- Bernadette Casket / *St. Bernadette* — by Leonard Von Matt, Courtesy Regnery Publishing
- Convent Chapel — © Robert F. Ringel
- Carroll Hall across St. Mary's Lake — © Robert F. Ringel
- Mother Mary of the Ascension — from *Pioneers and Builders Chronicles of the Sisters of the Holy Cross, 1841-1941*— Courtesy Sisters of the Holy Cross

Chapter 6
- 1916 Grotto Painting — by Joseph P. Flynn, *The Dome*, 1916
- Sorin and statue on table — Courtesy University of Notre Dame Archives
- Sorin Stained Glass Window — © Robert F. Ringel
- Close-up Stained Glass Window — © Robert F. Ringel
- Rev. Wm. Corby, C.S.C.— Originator of the Grotto — Courtesy University of Notre Dame Archives
- Notre Dame's Blue and Gold colors — © Robert F. Ringel
- Rev. Thomas Carroll C.S.C.— Grotto donor — University of Notre Dame Archives
- Huge Bell in Church — © Steve Moriarty, Courtesy UNDA
- Mary Kintz — by Barbara Allison / Courtesy *South Bend Tribune*

Chapter 7
- Talley House Sketch from 1875 Atlas — Courtesy Hesburgh Library Rare Books & Special Collections
- White marble with words "thday Gift" on it — (c) by Robert F. Ringel
- Merritt Metras — Courtesy of Sr. Helen Therese, C.S.C.
- Tally / O'Connor House on Juniper Road — by Dorothy V. Corson
- Haney House / The Pie House — *The Dome*, 1911
- Conyer's Cottage — By Dorothy V. Corson
- Stained Glass / *Spire of Faith* © Steve Moriarty — Courtesy Notre Dame Alumni Association

Chapter 8
- Builders of Grotto — Courtesy University of Notre Dame Archives
- Holy Cross Cemetery — © Robert F. Ringel
- Sullivan Cottage — by Dorothy V. Corson
- 1916 Lake Painting — by Joseph P. Flynn, *The Dome* 1916
- Swans on St. Mary's Lake — © Robert F. Ringel
- Robert Braunsdorf Family — Courtesy James Braunsdorf
- St. Stanislaus Grotto — © Michael P. Kelly
- Copshaholm — from *Copshaholm, The Oliver Story* by Joan Romine — Courtesy of the Northern Indiana Center for History
- Ivy covered Grotto — © Bro. Martinus Bombardier, C.S.C. Midwest Province

Chapter 9
- 1896 Grotto Dedication (minims) — Courtesy University of Notre Dame Archives
- Choir boys at the Grotto — Courtesy University of Notre Dame Archives
- Backyard pump at Grotto — Courtesy University of Notre Dame Archives
- 1912 Grotto Postcard — Courtesy Dorothy V. Corson — University of Notre Dame Archives

Chapter 10
- Kilmer as Soldier — From *Joyce Kilmer* by Robert C. Holliday
- Joggers on the lake path — © Richard Stevens
- Autumn trees at St. Mary's Lake — © Robert F. Ringel
- Sketch of Joyce Kilmer — © Carolyn Jagodits
- Photograph of Painting of Mother Madeleva, C.S.C. — by Robert F. Ringel
- Autumn trees on Notre Dame Campus — © Robert F. Ringel
- St. Mary's Lake, the Dome, and Redbuds — © Robert F. Ringel

Chapter 11
- Student Study Break in Tree — © Jim Rider
- Legendary Sycamore in the Winter — © Robert F. Ringel
- Tepees by Sr. Paraclita — Courtesy Sisters of the Holy Cross
- Cedar Grove Cemetery in Fall — © Robert F. Ringel

- Plaque on Stone in Cedar Grove Cemetery — by Dorothy V. Corson
- Bro. Frederick — Courtesy Indiana Province Archives Center
- Summer Sycamore — © Greg A. Corson
- St. Mary's Lake "like a magic mirror" — © Robert F. Ringel
- Summer Log Cabin — © Robert F. Ringel
- Mrs. Coquillard — Courtesy of the Northern Indiana Center for History
- Chief Topinabee — Courtesy of the Northern Indiana Center for History
- Badin Engraving — Courtesy University of Notre Dame Archives
- Badin documents — Courtesy University of Notre Dame Archives
- Log Cabin, Old College and Lake — © Robert F. Ringel
- "Clear water mirror of the lake. . ." — © Robert F. Ringel
- Kids in Tree — Courtesy Patrick Holmes Family

Chapter 12
- Niche in St. Mary's Glen — By Dorothy V. Corson
- St. Angela's Island — Courtesy Saint Mary's College Archives
- St. Angela's Island in the River — *The Dome*, 1915
- Avenue of trees in the glen — by Dorothy V. Corson
- The island today — by Dorothy V. Corson
- Racing Galleys ca 1870s — Courtesy UNDA
- Ducks at Lake Marian, Saint Mary's — © Robert F. Ringel

Chapter 13
- A Little wooded Dell — © Bro. Martinus Bombardier C.S.C., Midwest Province
- Grotto Statue and Fall Leaves — © Robert F. Ringel
- Picture Rev. John O'Hara, C.S.C. — Courtesy University of Notre Dame Archives
- Bernadette's statue at the Grotto — © Robert F. Ringel
- One candle at the Grotto — © Robert F. Ringel
- Fred Snite at Notre Dame Football Game — *Scholastic*, 1946
- Snite Family — Courtesy of Snite Museum, 1949 Photograph Courtesy of South Bend Tribune
- Winter at the Grotto — © Patrick C. Ryan
- View from cave of Grotto — © Robert F. Ringel

Chapter 14
- Bernadette's first apparition at Lourdes — Watercolor by Hoffbauer from *Lourdes: Yesterday, To-day and To-morrow* by Daniel Barbé
- Lourdes before the apparition — *Lourdes*, Watercolor by Hoffbauer
- Lourdes March 28 apparition — *Lourdes*, Watercolor by Hoffbauer
- Lourdes Rosary Church — *Lourdes*, Watercolor by Hoffbauer
- Rosary Church Interior — *Lourdes*, Watercolor by Hoffbauer
- Photograph of Henri Lasserre — *The Wonders of Massabielle at Lourdes* by Rev. S Pruvost
- Young Bernadette — *St Bernadette* Courtesy Regnery Publishing
- Processions at Lourdes —*The Wonders of Massabielle at Lourdes* by Rev. S Pruvost
- George Seaton signature — Courtesy Saint Mary's College Archives
- Young Bernadette — *St Bernadette* Courtesy Regnery Publishing
- Statue of Blessed Virgin at Notre Dame Grotto — © Jennifer Jones
- Lourdes Basilica, Grotto and Gave River — *Lourdes: Les Guerisons* by Prosper Gustave Boissarie

Chapter 15
- Student and black stone — © Luke Woods and Mark Pledger — *The Dome* 1993
- Grotto sketch, Seniors Last Visit — © Kathleen Mapes Turner '95
- Dome Reliquary / *Dome of Learning* — Courtesy Notre Dame Alumni Association
- Black Stone at Grotto — by Joseph Wentland, Courtesy *Our Sunday Visitor*
- Student Praying at Black Stone —*Scholastic*, 1958
- Notre Dame Grotto in autumn — by L. K. Dunn, Courtesy Notre Dame Photography

Chapter 16
- Summer Grotto / Hesburgh Tree — by L. K. Dunn, Courtesy Notre Dame Photography
- Dr. Thomas Dooley — Courtesy University of Notre Dame Archives
- House With Three Flags — © Matt Cashore, Courtesy Col. Richard E. Lochner
- St. Stanislaus Grotto — © Michael P. Kelly
- Rudy at Hesburgh Library Penthouse — Courtesy University of Notre Dame Archives
- Summer Gathering at the Grotto — © Rev. Wm. Blum, C.S.C.

- Rev. Theodore Hesburgh, C.S.C. — Courtesy Notre Dame Photography
- Hesburgh at the Grotto — by L. K. Dunn, Courtesy Notre Dame Photography
- Grotto Painting with Bro. Rod — © Franklin McMahon
- Bro. Cosmas on bench — *The Dome*, 1990

Chapter 17
- Student praying after Fire — by Joe Raymond / Courtesy *South Bend Tribune*
- 1985 Grotto Fire — by Ed Ballotts / Courtesy *South Bend Tribune*
- Autumn at the Grotto — © David C. Berta
- Lighting a Candle of Hope — © Meredith Salisbury
- Dooley's Statue at Grotto — © Paul Wieber / Courtesy Campus Ministry
- Summertime Grotto — © Robert F. Ringel
- Flowers and Candles at the Grotto — © Robert F. Ringel
- Sunrise over St. Mary's Lake — © Rev. Wm. Blum, C.S.C. enlargements available in five sizes with proceeds going to benefit
Holy Cross Missions. To order-contact: Father James T. Rahilly C.S.C., P.O. Box 543, Notre Dame, In 46556 Phone: (219) 631-5477.
- Rainbow over the Grotto — © Richard L. Spicer

Keystone —
- Wm. Buckles, Builder of St. Stanislaus — Courtesy Buckles Family
- Rev. Sigmund Jankowski, C.S.C. — Courtesy Indiana Province Archives Center
- St. Stanislaus Grotto — © Michael P. Kelly

Author's Personal Epilogue —
- Dorothy Corson and Legendary Sycamore — by Sue Lowe — Courtesy *South Bend Tribune*
- Lourdes Basilica — Watercolor by Hoffbauer from *Lourdes*, 19th Century
- Lourdes Procession — Watercolor by Hoffbauer from *Lourdes*, 19th Century
- Lighting a Candle of Hope — © Meredith Salisbury
- Angel Light at St. Mary's Lake — © Robert F. Ringel
- Dove Above the Presbytery Sign — © Robert F. Ringel
- Squirrel on a Tombstone — © Robert F. Ringel
- Baby Robin on a Cozy Perch – © Robert F. Ringel
- Raccoon's Lookout – © Robert F. Ringel
- The First Sign of Spring — © Robert F. Ringel
- A Robin's Home — © Robert F. Ringel
- Sunrise over St. Mary's Lake — © Robert F. Ringel

Notre Dame Chronological Chart —
- Log Chapel at Notre Dame © Robert F. Ringel.

Photo Credits Page —
- St. Mary's Lake at Notre Dame © Robert F. Ringel.

Excerpts

The following publishers and copyright holders have generously given their permission to use excerpts from copyrighted works. Please report any errors or omissions; we will gladly make amends.

Chapter 1 — Note 4 — Edward Sorin, C.S.C., excerpts from *Chronicles of Notre Dame du Lac* by Edward Sorin, edited and annotated by James T. Connelly. (c) by University of Notre Dame Press. Used by permission of the publisher.

Chapter 1 — Note 7 — Rev. Eugene P. Burke, *Our Lady and the University of Notre Dame: The Mystery of the Woman*, by Rev. Eugene P. Burke (c) 1956 by University of Notre Dame Press. Used by permission of the publisher.

Chapter 1 — Note 9 — Edward Sorin, C.S.C., excerpts from *Chronicles of Notre Dame du Lac* by Edward Sorin, edited and annotated by James T. Connelly. (c) by University of Notre Dame Press. Used by permission of the publisher.

Chapter 1 — Note 12 — Sisters of the Holy Cross, excerpts from *Fruits of the Tree*, V. 1, 1843, Sisters Of Holy Cross Sesquicentennial (c) 1988 Ave Maria Press. Used by permission of the Sisters of the Holy Cross.

Chapter 1 — Note 15 — Edward Sorin, C.S.C., excerpts from *Chronicles of Notre Dame du Lac* by Edward Sorin, edited and annotated by James T. Connelly. (c) by University of Notre Dame Press. Used by permission of the publisher.

Chapter 1 — Note 18 — Sisters of the Holy Cross, excerpts from *Pioneers and Builders, Centenary Chronicles of the Sisters of the Holy Cross*, St. Mary's of the Immaculate Conception, Notre Dame IN 1941. Used by permission of the Sisters of the Holy Cross.

Chapter 1 — Note 19 — Thomas J. Schlereth, excerpts from *A Dome of Learning, The University of Notre Dame's Administration Building* by Thomas J. Schlereth, University of Notre Dame Alumni Association 1991. Used by permission of the publisher.

Chapter 2 — Ft.. 21 — Joseph M. White, excerpts from *Sacred Heart Parish at Notre Dame, A Heritage and History* by Joseph M. White (c) 1992 Sacred Heart Parish. Used by the permission of the publisher.

Chapter 2 — Note 25 — Colleen McDannell, excerpts from *Material Christianity: Religion and Popular Culture in America* by Colleen McDannell [Working Paper Series 24, No. 3] (c) 1995 New Haven: Yale University Press. Used by permission of the publisher.

Chapter 2 — Note 45 — Bro. Killian Beirne, C.S.C., Eastern Province, excerpts from *From Sea to Shining Sea*, by Bro. Killian Beirne, (c) 1966 Holy Cross Press. Used by permission of the publisher.

Chapter 3 — Note 61 — Thomas J. Schlereth, excerpts from *A Spire of Faith, The University of Notre Dame's Sacred Heart Church* by Thomas J. Schlereth, (c) 1991 University of Notre Dame Alumni Association. Used by permission of the publisher.

Chapter 3 — Note 62 — Sister M. Georgia Costin, C.S.C., excerpts from *Priceless Spirit: A History of the Sisters of the Holy Cross, 1841-1893* by Sister M. Georgia Costin, C.S.C. (c) 1994 by University of Notre Dame Press. Used by the permission of the publisher.

Chapter 3 — Note 64 — Joseph M. White, excerpts from *Sacred Heart Parish at Notre Dame, A Heritage and History* by Joseph M. White (c) 1992 Sacred Heart Parish. Used by the permission of the publisher.

Chapter 3 — Note 68 — Edward Sorin, C.S.C., excerpts from *Chronicles of Notre Dame du Lac* by Edward Sorin, edited and annotated by James T. Connelly. (c) by University of Notre Dame Press. Used by permission of the publisher.

Chapter 3 — Note 69 — Sister M. Georgia Costin, C.S.C., excerpts from *Priceless Spirit: A History of the Sisters of the Holy Cross, 1841-1893* by Sister M. Georgia Costin, C.S.C. (c) 1994 by University of Notre Dame Press. Used by the permission of the publisher.

Chapter 4 — Note 71 — Thomas J. Schlereth, excerpts from *A Dome of Learning, The University of Notre Dame's Administration Building* by Thomas J. Schlereth, University of Notre Dame Alumni Association 1991. Used by permission of the publisher.

Chapter 4 — Note 81 — Marion McCandless, excerpts from *Family Portraits* by Marion McCandless, Notre Dame IN, (c) 1952. Used by permission of the Sisters of the Holy Cross.

Chapter 4 — Note 82 — Thomas J. Schlereth, excerpts from *A Dome of Learning, The University of Notre Dame's Administration Building* by Thomas J. Schlereth, University of Notre Dame Alumni Association 1991. Used by permission of the publisher

Chapter 4 — Note 83 — Sister M. Georgia Costin, C.S.C., excerpts from *Priceless Spirit: A History of the Sisters of the Holy Cross, 1841-1893* by Sister M. Georgia Costin, C.S.C. (c) 1994 by University of Notre Dame Press. Used by the permission of the publisher.

Chapter 4 — Note 94 — Thomas J. Schlereth, excerpts from *A Dome of Learning, The University of Notre Dame's Administration Building* by Thomas J. Schlereth, University of Notre Dame Alumni Association 1991. Used by permission of the publisher.

Chapter 5 — Note 102 — Thomas J. Schlereth, excerpts from *A Spire of Faith, The University of Notre Dame's Sacred Heart Church* by Thomas J. Schlereth, (c) 1991 University of Notre Dame Alumni Association. Used by permission of the publisher.

Chapter 5 — Note 111 — Alain Woodrow, excerpts from "Lourdes, More Popular Than Ever," reprinted from *The Tablet* by the Catholic Digest , July 1994. Used by permission of the publisher, The Tablet..

Chapter 5 — Note 113 — Sisters of the Holy Cross, excerpts from *Pioneers and Builders, Centenary Chronicles of the Sisters of the Holy Cross*, St. Mary's of the Immaculate Conception, Notre Dame IN 1941. Used by permission of the Sisters of the Holy Cross.

Chapter 6 — Note 121 — J. C. Cooper, *An Illustrated Encyclopaedia of Traditional Symbols* by J. C. Cooper, (c) 1978 by Thames & Hudson. Used by permission of the publisher. (Correct text)

Chapter 7 — Note 139 — Bishop John M. D'Arcy, excerpts from "Stories of two remarkable priests — Benoit and Sorin," *Today's Catholic* 7 March 1993. Used by permission of the publisher.

Chapter 8 — Note 152 — Joan Romine, excerpts from *Copshaholm, The Oliver Story*, by Joan Romine, Northern Indiana Historical Society (c) 1970, Used by permission of the publisher.

Chapter 8 — Note 153 — Jeanne Derbeck, "3 Buildings Exemplify Stonemasonry," *South Bend Tribune*, 14 December 1970. Used by permission of the publisher.

Chapter 10 — Note 173 — Used by permission of the publisher, Macmillan Publishing, A division of Ahsuog, Inc. Excerpts from: *My First Seventy Years* by Sister M. Madeleva, C.S.C. (c) Sister M. Madeleva, C.S.C., 1959.

Chapter 10 — Note 174 — Used by permission of the publisher, MacMillan Publishing, A division of Ahsuog, Inc. Excerpts from: *Collected Poems* by Sister M. Madeleva, C.S.C. Copyright, 1923, 1927, 1935, 1936, 1938, 1939, 1941, 1946, by Sister M. Madeleva.

Chapter 10 — Note 177 — Thomas Stritch, excerpts from *My Notre Dame: Memories and Reflections of Sixty Years*, by Thomas Stritch (c) 1991 by University of Notre Dame Press. Used by permission of the publisher.

Chapter 11 — Note 183 — R. David Edmunds, excerpts from *The Potawatomis, Keepers of the Fire* by R. David Edmunds, (c) 1978 University of Oklahoma Press. Used by permission of the publisher.

Chapter 11 — Note 187 — Edward Sorin, C.S.C., excerpts from *Chronicles of Notre Dame du Lac* by Edward Sorin, edited and annotated by James T. Connelly. (c) by University of Notre Dame Press. Used by permission of the publisher.

Chapter 11 — Note 192 — Edward Sorin, C.S.C., excerpts from *Chronicles of Notre Dame du Lac* by Edward Sorin, edited and annotated by James T. Connelly. (c) by University of Notre Dame Press. Used by permission of the publisher.

Chapter 12 — Note 213 — Eugene O'Neill, excerpts from *Long Day's Journey Into Night* by Eugene O'Neill (c) 1956 Yale University Press, New Haven, Connecticut, Used by permission of the publisher.

Chapter 12 — Note 214 — Edward Fisher, excerpts from *Notre Dame remembered: an autobiography*, by Edward Fischer, (c) 1987 by University of Notre Dame Press. Used by permission of the publisher.

Chapter 13 — Note 222 — Rev. Eugene P. Burke, *Our Lady and the University of Notre Dame: The Mystery of the Woman*, by Rev. Eugene P. Burke (c) 1956 by University of Notre Dame Press. Used by permission of the publisher.

Chapter 13 — Note 226 — Milton Lomask, excerpts from *The Man in the Iron Lung*, by Milton Lomask (c) 1956 by Doubleday. Used by permission of Shirley G. Cochrane, Literary Executor of Milton Lomask estate.

Chapter 14 — Note 237 — David Cherichetti, excerpts from a 1977 oral history interview of George Seaton, Hollywood director and screenwriter by David Cherichetti for the *New York Times* Oral History Program. Used by permission of the American Film Institute, Louis B. Mayer Library, Oral History Collection, Part 1.

Chapter 15 — Note 246 — Carl J. Jung, excerpts from *Man and His Symbols*, by Carl J. Jung (c) 1964. Current copyright holder Ferguson Publishing Co. Used by permission of the publisher.

Bibliography

An Illustrated Historical Atlas Of St. Joseph County Indiana, 1875, (Biggins Belen & Co.).

Ave Maria, Serial, (Notre Dame, IN., Congregation of Holy Cross, 1866-1970)

Barbe, Daniel, *Lourdes, Yesterday, Today and Tomorrow*, (Burns & Oates, London, no date).

Barthez, Antoine, *The Empress Eugenie and Her Circle*, (New York: Bretano's, 1913).

Benson, Robert Hugh, *Lourdes*, (London: Manresa Press, 1914).

Bergman, Ingrid, *Ingrid Bergman, My Story*, (Delacorte Press, N.Y., 1972).

Beirne, C.S.C., Bro Kilian *From Sea to Shining Sea*, (Holy Cross Press, 1966).

Brother Founders of Notre Dame, 1841-1849, *Adapted to the Lake*, Editor and Translated by George Klawitter, (Peter Lang Publishing, Inc. 1993).

Brown, John Gary, *Soul In The Stone: Cemetery Art from America's Heartland*, (University Press of Kansas, 1994).

Burton, Katherine, *Three Generations*, (Longmans Green & Co., 1947).

Cooper, J. C., *Illustrated Encyclopedia of Symbolism*, (James Hames & Hudson, 1978).

Coquillard, Mary Clarke, *Alexis Coquillard — His Times*, (Northern Indiana Historical Society, 1931).

Costin, C.S.C., Sr. M. Georgia, *Priceless Spirit*, (University of Notre Dame Press, 1994).

Edmunds, David R., *The Potawatomis, Keepers of the Fire*, (University of Oklahoma Press, 1978).

Eleanore, Sister M., *On The King's Highway*, (D. Appleton & Co., 1931).

Fischer, Edward, *Notre Dame Remembered: An autobiography*, (University of Notre Dame, 1987).

Francesca, Sister M., *Our Mother House*, (W. B. Conky Company, 1941).

Hawkins, Leonard C., *Man in the Iron Lung*, (Doubleday, 1956).

History Of Laporte County Indiana, (C. C. Chapman & Co. 1880).

Hope, C.S.C., Arthur J., *Notre Dame: One Hundred Years*, (The University of Notre Dame Press, 1948).

Hope, C.S.C., Arthur J., *Sisters of Holy Cross at Notre Dame*, (Notre Dame, 1958).

Howard, Timothy E., *A History of St. Joseph County Indiana*, (The Lewis Publishing Co., 1907).

Howard, Timothy E., *A Brief History of the University of Notre Dame du Lac*, (Warner, 1895).

Indiana Historical Collection, (Indiana Historical Commission,1922).

Indiana Magazine of History, (Bloomington, IN 1934).

Jankowski, C.S.C., Rev. Sigmund A., *When Dreams Come True*, (Notre Dame, IN, 1970).

Jones, C.S.C., Rev. Thomas P., *Development of the Office of the Prefect of Religion at Notre Dame: 1842-1952*.

Jung, Carl G., *Man and His Symbols*, (Doubleday, 1964).

Kappler, C. C., *Indian Treaties 1778-1883*, (Interland Publishing, 1972).

Kilmer And Campion, (Campion Jesuit High School, 1937).

Kilmer, Joyce, *Joyce Kilmer, Poems, Essays and Letters*, With a Memoir, Edited by Holliday, Cortes, Robert (George H. Doran Company 1918).

Kurtz, Harold, *The Empress Eugenie*, (Houghton Mifflin, 1964).

Lasserre, Henri, *Our Lady Of Lourdes*, (D. & J. Sadlier, 1875).

Lasserre, Henri, *Miracles at Lourdes*, (John Murphy & Co., 1884).

Lyons, Joseph A., *Silver Jubilee of the University of Notre Dame*, (E. B. Meyers & Co., 1869).

Madeleva, C.S.C., Sister M. *My First Seventy Years*, (The MacMillan Company, 1959).

Mayer, Louis B., Oral History Collection, (The American Film Institute, 1977).

McAllister, Anna, *Ellen Ewing, Wife of General Sherman*, (Benziger Brothers, 1936).

McAvoy, C.S.C., Rev. Thomas T., *The Catholic Church in Indiana, 1789 - 1834*, (Columbia University Press, 1940).

McCandless, Marion, *Family Portraits*, (Saint Mary's College, Notre Dame, IN, 1952).

McDannell, Colleen "Lourdes Water and American Catholocism," Working Paper Series 24, No. 3, (Cushwa Center, University of Notre Dame, Fall, 1992).

McKee, Irving, *Trail Of Death, Letters of Benjamin Marie Petit*, (Indiana Historical Society, 1941).

Meginness, John F., *The Biography Of Frances Slocum , Lost Sister of Wyoming*, (Heller Brothers Printing House, Williamsport, PA, 1891).

Notre Dame Alumnus, Serial, (University of Notre Dame 1923-).

Notre Dame Magazine, Serial, Sesquicentennial Edition, Summer 1991

Notre Dame Scholastic, Serial, (University of Notre Dame, 1867-)

O'Connor, C.S.C., Rev. Edward D., Edited by, *The Mystery of the Woman*, (University of Notre Dame Press, 1956).

O'Neill, Eugene, *Long Day's Journey Into Night*, (New Haven, Yale University Press, 1956).

Reflections in the Dome, Edited by James S. O'Rourke, (James S. O'Rourke, 1988).

Phelps, Martha, *Lost Sister Of Wyoming*, (Published by the author, Wilkes Barre, Pa., 1916).

Poetry: A Magazine of Verse, (Modern Poetry Association, 1913).

The Pokagons, 1683-1983, (University Press of America, 1984).

Post, Erma Helmen, *Gleanings of Clay Township, St. Joseph County Indiana, For My Own Pleasure*, (Microfilmed by Allen County Public Library, 1973).

Roberto, Brother, *Death Beneath the Trees*, (Dujarie Press, 1967).

Romine, Joan, *COPSHAHOLM, The Oliver Story*, (Northern Indiana Historical Society, 1978).

Schlereth, Thomas, *University of Notre Dame, Portrait Of Its History and Campus*, (University of Notre Dame Press, 1976).

Schlereth, Thomas, *A Dome of Learning, The University of Notre Dame's Administration Building*, (Alumni Association, 1991).

Schlereth, Thomas, *A Spire of Faith, The University of Notre Dame's Sacred Heart Church*, (Alumni Assocation, 1991).

Schneider, Richard H., *Freedom's Holy Light*, (Thomas Nelson, Inc., 1985).

Sencourt, Robert, *Life Of The Empress Eugenie*, (New York, Scriber, 1931).

Sisters of the Holy Cross, Notre Dame, IN, *St. Mary's, A Story Of Fifty Years*, (Notre Dame: Ave Maria, 1905).

Sisters of the Holy Cross, Notre Dame, IN, *Pioneers and Builders, Centenary Chronicles of the Sisters of the Holy Cross, St. Mary's of the Immaculate Conception*, Notre Dame, IN, (W. B. Conkey Co. 1941).

Sorin,C.S.C., Edward Rev, *Circular Letters of Very Rev. Edward Sorin*, (Notre Dame, Indiana, 1885).

Sorin, C.S.C., Edward, *The Chronicles of Notre Dame du Lac*, Edited by James J. Connelly, C.S.C., (University of Notre Dame Press, 1992).

Standard Atlas Of St. Joseph County Indiana, (Geo Ogle & Co.1895 and 1911).

Stritch, Tom, *My Notre Dame: Memories and Reflections of Sixty Years*, (University of Notre Dame Press, 1991).

The Observer, Serial, (Student Government, University of Notre Dame, 1962-).

Trennert, Jr., *Robert A. Indian Traders of the Middle Border, The House of Ewing, 1827-54*, (University of Nebraska Press, 1981).

Von Matt, Leonard, *St. Bernadette, A Pictorial Biography*, (Longmans, Green, & Regnery, 1957).

Werfel, Franz, *The Song Of Bernadette*, (Viking Press, 1942).

White, Joseph M., *Sacred Heart Parish At Notre Dame, A Heritage and History*, (Sacred Heart Parish, 1992).

Who Was Who, (St. Martin's Press, 1971-1980).

Woodrow, Alain "LOURDES, More Popular Than Ever," Serial, (*Catholic Digest*, July 1994

Endnotes

1. "The Location of Old Fort St. Joseph," Thomas T. McAvoy, C.S.C., University Libraries of Notre Dame, Special Collections, RBSC, p. 1.

2. Until more recent times, the University of Notre Dame and Saint Mary's College were referred to, in early written sources, as Notre Dame and St. Mary's. For this reason, with a few exceptions, I will be using the earlier Notre Dame and "St." Mary's in referring them.

3. *Parade Magazine*, (Parade Publications Inc.), Lamar Alexander, "Find The Good and Praise it," 24 January 1993, p.5.

4. Edward Sorin, C.S.C., *The Chronicles of Notre Dame du Lac*, Edited by James J. Connelly, C.S.C., (University of Notre Dame Press, 1992), p. 309.

5. "Notre Dame and Lourdes," Confraternity of Lourdes News Letter, Circa 1956, Unprocessed, UNDA.

6. *Notre Dame Alumnus*, V. 20, March 1942, "The Character of Sorin," p. 7.

7. Rev. Eugene P. Burke, "Our Lady and the University of Notre Dame, *The Mystery of the Woman*, (University of Notre Dame Press, 1956), pp. 143, 144.

8. *Notre Dame Alumnus*, V. 20, March 1942, "The Character of Sorin," p. 8.

9. Edward Sorin, C.S.C., *The Chronicles of Notre Dame du Lac*, Edited by James J. Connelly, C.S.C., (University of Notre Dame Press, 1992), pp. 27, 315.

10. *The Columbian Jubilee*, 1892, PNDP, 101-1890, p. 493-94, UNDA. Also *Schol.*, V. 20,14 August 1886, p. 15.

11. "A Guide to the University of Notre Dame and the Academy of St. Mary of the Immaculate Conception," Near South Bend, IN (J. B. Chandler, Printer, 1865), PNDP 100-1865, p. 39.

12. Fruits of the Tree, V. 1, 1843, (Marianette Annals, 22), Sisters of Holy Cross Sesquicentennial, (Ave Marie Press, 1988), p. 36.

13. "A Guide to the University of Notre Dame and the Academy of St. Mary of the Immaculate Conception," Near South Bend, IN (J. B. Chandler, Printer, 1865), PNDP 100-1865, p. 40.

14. Joseph A. Lyons, *Silver Jubilee of the University of Notre Dame*, (E. B. Meyers & Co., 1869), pp. 20- 23.

15. Edward Sorin, *The Chronicles of Notre Dame du Lac*, (University of Notre Dame Press, 1992), Edited by James T. Connelly, C.S.C., p. 141.

16. "Our Lady of Lourdes," From the *London Lamp, Ave Maria*, V. VIII, 1 January 1870, p. 11, "Pilgrimages in the Pyrenees and Landes," Denys Shyne Lawlor, 28 May 1870, p. 341.

17. Maria (Maritza) Mestrovic, Biography of Ivan Mestrovic, UNDA etc.

18. *Pioneers and Builders*, Centenary Chronicles of the Sisters of the Holy Cross, St. Mary's of the Immaculate Conception, Notre Dame, IN, (W. B. Conkey Co. 1941), pp. 23,24,29,30.

19. Tom Schlereth, *A Dome of Learning,The University of Notre Dame's Administration Building*, (Alumni Association, 1991) p. 6.

20. *Ave Maria*, (Notre Dame, 1866), 6 October 1866, pp. 632, 633, 10 November 1866, p. 714, Administration Building, Dome: Statue of Virgin Mary, Gilding, 1860s-1900s, PNDP, 10 Ad-4.

21. Joseph M. White, *Sacred Heart Parish at Notre Dame, A Heritage and History*, (Sacred Heart Parish, 1992), p. 45.

22. The November 23, 1991 decree of Pope John Paul 11, was officially announced in *The Observer* on January 17, 1992, p. 1., (hereafter cited by its earlier name, Sacred Heart Church).

23. Fr. Granger to Fr. Sorin, January,1869, Fr. Granger's Correspondence, CGRA Box 1 of 1, 1st folder, p. 2,4, UNDA.

24. *Sisters of the Holy Cross at Notre Dame*, Rev. Arthur J. Hope, C.S.C. (Notre Dame, 1958), p. 17.

25. Colleen McDannell, "Lourdes Water and American Catholicism," Working Paper Series 24, No. 3, (Cushwa Center, University of Notre Dame, Fall, 1992), pp. 11, 12.

26. *Schol.*, V. VIII, 21 June 1873, p. 324. This publication was known as the *Scholastic Year* from 1867- 1869, the *Notre Dame Scholastic* from 1869-1962, and since 1962, the *Scholastic*. (hereafter cited as Schol.).

27. *Schol.*, V. VIII, 1 November 1873, p. 77.

28. *Schol.*, V. VIII, 13 September 1873, p. 23.

29. The Grotto at the House of the Sisters of Charity at Yonkers is the only one of the three still in existence.

30. *Schol.*, V. 11, 29 September 1877, p. 75.

31. *Schol.*, V. 12, 22 August 1878, p. 16.

32. *Schol.*, V. VIII, 26 December 1874, p. 189.

33. Class Day Book of 1880, PNDP 100-1880, p. 80- 81, UNDA.

34. Sister Georgia Costin, C.S.C., *Priceless Spirit*, (University of Notre Dame Press, 1994), p. 211.

35. *Schol.*, V. 13, 20 September 1879, p. 45.

36. "Our Lady of Lourdes," From the *London Lamp, Ave Maria*, V. VIII, 1 January 1870, p. 11., "Pilgrimages in the Pyrenees and Landes," Denys Shyne Lawlor, 28 May 1970, p. 341.

37. Map of Notre Dame University and St. Mary's Academy - -1878, Campus Maps 1870s—1940s, PNDP 10-Aa-05, UNDA.

38. Sanborn Fire Insurance Maps of Notre Dame, Farms and SMC, 1885-1941, UNDA 11/01-05, UNDA.

39. "Some Of St. Mary's Shrines," *Schol.*, V. 11, 13 October 1877, pp. 98-100.

40. *Schol.*, V. 13, 14 November 1874, p. 90.

41. Howard, Timothy, *A Brief History of the University of Notre Dame du Lac*, (Warner Co., 1895), p. 128.

42. *Schol.*, V. 8, 1 May 1875, p. 477.

43. *Schol.*, V. IX, 11 December 1875, p. 235.

44. Mariaphilos, "The Sanctuary Lamp of Notre Dame," *Ave Maria*, V. 10, 9 January, 1875, p. 19.

45. Bro. Kilian Beirne, *From Sea to Shining Sea*, (Holy Cross Press, 1966), p. 26.

46. Thomas Schlereth, *The University of Notre Dame, A Spire of Faith*, (Alumni Association, 1991), pp. 30, 64.

47. *Schol.*, V. VIII,14 & 21 November 1874, Death, pp. 88,89, Funeral, p.105.

48. *Schol.*, V. 12, 28 September 1878, pp. 63, 64.

49. *Ave Maria*, V. 13, 10 February 1877, p. 91.

50. *Schol.*, V. 9, 8 January 1876, pp. 297, 298.

51. *Ave Maria*, V. 17, 3 December, 1881, p. 967.

52. *Schol.*, V. 11, 29 September 1877, p. 75.

53. Schol., V. 11, 6 April 1878, p. 506.

54. *Schol.*, V. 12, 22 August 1878, p. 13.

55. *Schol.*, V. 30, 20 August 1896, p. 14.

56. *The Columbian Jubilee*, 1892, PNDP, 101-1890, p. 493-94, UNDA. Also *Schol.*, V. 20,14 August 1886, p. 15.

57. Thomas Schlereth, *The University Of Notre Dame, A Portrait Of Its History and Campus*, (University of Notre Dame Press, 1976), p. 44.

58. Photograph of Sorin's 1878 Grotto, 22 November 1886, GNDL Box 7 7/8, UNDA.

59. Edward Sorin, C.S.C., *Circular Letters of the Very Rev. Edward Sorin*, 1885 Edition, (Notre Dame, IN), Letter, "On Board the 'St. Germaine,' June 4, 1883, pp. 181, 182.

60. "An Indiana Academy," *Schol.*, V. 12, 22 August 1878, pp.17-18.

61. Thomas J. Schlereth, *A Spire of Faith, The University of Notre Dame's Sacred Heart Church*, (University of Notre Dame Alumni Association), 1991, p. 17.

62. Sr. M. Georgia Costin, C.S.C., *Priceless Spirit*, (University of Notre Dame Press, 1994), p. 79, 90.

63. *Schol.*, V. VIII, 30 August 1873, pp. 6,7.

64. Joseph M. White, *Sacred Heart Parish at Notre Dame, A Heritage and History*, (Sacred Heart Parish, 1992), p. 43.

65. *Notre Dame Magazine*, Summer '93, p. 15.

66. *Notre Dame Alumnus*, V. 20, March, 1942, "The Character of Sorin," p. 7.

67. CSHR, Box 8, Folder 12, Letters between Ellen Ewing Sherman and General Sherman, 23 April, 1873, UNDA.

68. Edward Sorin, C.S.C., *The Chronicles of Notre Dame du Lac*, Edited by James J. Connelly, C.S.C., (University of Notre Dame Press, 1992), p. 269.

69. Sr. M. Georgia Costin, C.S.C., *Priceless Spirit*, (University of Notre Dame Press, 1994) p. 221.

70. *Schol.*, V. 12, 7 June 1879, p. 610.

71. Tom Schlereth, *A Dome of Learning,The University of Notre Dame's Administration Building*, (Alumni Association, 1991) p. 8.

72. *Schol.*, V. 12, 24 May 1879, p. 579.

73. *Notre Dame Alumnus*, V. 20, March 1942., p. 7.

74. "Notre Dame and Lourdes," Confraternity of Lourdes News Letter, Circa 1956, Unprocessed, UNDA.

75. *Schol.*, V.13, 13 September 1879, p. 25,26.

76. PNDP-110-CAV, Notes of Early History, J.W. Cavanaugh, p. 23, 24.

77. *Schol.*, V. 13, 23 August 1879, p. 4., Obituary, *Schol.* V. 58, 19 March 1926, p. 678.

78. *Circular Letters of the Very Rev. Edward Sorin, 1885 Edition*, (Notre Dame, IN), 17 October 1882 Letter mentions other contributors to the Dome, pp. 173,174. Other details, pp. 174,175,184,185.

79. Correct measurement 197 feet, Administration Bldg., Dome: Statue of Virgin Mary, Gilding, 1870s to 1990s. PNDP 10- Ad-4, UNDA.

80. "The Statue for the Dome of the College," *Schol.*, V. 12, 12 July 1879, p. 688.

81. Marion McCandless, Family Portraits, (Notre Dame, IN 1952), p.14-16.

82. Thomas J. Schlereth, A Dome of Learning, The University of Notre Dame's Main Building, (Alumni Association, 1991), p. 25.

83. Sister M. Georgia Costin, C.S.C., *Priceless Spirit*, (University of Notre Dame Press, 1994), p. 215.

84. *Schol.*, V. 17, 13 October 1883, p. 88.

85. *University Statue Shrine Stories*, (Kerrville, Texas, 1943), p. 8, UQAC, UNDA.

86. "Circle of electric lights," 1906 Dome, and *Schol.*, V. XLVIII, 26 June 1915, p. 601.

87. PNDP-110-CAV, Notes of Early History, J.W. Cavanaugh, p. 24.

88. Howard, Timothy, *A Brief History of the University of Notre Dame du Lac*, (Warner,1895), pp. 179, 185.

89. *Schol.*, V. 17, 5 January 1884, p. 264.

90. Richard H. Schneider, *Freedom's Holy Light*, (Thomas Nelson, Inc., 1985).

91. *Reflections in the Dome*, Edited by James S. O'Rourke, (James S. O'Rourke, 1988), Introduction, Kerry Temple, p. 11.

92. *Schol.*, V. 17, 29 March 1884, p. 457.

93. *Schol.*, V. 17, 22 March 1884, p. 441.

94. Tom Schlereth, *A Dome of Learning,The University of Notre Dame's Administration Building*, (Alumni Association, 1991) p. 36.

95. Color picture of Our Lady on the Dome, Bill Mowle, photographer, *The Dome*, V. 84, 1993, p. 7.

96. *Schol.*, V. 57, April 1924, Poem, writer unknown, p. 193.

97. Sacred Heart Crowns — Description and theft of —10-6-1886, PNDP 10-Sb-8, UNDA. "Bold Burglary At Notre Dame," *South Bend Tribune*, 6 October 1886, PNDP 10-Sb-8, UNDA.

98. *Ave Maria*, (Notre Dame, 1866),10 November 1866, p. 714, Administration Building, Dome: Statue of Virgin Mary, Gilding, 1860s-1900s, PNDP, 10 Ad-4.

99. "A Monument to Our Lady, The Church of the Sacred Heart at Notre Dame," *Annals of Our Lady of Lourdes*, July, 1891, p. 104, RBSC, UNDA.

100. Full story, Empress Eugenie Crown, Unpublished manuscript, Journal of Notre Dame Grotto Research, Dorothy Corson Collection, UNDA.

101. Richard Gerbracht, "The Forgotten Crown," *Schol.*, V. 94, 16 January 1953, p. 20-21.

102. Thomas Schlereth, *The University of Notre Dame, A Spire of Faith*, (Alumni Association, 1991), pp. 30, 64.

103. *Schol.*, V. 22, 8 September 1888, p. 53.

104. *Schol.*, V. 22, 6 April 1889, p. 512.

105. *Schol.*, V. 12, 2 November 1878, p. 142.

106. *Schol.*, V. 22, 20 April 1889, p. 544.

107. *Schol.*, V. 22, 2 June 1889, p. 640.

108. *South Bend News Times*, 13 October 1933, also PNDP 10-Sb-8, UNDA.

109. Henri Lasserre, *Our Lady Of Lourdes*, (D. & J. Sadlier, 1875). Werfel, Franz, *The Song of Bernadette*, (Viking Press, 1942), pp. 406-407, 419.

110. Daniel Barbé, *Lourdes, Yesterday, Today and Tomorrow*, (Burns & Oates, London, no date, latest reference to date in text,1892), p. 103.

111. Alain Woodrow, "LOURDES, More Popular Than Ever," *Catholic Digest*, July 1994, pp. 106-109.

112. "Sister Lourdes Dies at 85," *Notre Dame Alumnus*, V. 14, February 1936, p. 122.

113. *Pioneers and Builders*, Centenary Chronicles of the Sisters of the Holy Cross, St. Mary's of the Immaculate Conception, Notre Dame, IN, (W. B. Conkey Co. 1941), pp. 23,24,29,30.

114. Arthur J. Hope, C.S.C., *Sisters of the Holy Cross at Notre Dame*, (Notre Dame, 1958), pp. 6,7.

115. Rev. John W. Cavanaugh, C.S.C., Unpublished manuscript, Notes on Early History of Notre Dame, p. 26, PNDP, 110-Cav, UNDA.

116. Arthur J. Hope, C.S.C., *Notre Dame One Hundred Years*, (University of Notre Dame Press, 1948), pp. 256,257.

117. Timothy Howard, *A Brief History of the University of Notre Dame du Lac*, (Warner, 1895), pp. 127, 212.

118. Rev. William Corby, C.S.C., Correspondence, Letter dated December 19, 1897, CCOR, Box 1/33, UNDA.

119. "Grotto of Lourdes at the Home of The 'Ave Maria," *The Annals Of Our Lady Of Lourdes*, (Notre Dame, 1896), hereafter cited as the Annals, V. X11 No. 5, May 1896, pp. 78-79, RBSC, UNDA.

120. Lelia P. Roby, "The School Question," *Daily Calumet*, 11 December, 1891, PNDP, 101-1890s, UNDA.

121. J. C. Cooper, *Illustrated Encyclopedia of Symbolism*, (James Hames & Hudson, 1978), pp. 39-42.

122. *The South Bend Tribune*, 12 January 1995, C5.

123. "Grotto of Lourdes at Notre Dame, Indiana," *Annals*, V. X11, No. 6, June 1896, p. 91, RBSC, UNDA.

124. Rev. Wm. Corby, C.S.C., Province Administration Papers, Letter from Carroll dated, 6 June 1896, Reply from Corby dated, June 8, 1896, Box 1, Folder 15, IPAC.

125. *Schol.*, V. 30, 14 November 1896, p.154.

126. *Schol.*, V. 30, 20 August 1896, pp. 15, 16.

127. *Schol.*, V. 46, 16 November 1912, p. 141.

128. *Notre Dame Alumnus*, V. 46, March 1968 April, "Right to the Tip-top," p. 26.

129. Rev. Joseph Maguire, *C.S.C. Collection*, Moreau Seminary letter, December 1953, Indiana Province Archive Center, (hereafter IPAC).

130. *Schol.*, V. 12, 7 June 1879, p. 610.

131. *Schol.*, V. 29, 23 May 1896, p. 547.

132. Ledger item #1300, June 6, 1896, Ledger 9, Journal 9, Cash Book 20, Early Notre Dame Student, Class, and Financial Record books, (hereafter cited as ULDG), UNDA.

133. By Coz, "A Hundred Years to Come," *Schol.*, V. 3, 5 February 1870, p. 82.

134. Log Cabin Marriage Records, 29 September 1856, Sacred Heart Church, MSHC, UNDA.

135. *An Illustrated Historical Atlas Of St. Joseph County Indiana*, (Higgins Belen & Co., 1875), Drawing of Talley House, p.42, St. Joseph County Public Library, History Room.

136. Charles Shober, *Map Of St. Joseph County Indiana*, (M. W. Stoke, 1863), St. Joseph County Public Library, History Room.

137. From the abstract of Victor Couch, a descendent of Peter Kintz and present owner of 10 acres of the original 80.10 acres on Kintz Drive.

138. *An Illustrated Historical Atlas Of St. Joseph Indiana, 1875*, and *Standard Atlas Of St. Joseph County Indiana*, (Geo Ogle & Co. 1895), Clay Township, p.35, St. Joseph County Public Library, History Room.

139. Bishop John M. D'Arcy, "Stories of two remarkable priests — Benoit and Sorin," *Today's Catholic*, 7 March 1993, p. 2.

140. Thomas Schlereth, *University of Notre Dame, Portrait of Its History and Campus*, (University of Notre Dame Press, 1976), p. 37.

141. *Schol.*, V. 3, 22 January 1870, p. 73.

142. *Schol.*, V. IX, 17 June, 1876, p. 667.

143. Work Ledger, 22 March 1884, Record of lay persons hired at the university and farm, 1872-91, Notre Dame *C.S.C. Community Collection*, IPAC.

144. *The South Bend Tribune*, 14 December, 1970, Sec. 2, p.17.

145. *South Bend Tribune, & South Bend News Times*, 8 August 1938.

146. *South Bend Tribune*, 6 May 1896.

147. *South Bend Daily Times*, 18 July 1896.

148. *South Bend Tribune*, 8 June 1896.

149. *South Bend Daily Times*, 23 June 1896.

150. Sister Eutropia to Dorothy Corson, 16 May, 1992, Grotto Sources file, *Dorothy Corson Collection*, UNDA. Unless otherwise noted, all letters and copies of most source material associated the Grotto story are held by the University of Notre Dame Archives.

151. Sister M. Eleanore, C.S.C. *On The King's Highway*, (D. Appleton & Co., 1931), p.312.

152. Joan Romine, *COPSHAHOLM, The Oliver Story*, (Northern Indiana Historical Society, 1978), pp. 60-63.

153. Jeanne Derbeck, "3 Buildings Exemplify Stonemasonry," *South Bend Tribune*, 14 December 1970, Sec. 2, p. 17.

154. "Grotto of Lourdes at Notre Dame, Indiana," *Annals*, V. X11, No. 8, August 1896, p.126, RBSC, UND.

155. "A Modern Monastery," PNDP 10/101-190 1917, republished, UNDA.

156. Johnny Walker, "I Am The Immaculate Conception," *Schol.*, V. 87, 3 May 1946, p.14.

157. "Grotto of Lourdes at Notre Dame, Indiana," *Annals*, V. XII, No. 6, June 1896, p. 91, RBSC, UND.

158. Peter Joseph Chandlery, *A Pilgrim Walks in Rome*, (B. Herder Book Co. & London Manresa Press, 1924).

159. "Grotto of Lourdes at Notre Dame, Indiana," *Annals*, V. X11, No. 9, Grotto Dedication, September 1896, pp. 141-42, RBSC,UND.

160. *Schol.*, V. 30, 20 August 1896, p. 15.

161. *South Bend Tribune*, 12 August 1896.

162. *The Kalamazoo Augustinian*, V. VIII. No. 10, 22 August 1896, Available in UNDA.

163. *Schol.*, V. 30, 26 September 1896, p. 47.

164. *Schol.*, V. 31, August 1897, p. 24.

165. *Schol.*, V. 32, 17 September 1898, p. 48.

166. "Noted Builder Dead," *South Bend Sunday News Times*, Robert Braunsdorf's Obituary, 29 December 1901, South Joseph County Public Library, History Room clipping file.

167. "University Statue Shrine Stories," (*The Kerrville Times*, 1943), all quotes, p. 24, UQAC, UNDA.

168. "Lecture By Joyce Kilmer," *Schol.*, V. 50, 10 March 1917, p. 358.

169. Joyce Kilmer, *Joyce Kilmer, Poems, Essays and Letters*, Edited by Robert Holliday, (George H. Doran, 1918), V. 1, p. 36, 64-65, 70, 89, 100, 115.

170. Sister Mary Roberta Bresnan, Thesis, "Home Life as a Theme in the Poetry of Joyce Kilmer", Summer 1927, RBSC, University of Notre Dame.

171. *Daily Local News*, West Chester, Pa., 14 August 1886, PNDP 101-1880s, UNDA.

172. Rev. Sigmund A. Jankowski, C.S.C., *When Dreams Come True*, (Notre Dame, IN, 1970), p. 118.

173. Sister M. Madeleva, C.S.C., *My First Seventy Years*, (The Macmillan Company 1959), p. 46.

174. S. M. Madeleva, *Collected Poems*, (The Macmillan Co., 1954), "Candlelight," p. 110.

175. *Kilmer And Campion*, (Campion Jesuit High School, 1937), p. 76.

176. Kenton Kilmer letter in in Grotto Sources file in *Dorothy Corson Collection*, UNDA.

177. Tom Stritch, *My Notre Dame: memories and reflections of sixty years*, (University of Notre Dame Press, 1991), pp. 234-236.

178. Kerry Temple, "A River Runs Through it," *Notre Dame Magazine*, Sesquicentennial Edition, Summer 1991, p. 16.

179. Rev. Thomas J. O'Donnell, C.S.C., "Man and the Moment," *Notre Dame Alumnus*, (Alumni Association) Yearend '63, V. 41, p. 11.

180. "Legendary Tree Stands in Rear of Corby Hall," *Schol.*, V. 68, 2 November 1934, p. 6.

181. Dr. Harvey A. Holt, Professor of Forestry, Purdue University, Letter,14 September 1993.

182. Daniel Vincent Casey, "The Walk To The Stile," *Schol.*, V. 29, 30 May 1896, p. 561-62.

183. R. David Edmunds, *The Potawatomis, Keepers of the Fire*, (University of Oklahoma Press, 1978), pp. 153-155, 261.

184. Robert A. Trennert, Jr., *Indian Traders of the Middle Border, The House of Ewing, 1827-54*, (University of Nebraska Press, 1981), p. 66.

185. For the act as passed by the general assembly and signed by the governor, see Acts 1907, p.623.

186. Timothy Howard, *History of St. Joseph County, Indiana*, (Lewis Publishing Co., 1907), V. 2, Excerpts on pp. 54-55.

187. Edward Sorin, C.S.C., The Chronicles of Notre Dame du Lac, Edited by James J. Connelly, C.S.C., (University of Notre Dame Press, 1992), p. 27.

188. McAvoy, Thomas T., *The Catholic Church in Indiana 1789 - 1834*, (Columbian University Press, 1940), p. 121.

189. *Schol.*, V. L, 14 April 1917, p. 426.

190. Obituary Ledger, 1847-1849, Item 31, ULDG - 3/1, UNDA.

191. *Schol.*, V. 74, 2 February 1941, p. 11.

192. Edward Sorin, C.S.C., *The Chronicles of Notre Dame du Lac*, Edited by James J. Connelly, C.S.C., (University of Notre Dame Press, 1992), p. 248.

193. Timothy Howard, *History of St. Joseph County, Indiana*, (Lewis Publishing Co., 1907), V. 2, p. 697.

194. Timothy Howard, *History of St. Joseph County, Indiana*, (Lewis Publishing Co., 1907), V 2, Excerpts on pp. 629,654.

195. *Schol.*, V. X11, 12 October, 1878, p. 93.

196. *A Guide To South Bend, Notre Dame du Lac, and St. Mary's Indiana*, (John Murphy & Co., 1859), UNDA

197. *History Of Laporte County Indiana*, (C. C. Chapman & Co. 1880), p.11, PNDP O1-Sa-1, UNDA.

198. *Indiana Historical Collection*, (Indiana Historical Commission, 1922), "Harrison: Messages and Letters," p. 579.

199. *Schol.*, V. 24, 14 March 1891, p. 412.

200. *South Bend Tribune*, 5 August 1932, Sec. 2, p. 1.

201. *Schol.*, V. VIII, 6 February, 1875, p. 282.

202. *Schol.*, V. 20, 14 August 1886, p. 24.

203. Administration Bldg., Dome: Statue of Virgin Mary, Gilding, 1870-1990s, PNDP 10-Ad-4, UNDA.

204. *Schol.*, V. 50, 3 February 1917, Brother Frederick's obituary, p. 277.

205. William Farrell, "The Legend of the Sycamore," *Schol.*, V. 50, 3 February 1917, pp. 272-273.

206. *The Dome*, 1926, (From a later version of the Legend), pp. 344,345.

207. Badin to the Potawatomis, 29 June 1832, and notes dated 30 October 1832, sent to Bishop Fenwick, Cincinnati, 11-4- e, UNDA.

208. *Skizzen aus Nord-Amerika* (1845), description Early Michiana area, ca. 1840; I quote from a manuscript translation made by Notre Dame archivists, which is filed with pages photocopied from the original German book, PPOT, UNDA.

209. Color picture of sycamore by Bill Mowle, *The Dome*, 1992, p. 15.

210. Eugene O'Neill, *Long Day's Journey Into Night*, (Yale University Press, 1956).

211. *A Guide To Notre Dame du Lac, and Saint Mary's Academy*, PNDP 100-1865, p. 58, UNDA.

212. Sister M. Francesca, C.S.C., *Our Mother House*, (W. B. Conky Company, 1941), pp.46-51 and Sister M. Eleanore, C.S.C. *On The King's Highway*, (D. Appleton & Co., 1931), p. 214.

213. Eugene O'Neill, *Long Day's Journey Into Night*, (Yale University Press, 1956).

214. Edward Fischer, *Notre Dame Remembered*, (University of Notre Dame Press, 1987), p.118.

215. Photograph, St. Mary's Academy & Grounds, *Yesteryear In South Bend,1905*, (Duley Press, Inc., Printed in 1966).

216. *Schol.*, V. VIII, 30 August 1873, p. 2.

217. *Schol.*, V. IX, 9 October 1875, p. 90.

218. *Schol.*, V. 66, 30 September 1932, p.12.

219. Rev. Thomas P. Jones, *Development of the Office of the Prefect of Religion at Notre Dame: 1842-1952*, p. 123, PNDP 3300, P3, UNDA.

220. Arthur J. Hope, C.S.C., *Notre Dame, One Hundred Years*, (Icarus Press, Inc., 1978), p. 444.

221. John F. O'Hara, Religious Bulletin, June 1, 1925, UNDA.

222. Rev. Eugene P. Burke, C.S.C.,"To Our Lady of the Lakes," *The Mystery of the Woman*, (University of Notre Dame Press, 1956), pp. 146-149.

223. *Reflections in the Dome*, Edited by James S. O'Rourke,(Published by James S. O'Rourke, Notre Dame, 1988), "A Concentration of Goodness," Edward Fischer, p. 18.

224. *Schol.*, 6 December 1946, p. 52.

225. *Notre Dame Alumnus*, V. 33, January-February, 1955, Snite Obituary, p. 9.

226. Leonard C. Hawkins, *Man in the Iron Lung*, (Doubleday, 1956), pp. 20, 76, 134, 141.

227. *Schol.*, V. 73, 1 January 1939, p. 9, 26.

228. *The Dome*, 1953, p. 172.

229. *Schol.*, V. 74, 13 December 1940, p. 7.

230. UDIS, 133/17, UNDA.

231. *Schol.*, V. 81, 12 May 1944, p. 7; *Notre Dame Alumnus*, V. 21, August 1943, War Dead Page 24.

232. MDEV 24.217, Development, Master Files, (microfilm), UNDA.

233. Maurice Francis Egan, *The Glories of the Catholic Church in Art, Architecture, and History* (Chicago, D.H.McBride & co., 1895), pp. 28, 110 and Leonard Von Matt, *St. Bernadette, A Pictorial Biography*, (Longmans, Green, & H. Regnery, 1957).

234. Henri Lasserre, *Our Lady Of Lourdes*, (D. & J. Sadlier, 1875).

235. Franz Werfel, *The Song Of Bernadette*, (Viking Press, 1942), pp. 488, 503.

236. George Seaton, *Who Was Who in America with World Notables*, V. 7, (Marquis Publishing,1971-1981), p. 512.

237. Oral History interview of Hollywood producer, George Seaton by David Cherichetti, New York Times Oral History Program, *The American Film Institute, Louis B. Mayer, Oral History Collection, Part 1.*, excerpts, pp. 1-14, 44-109. (Microfilming Corporation of America, 1977).

238. Ingrid Bergman and Alan Burgess, *Ingrid Bergman, My Story*, (Delacorte Press, N.Y., 1972).

239. *Notre Dame Alumnus*, V. 36, November 1958, p. 16.

240. Dorothy Corson, "The Mystery of Sister Paraclita's Album," 1992, Album and story, *Dorothy Corson Collection*, UNDA.

241. *Notre Dame Alumnus*, (University of Notre Dame), V. 36, November 1958, p. 45.

242. *Notre Dame Alumnus*, V. 36, August- September, 1958, page 11.

243. John Laughlin, "Our Lady Of Lourdes At Notre Dame," *Our Sunday Visitor*, 11 February 1968, p. 3.

244. "The Confraternity Of Our Lady of Lourdes," *Schol.*, V. 99, 21 March 1958, p.13.

245. Mary Catherine Rose, Grotto story for *The New World*, Grotto folder, Notre Dame Public Relations and Information, Drop File.

246. Carl G. Jung, *Man and His Symbols*, (Doubleday, 1964), pp. 209-210.

247. An exact copy of Tom Dooley's letter is in an appendix of *A Cave of Candles*.

248. Thomas Dooley Collection, Letter, May 25, 1959, UNDA.

249. *Notre Dame Alumnus*, V. 42, February/March 1964, "Man and the Moment," Thomas O'Donnell, C.S.C., p. 12.

250. Rev. Sigmund A. Jankowski, C.S.C., *When Dreams Come True*, (Notre Dame, IN, 1970), Copy UNDA.

251. *Chicago Tribune*, Joseph Tiber, "Dream Merchant," Sports, Section 4, p. 1.

252. "University Statue Shrine Stories," (*The Kerrville Times*, 1943), UQAC, UNDA.

253. *Joliet Catholic Explorer*, Fr. Joseph M. Champlin, "Devotion to Mary strong at ND", 26 June 1981, p.10.

254. Mike Wilkins, "Fire at Grotto reveals its importance to many," *The Observer*, 4 October 1985, p. 6.

255. *The Observer*, 16 October 1985, pp. 1,3.

256. Timothy Howard, *A Brief History of the University of Notre Dame du Lac*, (Warner, 1895), p 662.

257. *The Observer*, Accent, Kathy Martin, "A special place at Notre Dame," 13 February 1986, p. 8-9. "What Does the Grotto mean to you?" Doug Anderson, p. 9.

258. *Schol.*, V. 91, John E. Fitzgerald, ". . . From Thy Heavenly Height," 12 May 1950, pp. 12-13.

259. *Chicago Tribune*, 23 July 1899, Descriptions of Notre Dame, PNDP, 101-1890s, UNDA.

260. *Schol.*, V. 30, 17 October 1896, pp.. 92-93.

261. Blessing engraved on the plaque at St. Stan's Grotto, a replica of the Grotto at Notre Dame erected by Rev. Sigmund Jankowski in 1962 at St. Stanislaus Church, South Bend, Indiana. Were Father Jan here today to celebrate its centennial, I know, he would bestow the same blessing on the Grotto of Lourdes at Notre Dame.

262. Originals of both stories, "Always Have a Dream," and "Friendship is a Chain of Gold," with photographs, are in Rev. Sigmund Jankowski's file at the Holy Cross Province Archives Center and the *Dorothy Corson Collection* at the University of Notre Dame Archives.